TOUCHING PEACE

TOUCHING PEACE

*From the Oslo Accord
to a Final Agreement*

Yossi Beilin

Translated from the Hebrew
by Philip Simpson

Weidenfeld & Nicolson
LONDON

First published in Great Britain in 1999
by Weidenfeld & Nicolson

A CIP catalogue record for this book is
available from the British Library.

ISBN 0 297 64316 9

Filmset by Selwood Systems, Midsomer Norton

Printed in Great Britain by Butler & Tanner Ltd, Frome and London

Weidenfeld & Nicolson
The Orion Publishing Group Ltd
Orion House
5 Upper Saint Martin's Lane
London, WC2H 9EA

Contents

Contents

Preface

This book was born the morning of 30 May 1996. It had been in me a long time, but I had not had the opportunity before then to sit down at my desk and transfer my thoughts on to paper, along with the question marks and exclamation marks, interim conclusions and lessons for the future. The four years 1992–6 were the most fascinating and stimulating years of my political life, a time in which I exploited all the contacts at my disposal, all the expertise that I had accumulated, both in academia and in national and international politics, in the effort to realise my hopes for this country. On several occasions I dared to deviate from the norms of diplomacy which are conventionally taken for granted. This I did in the Oslo track, in the Stockholm track and in conversations with the Vatican, which were – as far as I was concerned – remarkable and particularly challenging.

These were four years that seemed to pass in an instant; conversation pursued conversation, agreement pursued agreement, journey pursued journey. This book has been written to a great extent for myself; it is like climbing to the top of a hill while a battle is in progress, to study what is happening from all angles and form a more accurate assessment of the likely outcome.

In May 1996, after the Labour Party's defeat in the Prime Ministerial election, at that time of bitter and sudden stalemate when what had begun in hope ended in disillusionment, I came to the conclusion that the effort to understand what had happened during this turbulent period was likely to be easier, and more successful in relation to longer-term prospects, if this were to be not a volume of reminiscences but one focused on specific issues, pointing the way to specific solutions.

The First Section of this book deals with political activity directed towards the Palestinians of the West Bank and Gaza and East Jerusalem in the 1980s and early 1990s, activity that made the Oslo process possible and laid the foundations of realistic dialogue. The Second Section addresses the Oslo process, from the eve of the 1992 elections to the moment of the signing of the Accord on a warm summer day, 13 September 1993, on the lawn of the White House, when the Prime Minister of Israel, the late Yitzhak Rabin, shook the hand of the PLO leader, Yasser Arafat. The Third Section is an account of the Stockholm process; beginning with a conversation between Arafat and myself in October 1993, continuing with some twenty conversations between two of the Oslo negotiators – Dr Yair Hirschfeld and Dr Ron Pundak – and two Palestinian academics, Dr Ahmed Khalidi and Dr Hussein Agha, associates of Mahmud Abbas (also known as Abu Mazen), and concluding five days before the murder of Rabin. The Fourth Section is devoted entirely to the future, setting out the solutions required, in my opinion, for the political problems that lie before us, and taking the liberty of suggesting ideas for a more just social policy, facing up to the tensions existing within Israel; these tensions will be further aggravated when we are living at peace with our neighbours and the threat to our survival has been largely averted. The common denominator of these political and social proposals is a profound belief in the equal value of all human beings, and my object here is to refute the very superficial notion according to which the political left in Israel is the social right. The fifteen years that I have spent since September 1984 in the government and the Knesset have shown me some splendid examples of commitment and sincere idealism, efficiency and pragmatism; on the other hand I have seen much anachronism, waste, duplicity and pathological fear of change. My conclusions from these years are set out in this section of the book.

This book has one serious flaw: it is written by me. It is not a scientific quest after the truth, but a subjective attempt to portray certain events the inception of which I witnessed, in the most objective manner of which I am capable. Every story such as this has a second and a third side, and each side in itself has several different versions; anyone who seeks an in-depth analysis of the truth and a precise account of all that has happened is likely to be disappointed by my book.

The people who worked beside me during these four years are those who really made possible the turnaround that we brought about. I owe them all a deep debt, for their initiative, discretion and willingness to invest long hours, energy and commitment in the project: my office chiefs – Shlomo Gur, Haim Divon and Aviv Shiron, the office director Orit Shani and their staff.

Dr Yair Hirschfeld, Dr Ron Pundak and Boaz Karni, representing the Economic Co-operation Foundation, worked tirelessly for the advancement of the peace process; they have not always received adequate recognition but there can be no doubt that without their sterling efforts it would have been impossible to pursue either the Oslo track or the Stockholm track.

And finally my nearest and dearest – Helena, Gil and Ori, who gave me a free hand and never complained about my eccentric hours and hectic daily schedule, Sabbaths and festivals included, and were always prepared to offer support, advice and criticism.

Yossi Beilin   November, 1998

LEBANON

SYRIA

Golan
Heights

Acre

Haifa

Sea of
Galilee

Nazareth

Mediterranean Sea

Jenin

WEST
BANK

SAMARIA

Tel Aviv
Jaffa

Lod

Ramalla

River Jordan

Amman

Ashdod

Jerusalem

Jericho

Bethlehem
JUDAEA

Dead Sea

Gaza

Hebron

JORDAN

GAZA STRIP

Beersheba

ISRAEL

EGYPT

0   15   30 Miles

0   25   50 Km

Eilat   Aqaba

Gulf of Aqaba

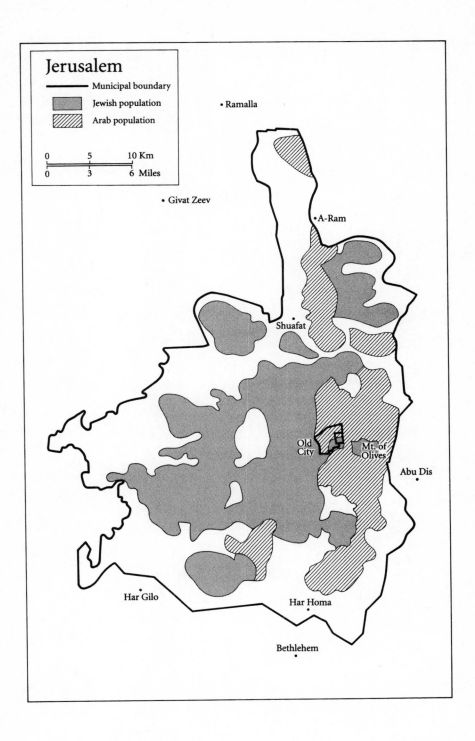

Jerusalem

— Municipal boundary

Jewish population

Arab population

0 5 10 Km
0 3 6 Miles

• Ramalla

• Givat Zeev

•A-Ram

Shuafat

Old
City

Mt. of
Olives

Abu Dis

Har Gilo

Har Homa

Bethlehem
•

Prologue

Frustration is an integral part of our lives because our lives are so short. From a historical perspective our lives are no more than an episode, a passing flash. They are so short that many people, more perhaps than we are prepared to admit, need constant reassurance in the form of belief in reincarnation or resurrection of the dead, in order to sweeten the pill just a little. All of us would like our lives to be longer and more meaningful, and they can be so the more we exert ourselves, acquiring better understanding of our surroundings and leaving an impression in the minds of others.

The role of the statesman is to reduce the risk of war to the minimum possible, on condition that prevention of war does not increase the danger of it in the longer term. It is also his duty to minimise the danger of deaths arising from other circumstances such as crime or traffic accidents, and to encourage scientists to lengthen life-expectancy and reduce the individual's need to waste an appreciable portion of his short life on 'maintenance'. If I compare our lives today with those lived in the early years of the State of Israel and consider how much time was wasted warming food on a primus, getting ice for the ice-box, buying wood to heat water for baths, travelling from place to place, I have no doubt that we live longer today solely because some of the tasks which we were compelled to perform in the past have already been consigned to history. Of course, credit for this is not due entirely – or even largely – to statesmen, but sometimes it is enough that the statesman does not impede the processes which improve the standard and quality of our lives.

In modern democratic society, the role of the statesman is to enable every individual in society to make the most of his potential and fulfil himself in a way that is beneficial both to himself and to his environment. As long as survival is threatened, it is very difficult to achieve this. It has been the aspiration of the peace camp in Israel to do everything necessary for the creation of normality in our society, thereby facilitating the attainment of these goals.

*

The elections of 1992, it must be admitted, resulted in *accidental* victory for the peace camp. It is true that Labour under Yitzhak Rabin's leadership obtained forty-four seats in the Knesset while Yitzhak Shamir's right-wing Likud Party won only thirty-two, but the total number of votes polled by the left: Labour, Meretz, Hadash and Mada – was several thousand short of the tally scored by the right and the religious parties. Had it not been for the raising of the exclusion-threshold, whereby parties which failed to win 1.5 per cent of the vote were granted no seats, and which prevented Tehiyya from entering the Knesset, Shamir could have formed a government.

I sensed that this was a rare opportunity that should not be allowed to pass without leaving an indelible imprint and creating in our lives the great change towards peace with the Arab world – in the first instance, peace with the Palestinians. So, I thought, let us fulfil our destiny as those responsible for the quality of life in Israeli society.

I was haunted by the many opportunities for peace that had been missed in the past. I had learned about them, taught about them, written about them and sworn to myself that I would never let such an opportunity slip through my hands, should I ever be in a position of influence. I had heard and seen how reasonable men, pursuers of peace, had contributed in the past to quite appalling neglect of opportunities and then wrung their hands helplessly as the prospects for peace evaporated: with Hosni Zaim of Syria in 1949, with Anwar Sadat of Egypt in 1971, with King Hussein of Jordan in 1987 and with Yasser Arafat of the PLO in 1988. This time, I assured myself, we are dealing with a unique combination of factors – a peace government formed by Labour–Meretz–Shas, an American administration interested in helping the process along, a Russian government prepared to co-operate with the USA and no longer underwriting Arab militarism, and pragmatic Arab regimes. This was not an occasion for letting time slip by or for more shuffling of feet in dreary Washington talks.

Shortly after the elections I met the leaders of Peace Now in the USA. They had about them the air of those who are already home and dry; a peace-seeking government had come to power in Israel and now matters would resolve themselves. When they realised that I did not share their euphoria, they seemed surprised. I told them that nothing ever happens by itself. Four years, our term in office, is both a short and a long time. In such a space of time you can turn the world upside down or continue, more or less, along the smooth path that leads to nowhere. I wanted to be sure that we were doing enough every day to advance the peace process, and I could not tell myself that this was indeed the case.

The Oslo process began as a very modest attempt to establish a secret conduit, to facilitate progress in the Washington talks, and within a few months it had developed to dimensions that we had never anticipated. It led to mutual recognition between Israel and the PLO, made peace with Jordan possible, opened the way for the majority of the states of the Arab League to establish official and unofficial relations with Israel, brought about the virtual lifting of the Arab boycott and attracted inward investment from all over the world.

As things have turned out, it is hard to believe that all these changes were created as the result of an almost accidental encounter in 1992. It is reasonable to suppose that, had it not been for this meeting between Terje Larsen and myself, a similar encounter would have taken place and would have led to the opening of the secret track. And yet the fact that the daughter of Lord Mishcon was a schoolfriend of King Hussein's sister enabled Mishcon to host the meetings between us and King Hussein and his Prime Minister in the mid-1980s; the encounter in 1992 in Tel Aviv likewise engendered a whole series of actions. The coincidence of people, time and place is often crucial to the success of political processes, wielding – it has to be admitted – inexorable and sometimes disproportionate influence.

It seems that the change was accepted too easily, and this misled us. The handshake between Rabin and Arafat did not cause the pillars of the universe to sway. In the government, the decision was accepted without opposition; in the Knesset the Declaration of Principles was passed with a large majority, and with the abstention of three Likud members. Opinion polls showed enthusiastic support from the public. We thought all was ripe for ideological revolution, the positive response being more sensational than the agreement itself. We thought we were absolved of the need to continue moulding public understanding, and in this we were wrong.

We were also mistaken in that we didn't show the public what we envisaged at the end of the process, and we thereby exposed ourselves to unnecessary accusations and questions. The combination of a firm agreement on principles and an effort to explain things even among circles remote from the peace camp could have changed perceptions of the political process.

I hope that comprehensive peace will be concluded in the coming years. In our activities over the past few years we have tried hard to prevent the process going into reverse, but to say that it is unstoppable, that there is no going back from it – such assertions are simply unrealistic. They are wishful thinking, not statements of fact.

We are not ready for peace. We are so used to non-peace and perpetual danger that we shall have to accustom ourselves to the new situation. You could compare our predicament to that of a man who has suffered an accident and been confined to a wheelchair for many years. One day he undergoes surgery and can begin to walk again, but even as he stands and tries to take a few steps, he misses the security of the chair to which he has grown so accustomed. At this moment the chair seems to him much more comfortable than standing upright; he needs a period of transition before he can feel confident in his ability to walk.

We, the generations born in this land of Israel, simply do not know what peace is. It is the height of paradox that there are those who fear the peace process, on the grounds that it will reduce the motivation of the young to fight in the next war. This is the wheelchair syndrome in a nutshell. We shall need to confront problems which, for considerations of security, have previously been ignored, but the most acute of all questions will surely be this: will Israeli society have a *purpose* when the problem of survival itself is no longer so high on our list of priorities?

The religious element can always recommend return to the synagogue, and this is of course entirely legitimate, but the secular majority must ensure that it too will not be devoid of values. In my opinion, Rabbi Avraham Yeshayhu Karelitz (known as Hazon Ish) was wrong when he told David Ben-Gurion that the empty wagon of the secular should give way to the laden wagon of the religious, the meaning of this being that the secular must make all kinds of concessions to the religious because they themselves have no values. In fact, the wagon of secular Zionism was heavily laden with values, Jewish and universal alike. But the secular wagon needs to be loaded afresh in time of peace, because until now an appreciable portion of secular values has been tied to the mutual responsibilities of warfare. Can we find a Jewish-national identity, which will characterise our lives here in the future? Are we to become a state that gives aid to the Third World and plays a central role in the international arena, in peace-keeping forces, in resolving international disputes? Can we exploit our ever increasing leisure, training ourselves to meet the new challenges of the next century?

I take the liberty of offering some suggestions for the character of Israeli society in time of peace. They are based on solid values, but are not immune to criticism. I have always been more worried by lack of response than by controversy, and I hope that the ideas expressed in this book, in both the political and social spheres, will stimulate a debate from which it will be possible, perhaps, to draw conclusions with which broad sections of Israeli society will be able to identify.

PART ONE

Nobody to Talk to,
Nothing to Discuss

THERE IS NO event more formative than war. Nothing else marks generations as war does. I was born during the War of Liberation of 1948–9, I experienced the Sinai Campaign of 1956: the black-out and the shelters, father and brother in the army. Ten months after I was conscripted, at the end of the quietest decade in Israel's history, I found myself embroiled in the Six Day War of 1967, in 8 Division, in the conquest of Sinai and the Golan Heights.

I was far from thinking then that the great victory of 1967 would turn out to be the heaviest of curses. Hearing news of the conquest of Jerusalem on my transistor radio, I was moved to tears. The defeat of Nasser's army in the Sinai was relatively easy, and gave a decisive answer to the Egyptian dictator, who had instructed UN Secretary-General U. Thant to evacuate the 6,000 soldiers of the UN Emergency Force from the Israel–Egypt border. The conquest of the Golan Heights was a sharp and smooth – though hard-fought – response to the Syrians, who had been firing on the tractor-drivers down below and injuring the residents of Shaar Hagolan, Tel-Katzir, Dishon and other settlements.

From the Heights we travelled, a few days after the war had ended, to the West Bank. The silence was eerie. The villas of Ramallah seemed to belong to another country, 'abroad'; in Old Jerusalem, seeing the Wall was a heart-stopping experience. It was impossible to believe all this was happening to us, long after we had resigned ourselves to frontiers and partitions. This was a prolonged sigh of relief, like a surgical operation successfully eradicating a chronic disease.

My father never forgave himself for being too old, at almost sixty, to wear uniform this time. A veteran of the Haganah and the 'Rangers', an admirer of Zeev Vilnai, he consoled himself with touring the occupied territories, sometimes accompanied by my equally emotional mother, one of the leading lights of the Society for Scriptural Research, a radio commentator on Biblical texts and an archaeological expert.

At the time it seemed that all the problems which had oppressed us for the past nineteen years had been solved, that from now on the natural borders of the State of Israel would be permanently fixed as a result of the folly of the Arabs, whose threats and promises towards Israel had been frustrated; the Arabs at last appreciated our invincibility and – if they had any interest in making peace with us – they should show some respect and ask for it politely, and we would decide with whom to make peace and when.

I did not know then of the Israeli government's secret decision to withdraw to the international frontiers (delineated by the Superpowers of the beginning of the twentieth century) in exchange for peace with Egypt and Syria, a decision taken one week after the end of the war, but the Khartoum Conference, which ended on 2 September with its three noes – no recognition, no negotiation and no peace with Israel – was enough to convince me that there was nobody to talk to, and perhaps this was not such a terrible thing.

A month at Kantara in the northern Canal Zone showed me that the issue was rather more complex, that our position was still far from secure and the War of Attrition could yet prove more traumatic and costly than the Six Day War itself. But there was no one to protest to. On 1 October 1967 the UN Security Council called on Egypt to open direct negotiations with Israel, and it refused.

I was never a hawk. I always believed that all human beings were created of the same matter and that my rights were in no way superior to those of the boy offering to black my army boots in exchange for a few coppers on my way through Gaza, but nor was I numbered among those who were so impetuously calling for unilateral withdrawal in the immediate post-war period.

In 1969 I was discharged from the army and hastily embarked on the process of consolidating my future. During my demobilisation leave I married Helena, and on 1 September I began working as a journalist on *Davar*. The following month I commenced my studies at Tel Aviv University. I believed then, as I have continued to believe throughout my life, that time was my greatest enemy, and that I had to attain my objectives with the minimum possible delay. I continued to practise religious obligations as I had done from an early age as a part of my 'rebellious youth': I put on *tefillin* every morning and observed dietary regulations and the Sabbath meticulously. I continued to support the Labour Party and even joined it in 1972, but I did not engage in any activism at all, not even student activism, having a job as well as studies to occupy me, also a home and a son born in 1972. I did not hate the Labour Prime Minister Golda Meir, although her image of motherly understanding failed to impress me. Nor did I care for her disingenuousness on the Palestinian issue ('I am a Palestinian') or her attitude towards the Black Panthers ('They're not nice boys'). I believed however that she was doing everything necessary to guarantee our security, keeping vigilant watch and missing no opportunity to advance the cause of peace.

The Yom Kippur War of 1973, which caught me in the synagogue, and during which (as for the remainder of my six months of reserve service) I was stationed at staff headquarters and not in the field, turned out in the end to be the war which moulded my perceptions more than any other episode in my life. In retrospect, I realised that until then I had lived in a secure and predictable world. Even the Six Day War, in which we had simply struck the first blow at those intent on killing us, had been included in this complacent view of things. Elementary school, high school, university, journalism, synagogue, government policy – all these had nourished my feeling that all was in order, that there was someone watching over us, someone understanding us. The Yom Kippur War exposed the nakedness of the whole apparatus, and when thousands of soldiers were killed and many more wounded and maimed, I became another person. I saw that the settlements on the Golan Heights were only a hindrance to the defence of Israel, and that evacuation of their residents was going to be the fundamental problem, I saw how unimportant the occupied territories were to us, and how to a great extent we had become the prisoners of our own conquests. I learned now that in 1971 Golda Meir had foolishly missed the opportunity to make peace with Egypt in exchange for the evacuation of Sinai. My disillusionment was such that I abandoned all religious observance and, after release from my long stint of reserve service, I decided to work inside the Labour Party towards strengthening the peace camp within it. I understood that the concept 'Nobody to talk to, nothing to discuss' developed after the Khartoum conference as a new Israeli consensus was correct only in part, and when there *had* been someone to talk to and something to discuss, we had still been trapped in a different mind-set.

In the Young Guard of the Labour Party I edited the monthly *Traffic Light*, joined the administrative staff of the organisation and, together with Haim Ramon and other youngsters, headed the camp believing in the existence of a Palestinian people as a distinct national group and not just as Arabs. In 1977, following the upheaval which brought Menahem Begin and the Likud Party to power, I decided to devote most of my time to the political issue. In response to a request from Shimon Peres (then the leader of the Labour Party and the Opposition), I left *Davar* newspaper and became the Labour Party spokesman. At the same time, with the appointment of Haim Ramon as secretary of the youth movement, I was elected to the post of international secretary of the movement and chairman of its policy committee.

The leadership of the Young Guard was more dovish than the majority of branch members. The proposals that we raised in plenary sessions were passed with great difficulty or not passed at all. Even in the social context the views of the organisation as a whole were far more conservative than the programme of socio-liberal policies that we presented, which called for separation between the trade unions and the health service – after so many decades in which the big Sick Fund was owned by them – and the liberation of workers' groups from centralised trade union dominance. For these and for other reasons, in 1981 I established the Mashov (which stands for feedback in Hebrew) caucus.

In the new caucus I felt quite different. By the nature of things it was more homogeneous, and it gave us a context for the shaping of political and social conceptions without having to spend most of the time engaged in internal wrangling, or in attempts to form coalitions before any draft had even been produced. In the course of less than three years, up to the establishment of the national unity government in 1984, we had moulded our political and social conceptions, moving beyond general principles to the adoption of more dovish political priorities. In the economic sphere we called our approach 'market socialism', advocating the privatisation, with selective subsidies, of national insurance, and social legislation offering the individual access to education, health, housing and pensions, with service-providers competing among themselves and not constituting a monopoly. In international politics we supported the application of the Camp David principles to the issue of peace with Syria as well, and the establishment of a Palestinian state in the West Bank and Gaza, on the basis of territorial compromise and an indivisible Jerusalem.

But we were not content merely with determining policy for ourselves.

We did a lot of work addressing day-to-day problems in the occupied territories, tackling legal and economic issues and organising meetings. The structure of the caucus facilitated activities of this kind, and in some respects it was reminiscent of a Fabian club. It was joined by faculty members and graduate students from several universities, alongside party members who needed a break from the constant wrangling in the sub-branches and who were unhappy with the power-plays endemic in the life of the party. We were accused in some quarters of running an elitist clique, and it is true that, while any Labour supporter was entitled to join the Mashov caucus, we for our part made no attempt to swell our ranks beyond the 700 or so registered members. We did not aspire to represent all shades of opinion in the party, thereby having to pay the price of pandering to the lowest common denominator. We wanted to be the party's research and development section.

As a first stage we succeeded in harassing and pressurising the party into taking notice of the stances that we had adopted and the reports we had prepared – such as the report of the committee headed by Imik Levi on the health service, submitted in the wake of the doctors' strike of 1983, or the outright opposition that we expressed to Reagan's invasion of Grenada in the same year. We learned how to operate and became aware of one of the best-kept secrets in the world – if you know what you want and you come prepared for debate and you have a paper, your potential influence is immeasurably greater than that of someone who comes to a meeting and, at the most, raises a finger and exercises the right to speak after he has heard the others. The more prepared you are, the less scope others have to change the formula that you have devised.

Dr Yair Hirschfeld was born in New Zealand, where his parents had taken refuge from the Nazis, and grew up in Vienna, to which they returned after the war. At the age of twenty he arrived in Israel as an organiser of the Zionist youth movement. His sister Miriam also emigrated to Israel, where she took a PhD in nursing; Yair obtained a doctorate in oriental studies and lectured at Haifa University.

In 1979 Bruno Kreisky, then the Chancellor of Austria, saw a television programme in which Yair was analysing the significance of the Iranian revolution, and he invited Yair to meet him in Vienna. He was impressed by the breadth of his knowledge and suggested that he organise deputations of young Israelis, Palestinians and Jordanians to visit Austria, Germany and Denmark to discuss issues of economic co-operation. He asked Yair to pursue this idea in an informal consultation with King Hussein and Shimon Peres, two friends of his. When both had given their consent to setting up the deputations, Hirschfeld asked for a meeting with me, to inform me of developments. Thus we met for the first time.

He had made contacts with Palestinians in the territories in the context of organising the deputations, and from my point of view he played a central role in forging links with Palestinians, with whom I had previously had no contact. He joined the Mashov caucus and was my political ally from the early 1980s onward.

Yair headed a committee that operated through forging links between Israel and the territories, and was focused on the economic situation in the Gaza Strip and the West Bank. Boaz Karni, a member of Kibbutz Tzora'a and one of the founders of the caucus, was a key figure in this committee. We tried to examine the feasibility of developing local industry and thus reducing the dependence of the residents of the territories on Israel, and we discovered it was virtually impossible to set up factories in the territories, for fear of their competing with Israeli companies. This applied to the Palestinian proposal to establish a cement factory in Hebron, and to many other similar projects. When we raised the problem with the co-ordinator of industry in the territories, Fuad Ben Eliezer, we were surprised to hear him making no attempt to justify the policy. His message was unequivocal, simple and unvarnished: 'There *is* no Israeli government policy towards the territories, and since there's no policy, I don't know what to do . . .'

The Law of Association forbidding contacts with the Palestine Liberation Organisation was not yet in force at that time, but we did not meet representatives of the PLO. I do not remember any disagreement between us on this point, nor any occasion when we were faced with a dilemma. Perhaps we felt that such a meeting would have been a kind of betrayal of principle, although we all supported the idea of having a recognised opponent, and this was one of the issues that we referred for decision to the committee of the Mashov caucus.

Contacts with Palestinian people in the West Bank and Gaza were expanded, and in the course of conversations with them we were made aware of a picture vastly more complex than what we had previously envisaged. We were exposed to the divisions among them, to their conceptions of future solutions, and to the manner in which they analysed

Israeli policy and the differences between the various political elements in the state.

Some of these meetings were held in the territories. Usually it was Yair who drove and, as the only immigrant among us, he impressed us with his knowledge of the roads. There were also broader meetings held at Labour Party headquarters in Hayarkon Street in Tel Aviv. Thus for example we met, in plenary session of the caucus, with Ibrahim Karain, editor of *El Awda* and with the journalist Ramonda Tawil (we didn't know then that she was destined for renown as Arafat's mother-in-law) and heard from them a more pragmatic approach to resolving the conflict than that expressed in the slogans emanating from the PLO's networks.

The Lebanon war launched in June 1982 was perceived from the outset as a disaster and it seemed that among the Israeli public there was a growing awareness of the limitations of force. Accompanied by the entire PLO leadership, Arafat moved from Beirut to Tunis and in 1983 the organisation adopted the idea of Jordanian–Palestinian confederation. After years during which Israel had been unwilling to recognise the existence of a Palestinian people and of the PLO as its representative, and after years during which the PLO had embraced the notion of a secular democratic state in which there would be room only for Palestinians, a way towards settlement of the conflict was being signposted: Israel recognises the PLO, is willing to withdraw from the whole of Gaza and most of the West Bank, the Palestinians proclaim the Palestinian state and establish confederation with Jordan whereby the Palestinian refugee problem will be solved; the issue of Jerusalem will be discussed at a later date, and in the meantime the Palestinians in the city may live their lives in conditions of municipal autonomy. This was the framework of the solution that we saw at that time.

The elections of 1984 and the resulting government of national unity brought about far-reaching changes. Peres was to be Prime Minister for twenty-five months to be replaced, then, by Shamir with Yitzhak Rabin as Minister of Defence. Now at last it seemed it would be possible to decide and to implement things with our own hands, rather than just preparing policy statements and issuing press releases. The reality proved to be more complex. The system of administering the territories remained the same; no policy regarding the future of the territories was initiated by this two-headed government. Refusal to negotiate with the PLO and denial of the Palestinian state were among the fundamental tenets of the new administration. Shmuel Goren, co-ordinator of operations in the territories, succeeded in preventing senior politicians from meeting Palestinians in the territories who were identified with the PLO. Just as after the Six Day War people were expelled from the territories on account of connections with Jordan, the folly of the 1980s was to banish the supporters of the PLO. Thus for example both Prime Minister Peres and the then President Haim Herzog were denied the opportunity of meeting Rashad e-Shawah, the former mayor of Gaza and a man of peace.

During those years I was serving as secretary to the government (following the British model, it is a civil servant who is in charge of the Cabinet meetings and the implementation of its resolutions), and although I had a certain influence over the conduct of affairs, especially in the Prime Minister's office, I had great difficulty bringing about the changes which I believed necessary in the relations between the government and its leader and the Palestinians. I feared an imminent explosion on account of the dire economic conditions in the territories, their total dependence on Israel and the lack of hope for reaching a political solution. But Goren – who wasn't a politician and who later proved, from a policy point of view, to be unexpectedly sympathetic to our thinking on the permanent settlement – was a slave to antiquated notions of civil governance, introducing Peres to Palestinian individuals associated with the administration who represented only themselves.

During this period I took a break from partisan activity, staying away from party headquarters and not even playing much of a role in Mashov. Under a Labour-Likud government the potential for progress was limited: on the one hand, withdrawal from Lebanon, serious negotiation over Taba (the last disputed area between Israel and Egypt), conversations with King Hussein in which I took part, and on the other, arguments over the future of settlements, serious controversy on the issue of the international conference suggested by Hussein, and lack of progress in relation to the Palestinians, with even the replacement of army officers in municipal posts by Palestinian appointees proceeding at a snail's pace for fear of provoking a backlash by Jewish settlers (especially in Hebron where the most extreme settlers live).

In the wake of the murder of two teachers from Afula, the government decided to return to a policy of administrative detentions and expulsions, and in August 1986 a misguided understanding was reached whereby

Likud supported the exclusion of racial movements from the Knesset while the leadership of the Labour Party backed a new law banning any contact whatsoever with PLO members. The final draft of the bill received government approval and, though opposed in the Knesset by a majority of Labour members, it passed into law.

At the very last moment amendments were made, for example authorising medical treatment or permitting a mother to visit a son belonging to the PLO, but there can be no doubt that this was one of the most reactionary and shameful laws ever to appear on our statute book. Through our own stupidity we prevented ourselves from even sitting down in television debates or symposia with PLO representatives and reacting to their demands.

In the course of many conversations with my friend Ephraim Sneh, then head of the civil administration in Judaea and Samaria, I was able to form an accurate assessment of what was going on in the territories. I continued to meet Palestinian leaders and here and there I succeeded in wielding some influence – over the accelerated appointment of Palestinians to positions of civic authority, the opening of a branch of the Cairo-Amman Bank in the territories, preventing the excavation of a shaft to exploit the waters of the Herodion – but I knew that all this was just a drop in the ocean.

As government secretary I was obliged to speak on behalf of the entire government. My position as political director of the Foreign Ministry and number two to the Foreign Minister enabled me to exercise greater freedom of speech and I expressed my personal opinion on a number of issues – including the international conference. I visited the territories and met individuals from the economic and political spheres, and in particular I became acquainted with the Palestinian East Jerusalem group, which over the years was to prove the most important factor in the leadership of the territories. The eminent *New York Times* columnist Tom Friedman introduced me to Dr Sari Nusseibeh and thereafter we held many conversations, trying to locate points of agreement in relation to both the interim agreement of self-rule for the Palestinians for five years, and permanent settlement between Israel and its Palestinian neighbour.

Sari's father, Anwar Nusseibeh, formerly a minister in the Jordanian government, I had known years before when I was present at the talks he held with Peres and the then mayor of Jerusalem Teddy Kollek at his home in East Jerusalem. He was suffering from throat cancer and speech was difficult for him, but in conversation he showed himself reasonable, experienced and pragmatic, believing it possible to obtain an acceptable compromise between the two peoples. In Sari I found an interlocutor easy to talk to. A few months younger than me, a native of East Jerusalem who had studied at Oxford, gained his doctorate from Harvard and married a British woman, he was endowed with a lively sense of humour and a thorough knowledge of Israeli society and Israeli politics. He once confided to me that in his twenties he had adopted an extreme anti-Israel stance and was considerably less pragmatic than his father, but over the years he had begun to appreciate the complexity of the situation, coming to the conclusion that compromise was the only answer.

I appeared with Sari Nusseibeh on numerous occasions in the world's communications network, in particular the BBC, which even commissioned a special programme about the two of us, and I hoped that one day I would be able to sit down with him at the negotiating table and reach an agreement which met the requirements of both sides.

My conversations with Nusseibeh as with others were intended to give me a better understanding of what were likely to be the minimum demands of the Palestinian side. Together with Yair Hirschfeld I set up meetings with Ziyad Abu Ziyad, editor of *Gesher*, a journalist and lawyer who also represented the pragmatic wing of the Palestinian leadership in the territories, with Radwan Abu Ayyash, one of the most respected Palestinian journalists, with Hana Siniora, editor of *El-Fajar*, with Elias Freij, mayor of Bethlehem since 1977, with Hannan Ashrawi, the prominent Christian-Palestinian academic and leader and, after his release from detention, with Faisal Husseini, the most significant Palestinian leader in East Jerusalem.

Conversations with these last two were especially frequent. They were hosted by Hirschfeld and Boaz Karni in Tel Aviv, in Jerusalem at Faisal Husseini's home in the east of the city, in a private apartment in Jerusalem and at Hannan's house in Ramallah. Hannan was very cautious in Husseini's presence, and usually he did most of the talking. Husseini behaved like a natural leader, and at his house there was always a long queue of Palestinians waiting to consult him. At one of our meetings in his house he told us we would never guess what his last consultation had involved. We offered several possibilities, without success. Finally he said: 'There was a dispute here over the ownership of a chicken, and I had to keep a straight face and adjudicate.'

Imprisonment has left in him no legacy of hatred. He is a man of pragmatism and humour. Many of the talks with him concerned technical problems, entry permits to the territories, summer visits and the like. Ashrawi was more interested in issues of principle and her speeches gave an impression of profound bitterness.

After the elections of 1988 I entered the Knesset for the first time, but this was not a particularly exhilarating experience in view of the comprehensive defeat inflicted upon the Labour Party mandate. I was among the most extreme opponents of the establishment of a government of national unity. In the party political bureau, in a secret ballot, we succeeded in outvoting the combined position of Rabin and Peres, but in the central committee there was a majority for the supporters of Unity government, and in the government that was formed under the leadership of Likud's Yitzhak Shamir I served as deputy Finance Minister.

In government we felt somewhat constrained. Peres, who would have preferred the Foreign Ministry, accepted the Treasury portfolio under pressure from the kibbutzim, the trade unions and Rabin. Haim Ramon, who was one of the most vociferous opponents of Unity government, found himself head of the faction and deputy – in rotation – to Sarah Doron, chair of the coalition. I enjoyed my new role but I had difficulty reconciling myself to the situation into which I had been thrown, remembering that in the previous term Shamir had torpedoed the Hussein–Peres agreement, and now we were returning to government under his leadership, without even rotation and without any genuine ability to devise solutions to the new problems facing us, which included the *intifada*.

The episode of the negotiations between the PLO and the USA was illustrative, both of the difficulties of functioning within a Unity government and of the prodigious effort required for the changing of positions in response to a changing reality. On 14 December 1988, following the decision taken in November of the same year by the Palestinian National Council in Algiers, and following negotiations between the USA and the PLO which had taken place in Sweden through the intermediary of Foreign Minister Sten Anderson and with the participation of representatives of the American Jewish community, including Rita Hauser and Stanley Scheinbaum, Yasser Arafat – then the arch-enemy of Israel – appeared at UN headquarters in Geneva, where he informed a news conference of a change in the PLO's position. Arafat announced that the PLO accepted Resolutions 242 and 338 as a basis for negotiations, condemned all forms of terror and was ready to enter into negotiations with Israel in the context of an international conference. The following day the American Secretary of State George Shultz, himself on the verge of retirement with the end of Reagan's presidency, announced the opening of direct negotiations with the PLO. Prime Minister Yitzhak Shamir denounced the decision, Peres said this was a sad day for Israel, and I told a Voice of Israel interviewer that I saw this as the beginning of a new era. I was in the minority.

Rabin and Peres had agreed between themselves, on entry into government, that if within a year there were no political progress the Labour Party would leave the coalition. In the Knesset we constituted – members of the Mashov (Avrum Burg and myself) and members of a group called after the name of the agricultural school 'The Green Village' (Haim Ramon, Amir Peretz, Nawaf Massalhah and Haggai Merom) – the sextet of MKs (Member of Knesset) who, when joined by Nissim Zvilli, secretary of the moshavim (agricultural co-operatives) movement, acted together as a pressure group, campaigning for secession from the government and departure into opposition.

In the meantime, as an MK I continued with my political activities in the party and in the Mashov caucus, inviting Faisal Husseini to address members of the caucus at Labour Party headquarters. This was a quasi-historic event since appearances by Husseini in Israel were extremely rare, and he had never before been seen in such a setting. The media, electronic as well as print-based, were in attendance. I said a few introductory words and Husseini followed me. He began by saying: 'I am your enemy.'

I wondered why he chose precisely those words at this first meeting. Evidently he too had a public, and a public perplexed by his willingness to enter Labour Party headquarters and there address representatives of one of the two ruling parties. This was not a trivial episode. Husseini stressed his desire for a solution and the need for compromise, but his opening words resounded ominously in our ears.

Criticism of the event, both from the right and from within the Labour Party, was ferocious. The then secretary-general of the Labour Party, Micha Harish, denounced the caucus for entertaining Husseini and said that if he had had foreknowledge of the event he would have prevented it happening. The critics became reticent when asked to explain their objections. After all, Husseini was not reckoned – at least in legal terms – a member of the PLO. This was a spontaneous and widespread reaction, arising from the consensus that there was nobody to talk to and nothing to discuss, from the suspicion that the very fact of meeting the other side was tantamount to agreeing with the other side's point of view. Just as Husseini could not enter Labour Party headquarters in Tel Aviv without telling us he was our enemy, so Harish felt that, if he did not denounce the very meeting, someone would call him to account for it. He had a public too!

Criticisms are one thing, actions another. Husseini's appearance created a precedent. He continued to address gatherings in various parts of the country and was invited to debates at party conferences; dialogue with him came to be seen as legitimate. Plotting a course against the tide, knowing from the start that one's actions or words are sure to be unpopular, and, in spite of that, creating a fact that cannot possibly be ignored – this was my *modus operandi*. My objective at this stage was to increase as far as possible the number of 'kosher' interlocutors, to identify possible common denominators and arrive at informal accords with the Palestinian leadership, thus proving to Peres, Rabin and the institutions of the Labour Party that agreement really was attainable. My assessment was that abstention from dialogue, from contact with the PLO and even from talks with Husseini and Ashrawi derived from fear of arriving at a moment of truth and discovering that there really was nothing to discuss: the Palestinians being unwilling to separate interim from permanent settlement, and the permanent settlement demanded by the Palestinians – a Palestinian state with the 1949 (The Green-line which is the ceasefire borders at the end of the 1948 war) or even 1947 borders (that is, the original UN map) and Jerusalem as its capital, return of the Palestinian refugees to Israel and eradication of all Jewish settlements – being a prospect which the Labour Party obviously could not countenance.

On 15 February 1989 there was a lengthy meeting at the guest-house of the Notre Dame Church in Jerusalem between a Palestinian delegation led by Faisal Husseini and an Israeli delegation led by me. This was one of a series of meetings held by the Mashov caucus for purposes of formulating policy. Here we were exposed to Palestinian frustration, to their lack of trust in us and also to differences among them, since those participating represented various trends within the Palestinian camp: Ziyad Abu Ziyad, Mamduh Alakat, Ghasan el Khatib, Halil Marshi, Sari Nusseibeh, Hannan Michael and Samaan Khouri. Our team included Avrum Burg, Ephraim

Sneh, Nimrod Novik, Aryeh Ofri (formerly Novik's deputy in the Prime Minister's office), Boaz Karni and Yair Hirschfeld.

The Palestinians expressed disappointment at the insignificant role of the Labour Party in Yitzhak Shamir's new government. They wanted to understand the difference between the view of the party hierarchy and our approach, and to voice their opinions on the idea of elections in the territories for a Palestinian team which would negotiate with Israel.

Husseini was the first to speak. He said that on both sides there was fear and anxiety about the other, and it was our role to respond to the fear and show that anxiety was unnecessary. For this to be achieved, the Palestinians had to have a better understanding of Israeli society and not see it in terms of black and white, and the Israeli elite had to have a better understanding of what was really going on within the Palestinian leadership, the various trends within it and its relationship with PLO-Tunis. 'At the very least you need to understand that we are part of the PLO,' he said. 'From our point of view you could say that we represent the PLO, but according to your law, we are the ones you're allowed to sit down with, so let's carry on sitting...'

Husseini dismissed the notion of elections in the territories. According to him, the results would be a foregone conclusion, only giving legitimacy to an unsatisfactory situation. 'These elections haven't been planned for our benefit,' said Mamduh Alakat, 'they're supposed to stop the *intifada* or create an alternative leadership.' 'How can you talk about elections while denying freedom of assembly and freedom of political expression?' asked Ghasan el Khatib.

Ziyad Abu Ziyad was less dogmatic about the elections. He asked which law (Israeli or Palestinian) would cover arrangements for elections in the territories, and whether it would not be more appropriate to hold a referendum. Hannan Michael represented the traditional position regarding linkage of interim self-rule and permanent settlements: 'We need a defined objective for the end of the process. Partial steps will not be acceptable without recognition of identity, self-determination, the establishment of a Palestinian state.' And Halil Marshi added: 'When we have agreed on principles we can discuss the principle of elections. In the meantime even the Labour Party is saying no to the PLO, no to a Palestinian state. Even you, the doves, are not putting any new positions forward.' Mamduh Alakat suggested that members of the Mashov caucus should come and inspect Palestinian casualties in the hospitals; perhaps this might change their minds and lead them to espouse alternative policies.

Among the Palestinians there was a lot of hostility to Rabin. El Khatib claimed that, although the Rabin plan for Palestinian elections contained some positive elements, the latter were utterly negated by what the Minister of Defence was actually doing in the territories. The most important priority was to limit military repression, stop the deportations and open the universities. The PLO had taken a substantive step in November 1988 by adopting a moderate line and now a substantive step was needed from the Israeli side, not just a vague statement of willingness to hold elections in the territories. Ziyad Abu Ziyad said that Rabin's sole objective was to portray the Palestinians as trouble-makers, and that Israel had made a minimal response to the PLO's generous initiative.

In turn, we stated our positions. We criticised them for their attitude towards the *intifada*, while making a considerable effort to find ways of bridging the gap between the two sides. The meeting was too big and the issues too complex for substantial progress to be made, but we all sensed how vital this dialogue was. We discovered new things, they admitted they had discovered new things, and we agreed to meet again in a similar forum. In fact it was to be a long time before such a meeting would again be possible.

The holding of this meeting – which was never meant to be publicised – became public knowledge and again there was criticism that a deputy minister had participated in meetings with Palestinian groups such as these. According to the headlines I was the most senior government representative ever to have met these Palestinian individuals, and inevitably my boss Shimon Peres was held responsible. I had not in fact asked for permission to host the meetings since I did not see them as anything exceptional. In the end it was Rabin who came to my defence, declaring that any Palestinian not in prison was by definition not a member of the PLO, and therefore meeting such a person was absolutely legal.

Rabin believed in the need to maintain the Unity government, and his commitment to Peres to leave it if there were no real progress towards peace led him to put pressure on Prime Minister Shamir to adopt a political initiative which could be set before the Arabs and the Americans. What emerged was an initiative of a decidedly 'Likudite' nature, very much in the spirit of Camp David: an extremely narrow raft of proposals, incapable of facilitating a solution but just enough, perhaps, to lead to the opening of talks. As far as Rabin was concerned it was an achievement. The initiative was concerned not with settling the Israeli–Palestinian dispute, but with a solution to the refugee problem. Wherever Palestinians were mentioned the expression used was 'Palestinian Arabs, residents of Judaea, Samaria and the Gaza Strip'. It was stated explicitly that Israel would not engage in talks with the PLO and there was no question of an 'additional' state emerging in Gaza or between Israel and Jordan. The proposal was to initiate 'dialogue' with residents of the territories, with Jordan and with Egypt, leading to agreement on the form of elections to be held in Judaea, Samaria and Gaza. The representatives chosen in these elections would conduct negotiations over the five-year period of the interim settlement and would also manage internal Palestinian issues during these five years; they would constitute a crucial component of the delegation that would eventually negotiate with Israel over the permanent settlement. In these negotiations over the permanent settlement, there would also be participation by Jordan.

A few weeks before this, Peres had been taken ill during a visit to the north and had been admitted to the Valley hospital in Afula for treatment. As his deputy, I had to take full responsibility for financial affairs, and I did not have the time to follow political developments as closely as I usually did. When Peres returned to Tel Aviv, a cabinet meeting was held in his home and there the initiative was approved. It was ratified by the government on 14 May 1989. When I saw the document in its entirety, remarkably reminiscent of a Likud manifesto, I criticised it vehemently at a meeting of 'our ministers' (Labour ministers and their deputies) and said that I would have preferred no agreement at all to acceptance of such a vapid plan. 'A few years from now someone is going to read this, and wonder what could have possessed us to vote for a combination of Begin's dream of never reaching a settlement and Golda's belief that there's no such thing as a Palestinian people.' In spite of my protests, the plan went ahead.

Now that the proposal had become a fact, it was necessary to make the best of it, the first priority being elections in the territories, which were supposed to change the political picture and open a new chapter. I spoke to the Palestinian leaders in East Jerusalem and was relieved by their pragmatism. They were prepared to organise a Palestinian delegation if the PLO leadership in Tunis agreed to participate in the new game.

Because the 14 May plan had not succeeded in answering the question of with whom Israel was now going to speak to set the rules of the elections, the whole political debate turned into a rerun of the perennial query: 'Who to talk to?' The solution to this suggested by the Camp David accords was that negotiations over elections in the territories should be conducted between Israel and delegations from Jordan and Egypt which could include Palestinians from Judaea and Samaria and any other 'mutually acceptable' parties. Rightly, this sentence did not recur in the new initiative and what was envisaged was a separate but undefined Palestinian delegation.

The new American Secretary of State James Baker now came into the picture, working hard and with great professionalism to solve an apparently technical but age-old question. On the one hand this was being discussed with Israel, while on the other consultations had begun in Tunis between Yasser Abd Rabbo, a former member of the PFLP who had joined Arafat, and Robert Pelletreau, United States ambassador in Tunis. These consultations, which Israel criticised, were concerned at this stage with the establishment and composition of a delegation for talks with Israel.

The Middle Ages returned. Our ambassadors were prohibited from obtaining information on talks with the PLO. If an American diplomat tried to consult the Israeli ambassador on the status of the PLO in future negotiations, the ambassador was supposed to ask politely that the conversation be terminated. The law banning contacts of any kind with the PLO, the prohibition on receiving information on the status of the PLO and the government's absurd plan – all of these combined to create a blind alley. Shamir was quite at ease with the situation, Rabin still believed there was something to be gained from a position of strength, and Peres increasingly felt himself a prisoner of a government that did not inspire him and a job (he was still Finance Minister) that was not his lifelong aspiration.

It was my assessment that the clearer the components of the permanent settlement became to the PLO, the easier it would be for it to agree to the immediate opening of negotiations on elections in the territories. In March 1989, Max van der Stoll, the former Dutch Foreign Minister, appeared on the scene, suggesting to Shimon Peres that he establish secret lines of communication with the Palestinians in Holland. Peres refused, but Nimrod Novik proposed to Yair Hirschfeld and to me that we examine what was on offer. Van der Stoll initiated meetings between Yair and

Hannan Ashrawi, and it was agreed that a joint effort be made to prepare a Dutch-sponsored protocol which would be acceptable to Palestinian and Israeli elements, address the permanent settlement and improve the chances of obtaining agreement on the interim settlement. Van der Stoll wanted to introduce me to a representative of the PLO with a view to engaging in a marathon negotiating session. I told him I couldn't hold talks with a PLO representative as long as the law prohibiting contact with the organisation remained in force. He accepted this and asked to be informed in advance of my next visit to Holland.

In July I took advantage of a trip which had been planned for the purpose of examining a computerised tax system (as deputy Finance Minister, I headed a committee dealing with this at home) and informed him accordingly. Hirschfeld arrived separately and we met in the Hague. Van der Stoll told us that Abdullah Hourani, a member of the executive committee of the PLO was a guest in another hotel in the city, with Afif Safiya, PLO representative in Holland, and that he was interested in putting together a joint statement of principles for solving the Israeli–Palestinian dispute. All that day, a Saturday, van der Stoll was shuttling between the two hotels with proposals for reasonable compromise, realisation of Palestinian rights, security for Israel and Israeli withdrawal from territories in the West Bank and Gaza. The intention of the former Foreign Minister was to get a green light from both sides, to publish the paper as a Dutch protocol and obtain immediate support from the Israeli Labour Party and from the PLO leadership, so that this statement of principles could serve as a point of reference and enable the leadership of the PLO to agree to the opening of negotiations with Israel on the issue of elections in the territories, without receiving official guarantees from Israel relating to the permanent settlement.

The draft was signed by Max van der Stoll in his capacity as chairman of the Dutch Labour Party. In a preamble he referred to the series of conversations held over recent months, with senior representatives of the Israeli Labour Party and of the PLO, on the basis of which he had reason to believe that there existed between the two sides an understanding on the principles of a permanent solution: implementation of Security Council Resolutions 242 and 338; provision for Israel's security needs; recognition of the right to self-determination of the Palestinian people; willingness to accept the interim settlement as a part of the overall settlement; agreement that the permanent settlement would include a solution to the problem of the Palestinian refugees; opposition to all forms of terrorism; Palestinian readiness to hold elections in the occupied territories in a framework of agreed conditions; agreement that the permanent agreement should be signed in the context of an international conference.

In the draft of his document van der Stoll said that the leadership of the PLO had confirmed to him that these principles would be accepted by it, if confirmed by the Israeli government, and it demanded that elections be held both in the occupied territories and in East Jerusalem. If this demand were accepted, the PLO would authorise representatives of the territories to open dialogue with the Israeli government with the object of clarifying the principles of the elections and the linkage between them and the permanent settlement. These representatives could consult with whomever they liked. The Israeli spokesmen had expressed their willingness to canvass for broader acceptance of these principles within the Labour Party and in the public at large.

I felt this was a good paper, because it responded to Palestinian needs without requiring recognition of the PLO. Nor was there any reference in it to the status of Jerusalem. The main problem was recognition of the right to self-determination of the Palestinians. Personally I was quite at ease with the concept and I reckoned that a fair number of Labour members would join me. From the point of view of the government and even of the party leadership, this was likely to be a stumbling-block.

But in the end we were not put to the test. When we returned to Israel I showed the paper to some of my colleagues. Avrum Burg was aware of the process and had also met Van der Stoll. He concurred with the document, as did Uzi Baram (the former Secretary General of the Labour Party and a committed dove), but we soon heard from Holland that the PLO was not happy with it and would not support it if van der Stoll published it. They suggested a supplementary meeting to debate the protocol. We did not agree to a second trip. Nimrod Novik and Yair Hirschfeld were involved in attempts to evaluate other versions to overcome the dispute. I could not justify another visit to Holland, and the document was not published, although there were important elements in it which would be of use to me in the future and through which I could learn something of the PLO's thought-processes.

Hourani himself, whom I never met, later proved to be one of the extremists in the Palestinian camp. He vehemently opposed the Oslo Accord and resigned in protest from the executive committee of the PLO.

Later still he moved to Gaza and became one of Arafat's advisers.

In a speech which I delivered in Tel Aviv, in the context of the Germany–Israel Coexistence Fund, I decided to call for negotiations with the PLO and put an end to the pretence whereby we were declaring to the world that we would never negotiate with it, while in fact holding indirect talks with it through the intermediary of the Americans in Tunis. My speech infuriated Likud: how is it that a deputy minister in the government of national unity dares to call for talks with the PLO in contravention of the official policy of his government? Amid a barrage of calls for my dismissal, Haim Korfu, a former minister then serving as chairman of the House committee – which deals with the Knesset regulations – tabled an oral question to the Finance Minister concerning the statements of his deputy. Peres passed the question on to me, as though it were one of the many questions which I used to answer every week dealing with taxes and duties, prices of raw materials and a long list of other topics belonging to the day-to-day business of the Treasury.

The matter was brought before the Knesset on 26 July 1989, and when Haim Korfu saw me rising to answer the question, he lost his temper and demanded to know how it was that the Minister was appointing his deputy 'to answer questions directly concerning relations and trust between him and his deputy. It is tactless on the part of the Finance Minister to ask his deputy to answer the question.' The Speaker assured him that there was nothing unconstitutional about this, and Korfu put his question to the Finance Minister:

In an interview on IDF [Israel Defence Forces] Radio on 13 July 1989, the deputy Finance Minister, Yossi Beilin MK, stated that in fact Israel had been conducting negotiations with the PLO for the past two and a half months, through the intermediary of the USA. The same day a statement was issued on your behalf – that is on behalf of the Finance Minister and on behalf of the Prime Minister's office – denying these reports. In your broadcast on IDF Radio at 11.00 a.m. on the Sabbath, you pointed out that our refusal to speak to the PLO had achieved the result that the PLO had withdrawn from its original position and now favoured restraint. I should appreciate an answer from the honourable Minister: 1. Which of these statements is true? 2. If the statements of Mr Beilin are untrue, why don't you draw the obvious conclusions regarding his fitness to serve as deputy Finance Minister?

My answer was brief:

1. a) The only error in my statement was that the negotiations began on 14 May 1989, and on 13 July they had been in progress for only two months and not two and a half as I stated. b) Direct talks with representatives of the PLO in the territories have been proceeding somewhat longer. If anyone chooses to regard Jamal Taarifi [who had met Prime Minister Shamir at that time] as a representative of the consumer protection agency – that is his prerogative. c) Indirect contacts with the PLO are taking place not only through the intermediary of the USA but also through Egypt, Rumania and European states. All these parties are passing messages from one side to the other. d) In 1981 the government of Israel negotiated with the PLO through the intermediary of Philip Habib. Those negotiations brought about the ceasefire, which lasted from July 1981 to June 1982.

2. Since these statements are true, I see no reason why my fitness for office should be called into question.

Korfu was not satisfied. As a supplementary question he demanded clarification:

Am I to understand from your answer that the Finance Minister is telling me that for two and a half months direct negotiations have been conducted with the PLO, not only through the intermediary of the United States but also through other states? If this is the Finance Minister's answer, how is it possible that the same day, in a subsequent radio broadcast, he has the nerve to say the opposite, and the next day finds a reason why it is not necessary to talk to the PLO?

If the first question and first answer were read from a text, the supplementary question and the answer to it were definitely oral. I replied:

Regarding the alleged discrepancy between my statements and those of the Finance Minister – there is no such discrepancy. Direct negotiation with the PLO is not taking place. Indirect negotiations with the PLO have been taking place since the government's decision on the issue of elections in the territories. Any sensible person is aware of this. Whether you approve of it or deplore it, it cannot be denied that negotiation with the PLO on this issue is proceeding. It has one objective: to get from the PLO a 'green light' for elections in the territories. It seems to me there is no disagreement on this...

These words caused uproar in the debating chamber of the Knesset, in the country at large and abroad. For the first time a government official had confirmed that Israel was waiting for a green light from the PLO. The Prime Minister was apoplectic with rage. This was precisely the information he wanted to suppress. He could not reconcile himself to the fact that prolonged negotiations were proceeding between Israel and the PLO through the intermediary of the American State Department, and he continued to live in a world of his own in which the Palestinians were ignored, those who were recognised were only Jordanians and Israeli Arabs. My speech tore away the mask from a political fact that he could not live with. In a long and detailed letter to Peres he demanded my dismissal.

Naturally it did not occur to Peres to accede to this request. After all, I had merely exposed the true situation. The government which had inscribed on its flag its opposition to talks with the PLO now found itself waiting impatiently for a decision from Tunis. Peres wrote a detailed reply to Shamir explaining his decision. Shamir was not mollified, but there was nothing he could do – other than dismiss Peres himself, since, according to the law as it then stood, the Prime Minister had no powers to dismiss deputy ministers. This was a legal loophole which MK Tzachi Hanegbi made haste to plug, tabling a law which would enable the Prime Minister to sack deputy ministers. By the time this law came into effect we were already in opposition, but it was a very significant law, adding as it did to the many autocratic rights enjoyed by a Prime Minister elected directly by the people.

On 3 October 1989 Abbie Nathan, the 'peace sailor', was sentenced to six months' imprisonment, plus a year's imprisonment suspended for three years, on charges of making contact with PLO representatives. I went to visit him in Eyal prison, feeling thoroughly depressed. The law is the law even when it is a foolish law, and anyone who knowingly flouts it must expect punishment. Everything is as it should be – and yet there is something twisted. If there is a law in Israel which puts a peace campaigner like Abbie Nathan behind bars for the offence of meeting the Palestinian leadership, and if I am serving as a deputy minister in a government that is not prepared to repeal this law, then something has to change. Either the law is changed, or we withdraw our support from the government.

Abbie was in despair; having to endure prison life was torment to him. The injustice in the situation was shocking, but there was nothing I could do to help him. I promised him I would do everything in my power to get the law changed, but everything in my power did not amount to much at that time.

In January 1990 we – members of the sextet of Mashov–Green Village group – had the feeling that it would be preferable to leave the government and campaign in opposition for negotiations with the Palestinians, or to set up an alternative government which would agree on a formula and start immediate negotiations over elections in the territories. At the close of the Sabbath, the 6th of the month, our group convened at Peres's home in Tel Aviv. It was a very amicable session. All of us, with the exception of Amir Peretz, were reckoned his staunch supporters. We told him that we felt the unity government had come to the end of the road, the peace process had become a joke and it was obvious that Shamir had no interest in advancing it, while our presence in the government gave legitimacy and a peace-seeking façade to the Likud administration. We stressed to him that, if it were feasible to establish a minority government in alliance with the religious parties, this would be our preferred option. Otherwise, our first priority was to dissolve the government, and we preferred to go into opposition and fight our corner from there.

Peres heard us out but was not enthusiastic. Rather than answering, he asked questions. He was the experienced veteran leader, we the impatient Young Turks. The meeting dragged on and when it finally ended we sensed that Shimon understood our message and was himself unhappy with the way things were going, but was not convinced that departure into the wilderness of opposition was the right course. We agreed to meet again soon, telling him we intended to talk to Rabin as well.

I was unable to attend the meeting with Rabin, which took place soon afterwards, but according to my colleagues it had been a much more difficult session. Rabin did not believe it possible to advance the peace process by means of a minority government, even if this could be established under Peres's leadership, which he also doubted. He disagreed with our group's assessment that Shamir was not interested in peace and maintained that it was still worth waiting to see whether the 14 May initiative would facilitate talks with the Palestinians about the holding of elections. It was Rabin's habit to coin phrases for things that he didn't like, and from that time onward he took to calling us 'Demolitions Inc.'.

We didn't see this as an insult. To 'demolish' this misguided government was precisely what we wanted.

It was at about this time that the Ezer Weizmann episode occurred. Weizmann was Minister of Science in the national unity government headed by Shamir. At the end of December 1989 Shamir demanded of Peres that he agree to Weizmann's expulsion from the government on account of his meeting with Nabil Ramallawi, PLO representative in Geneva. Weizmann insisted this had been a chance encounter in a hotel, and not contact as such. Shamir met with Labour ministers and tried to convince them that the proposed expulsion was justified. I suggested that, if Weizmann were removed, all Labour ministers should resign in protest. Rabin thought otherwise. Both he and Shamir feared disintegration of the unity government and in January 1990 a compromise was proposed whereby Weizmann was expelled from the inner cabinet but remained in the government. I was vehemently opposed to this compromise. It was shameful to see a former Commander of the Air Force and Defence Minister of Israel excluded from the security cabinet on suspicion of contact with a PLO representative in Europe. But my protests were unavailing, and, when Weizmann himself accepted the compromise, it was confirmed.

This was not the end of the affair. The government's legal adviser, Yosef Harish, ordered an investigation into allegations that Weizmann had contravened anti-terrorism orders; it was not until mid-February, when no evidence against Weizmann had been found, that Harish decided to close the file.

It was an open secret that James Baker's questions to Shamir were proposed to the Secretary of State by no other than Moshe Arens, Shamir's foreign minister, who had thought that they were good questions for his boss. When Shamir replied negatively to these questions and when discussion was resumed on the issue of the composition of the Palestinian delegation which would hold talks with Israel on the choice of a delegation to negotiate – this was too much even for Rabin's patience and he lent his support, reluctantly but resolutely, to dissolution. Arye Deri, a minister from the Shas religious party, persuaded him that the prospects of forming an alternative government were good, and so he donned his skullcap and went to call on the rabbis.

We succeeded in dissolving the government, but failed to establish a new one. In March 1990, for the first time ever, a government in Israel fell as the result of a no-confidence vote. In April Labour's attempts to form a government in alliance with Agudat Israel foundered, and in June a right-wing–religious coalition took office. The Labour Party was in opposition. Rabin described the attempt to set up an alternative government as a 'despicable exercise', in spite of his own deep involvement in the project. In July he tried to undermine Peres's leadership by bringing forward the decision on the choice of the party's candidate for the premiership in 1992, and in this he failed. The old rivalry between him and Peres was rekindled, and the Labour Party looked forward with pessimism to the forthcoming elections.

In the meantime there was to be no neglect of the peace process. The minority Likud government had effectively halted the process, with the result that James Baker went so far as to remind Shamir, publicly, of the White House telephone number, just in case he might want to get in touch. Our role was to keep up the pressure of criticism on the government and try to crystallise policy directions of our own for the future.

Shortly after the installation of Shamir's new government (with David Levy as Foreign Minister, Moshe Arens as Minister of Defence, Ariel Sharon as Minister of Housing and Construction, Rafael Eitan as Minister of Agriculture, Yuval Ne'eman as Science Minister and, in a later appointment, Rehavam Zeevi as Minister without Portfolio), I began talking to Sari Nusseibeh with the object of obtaining a joint protocol which could be signed by MKs from Labour, Mapam, Ratz and Shinui and by Palestinian leaders in East Jerusalem and would prepare the way for future negotiations between the two sides. It was important to me to be sure that the Palestinian side hadn't lost hope and was aware that a very large section of Israeli society was in favour of reaching a historic compromise.

We drafted the protocol in a series of meetings in the Larom Hotel in Jerusalem, and on completion it was shown by both sides to those invited to attend the plenary session. This was convened in Notre Dame on 5 August 1990 and was the most important meeting we had held with Palestinians so far.

Faisal Husseini led the Palestinian group. Sari Nusseibeh, my collaborator in preparing the protocol, did not attend, being abroad at the time, and those present on the Palestinian side were Zahara Kamal, Sami Kilani, Salah Iyad, Ghasan el Khatib, Hannan Ashrawi, Faiz Kawasmeh, Abdel Rahman e-Turk, Ziyad Abu Ziyad, Radwan Abu Ayyash, Nicole Daabit and Rana Nashashibi. We were fifteen MKs from Labour, Mapam, Ratz and Shinui. Besides me, the Israeli team consisted of Navah Arad, Arieh (Lova)

Eliav, Amir Peretz, Avrum Burg, Amnon Rubinstein, Avraham Poraz, Ran Cohen, Dedi Zuker, Yossi Sarid, Shulamit Aloni, Mordecai Virschuvski, Yair Tzaban and Haim (Jumes) Oron.

If this meeting had taken place when originally scheduled, a week earlier, it would have been of a totally different nature. But we were unable to hold it then on account of an extended sitting of the Knesset. Three days after Iraq's invasion of Kuwait, with the PLO supporting Iraq, in the hot and stifling atmosphere of a hotel which had never heard of air-conditioning, it was not easy to focus on other issues. We saw the Iraqi incursion as a threat to Israel; those facing us – most if not all of them – were unhappy with Arafat's stance but were reluctant to criticise him. Hannan Ashrawi tried to walk a tightrope, explaining that the Palestinians opposed Iraq's invasion of Kuwait as they opposed any invasion, but the practicalities were much more complicated. For years Kuwait had served as a tool of the USA, she said, and as such it had played a negative role in Arab politics. Anyone who did not understand this would not understand the complex Arab reaction to recent events.

Husseini urged us all to turn to the issue of peace between us, which suddenly seemed much less controversial than the other topics on offer. He congratulated Sari and me on our success in producing an agreed protocol. Never, he said, had we reached consensus at such a senior level and over such a broad range of issues, and his assessment was that the efforts of the peace camp in shaping Israeli public opinion would help the Palestinian leadership to consolidate its position among the Palestinian public. 'Peace', he said, 'will not be built on a balance of forces, such as leads to a balance of fear. Genuine peace and security will be built only on the shared interests of the two peoples.'

Several of those present in that sauna were in years to come to play central roles in the peace process, but this was not known at the time. It seems to me that the only one who grasped the full significance of the meeting at the time was Ghasan el Khatib, who was very emotional. He said that this particular meeting represented a change in the level of willingness of the two peoples to institute dialogue between themselves. El Khatib admitted that the Palestinian position had shifted from insistence on rights at Israel's expense to a concept of compromise on the historic demands. 'That is correct!' Sami Kilani interrupted him. 'Palestinian demands have already been cut in half and the Israelis haven't budged at all. We're thinking about shared interests, but the government of Israel is concerned only with your interests.' Everyone talked about the international conference. Radwan Abu Ayyash said that such a conference would give an opportunity to all sides including Yitzhak Shamir's Israel to talk with the other Arab states, and this would be worth while whatever the eventual shape of the direct negotiations which should ultimately take place between Israel and the PLO. Husseini said that for peace to be assured international guarantees were required, and these would be given only in the context of an international conference.

The Israelis spoke at length. We said what we had to say about Iraq's invasion of Kuwait, about our expectations of the Palestinians, about the damage done by the *intifada* and the importance of the joint protocol. Many comments were raised concerning the document that we had prepared, but in the end it was endorsed by both sides. It was a short paper, entitled 'General Principles' and its content was as follows:

At a time of reconciliation between powers, when the Iron Curtain has been breached, when Europe is united after devastating wars, the Middle East dispute remains the longest-running unsolved political quarrel since the Second World War. This is a dispute between peoples whose roots spring from the same land, whose cultures and languages are similar and whose co-operation in all areas seems entirely natural.

The thousands of young men who have sacrificed their lives in the course of this dispute since the 1920s, out of passionate faith in the justice of their cause, the huge scale of resources dedicated to the acquisition of lethal weapons rather than to economic and social development – these have created our obligation to change the direction of the Middle East dispute and move towards peace.

Many mistakes have been made over the years by both peoples. We, representing the third generation of the conflict, feel an obligation to the fourth generation, to the future of our peoples and to the national interest of each of them, to advance the peace process.

The long years of violent struggle have proved that violence and terror have intensified the hatred but have solved nothing. We believe that a real solution can be based on peaceful measures without resort to violence of any kind.

Any solution will be based on the following principles:

1. The Israeli–Palestinian conflict is at the heart of the Middle East problem and it requires immediate resolution.

2. The Palestinians are entitled to self-determination like any other people, on

the basis of the UN Convention and the General Assembly resolution against colonialism (1960).

3. Any solution will be based on Security Council Resolutions 242 and 338, and any other resolutions bearing on the issue as may be agreed and implemented with immediate effect or in stages. Negotiation will take place between the government of Israel and the legitimate and internationally recognised representative of the Palestinian people. This negotiation may be assisted by the USA, the USSR, China and the European Community, in the context of an international conference, of a form to be mutually agreed, sponsored by the UN.

4. Neither side may determine on behalf of the other who is to represent the other in negotiations, and each side shall determine for itself who is to represent it, the only condition being that all participants accept the principles set out above.

The Israeli and international media were waiting for us in the lobby of the hotel. The document was presented as an important milestone; both sides felt that we had succeeded in moving the process forward and that the crisis in the Gulf would not interfere with long-term prospects.

But, as the crisis intensified, the process was pushed to the sidelines. During those dark days when Scuds were fired into the heart of Israel and we carried gas masks in the streets of Tel Aviv, when there were Palestinians who danced on the rooftops and celebrated the heroism of Saddam Hussein and what was perceived as our impotence, when Sari Nusseibeh was interned for – allegedly – reporting to the Iraqis on the accuracy of their missiles, it was hard to deal with James Baker's questions and with the composition of Palestinian delegations.

When the Gulf War was over Yossi Sarid published his article 'Don't Call Me!' in which he distanced himself from the leadership of the PLO on account of its support for the Iraqi despot. Soon after this I published an article rebutting Sarid's arguments. Anger with the PLO leadership was justified but the question remained: who was to replace it? No one seeking peace can say 'don't call me', as if he has more reasonable people to negotiate with, or alternatively is unconcerned by the stalling of the process. Punishing the PLO, in this instance, was punishing ourselves.

Paradoxically, it was the Gulf War which extricated the political talks from cold storage and led to James Baker's eight rounds of discussions in the region. In the Labour Party we took a preliminary decision on support for the establishment of a Jordanian–Palestinian confederation. This was preceded by a series of debates at Peres's home, leading to the acceptance of a formula which, though ultimately watered down somewhat, opened the way to this option. Although other confederations in the world (Switzerland, Canada) are one country, technically the term denotes association between two or more states; thus for the first time the Labour Party took a position which did not absolutely rule out the possible establishment of a Palestinian state.

In August 1991 the Labour central committee decided on the basis of the Baker talks, that residents of East Jerusalem could be elected to the future Palestinian Council if they had another address outside Jerusalem. All these decisions were designed to establish party obligations in readiness for the Israeli elections due in 1992, showing that the Labour Party was offering a genuine alternative to the policies of this right-wing administration.

In December of the previous year (1990) I had gone public with a proposal whereby Israeli forces would withdraw from the Gaza Strip, permitting the establishment of a Palestinian state in Gaza, on the assumption that the territory of such a state could be extended to include parts of the West Bank only when peace existed between Israel and its neighbours. The Palestinian state could establish confederation with Jordan, this being Israel's preferred solution.

With this proposal, worked out in collaboration with Yair Hirschfeld, I intended both to challenge the taboo on speaking of a Palestinian state and to revive the old notion of 'Gaza first', which had never taken on any substance, being understood simply as a proposal to initiate autonomy in Gaza before extending it to the West Bank.

When I put my plan forward, on the evening news on television, it attracted widespread criticism. In Likud it was alleged that Labour's secret agenda, to establish a Palestinian state, had finally been revealed, and within the Labour Party there were complaints that the proposal was at odds with the party's programme, and that such a state was likely to be hostile to us and at the service of foreign elements. Although the USSR was then on the verge of disintegration, the hawks in the party still dreaded the installation of a Soviet enclave in the heart of the Middle East. Even my good friend Haim Ramon spoke out in public against what he called 'the Balfour Declaration of the Palestinian state'; according to his preference, Israel should simply pull out of Gaza and avoid any involvement in its political future.

This public debate flared up on the eve of my departure for Cairo to attend a series of meetings. This was at the initiative of Dr Osama Elbaz, political adviser to President Mubarak, and I was on the point of flying to the Egyptian capital in a plane belonging to Danny Abram, an American Jew who had contributed a great deal to the peace process with shuttle flights to Cairo and Damascus. Some members of the Knesset, led by Dr Michael Bar Zohar, appealed to me not to go to Egypt, on the ground that the journey, coming so soon after the publication of my proposal, would create the impression that I was in Egypt specifically to discuss a Palestinian state.

The party secretary-general, Micha Harish, sent me a long letter which he also saw fit to publish, criticising what he called my 'two obsessions' – negotiating with the rabbis and negotiating with the PLO – and demanded I cancel the trip.

So my journey to Egypt, originally planned as a means of exchanging views and keeping communications open, assumed considerable political significance, against a background of intense controversy at home. Dr Elbaz told me that the proposal that I had raised, to allow the establishment of a Palestinian state in Gaza, was seen by him and his colleagues as an interesting possibility, on condition that there would be linkage between such a state and the West Bank. This linkage could be established by means of a referendum to be held in the West Bank five years after the inauguration of the Palestinian state, allowing the residents to decide which entity they preferred to belong to.

In retrospect, Elbaz's assessment of future events related to the PLO was all too accurate. He reckoned that the PLO's support of Saddam Hussein would weaken it but not wipe it off the map. In his view, there would be elements in the Arab world unsuccessfully calling for the replacement of Arafat with someone more amenable to them. In spite of its displeasure with the PLO and its leader, Egypt would not turn its back on him and, once tensions in the Gulf had eased, would help with the renewal of contacts for peace, in the context of an international conference sponsored by the USA and the USSR. A weakened PLO, he reckoned, could perhaps agree to compromises that it would earlier have rejected.

Osama Elbaz is one of the shrewdest and most perceptive members of the regional peace club. He has been following the process for years, is an expert in all its details, knows all the players and has clear opinions of them; he dislikes formality and avails himself of every opportunity to remove not only his tie but his shoes as well.

In the course of his career he has never wanted official appointments, and when he was offered the opportunity to serve as Foreign Minister he turned it down on account of the plethora of ceremonial duties associated with the post. He was content with the titles of political adviser to the President and deputy director-general of the Foreign Ministry. He is into his sixties but behaves and looks like a much younger man in spite of health problems. When I served as political director-general of Israel's Foreign Ministry and later as well, I used to meet him at regular intervals; I would invariably be treated to a profound analysis of the situation from an entirely unofficial perspective.

Osama was right about many things, but mistaken in his predictions regarding the Gulf crisis. He believed Saddam Hussein would not risk military confrontation with the USA and would try to appease the Americans by withdrawing in two stages – first from Kuwait City and then from the surrounding area. In any case, even if hostilities did break out, Saddam would not dare attack Israel.

The only one who offered an alternative analysis was the chairman of the foreign committee of the People's Assembly, Dr Muhammad Abdallah, whom I had known since the time of Sadat. He believed that we were on the verge of war in the Gulf and that, the moment the Americans attacked Iraq, Iraq would attack Israel, but it would all be over by March. He was right in every particular.

The Foreign Minister, Amr Moussa, I had known when he was his country's ambassador to the UN, and in a conversation with him I suggested that he invite David Levy to visit Egypt, as one who was more moderate in his views than most of his colleagues. I had a third meeting with Boutros Boutros Ghali, Secretary of State for Foreign Affairs (which means a senior deputy minister), whom I had first encountered, and befriended, in the late 1970s. He asked me how the peace camp in Israel could be encouraged in the current situation. I suggested that he invite our sextet of MKs to Egypt for in-depth political discussions. He liked the idea of entertaining the 'younger generation' and promised to set this in motion as soon as tension in the Gulf had eased. The outbreak of war – which took us completely by surprise – delayed the project for a few months.

One of the topics that I raised with him concerned an episode from the past. I asked him whether the Sadat–Begin meeting, which took place on the eve of the 1981 elections and dominated Likud's election broadcasts, had been coincidental or an intentional ploy to help Begin. Ghali laughed. 'Sadat was a Likudnik,' he told me. 'He was convinced by Ezer Weizmann that anyone prepared to withdraw from the whole of Sinai would pull out of the West Bank as well. He believed that, if Begin were re-elected, he could guarantee evacuation of Sinai and clearance of the West Bank settlements, and he wasn't sure that any other leader could deliver this. I'd read Begin's writings and I told the President, "Begin can't give up the West Bank, he's never going to do that." But Sadat ignored me and when Begin asked for a meeting in Sharm el-Sheikh just before the elections, he knew exactly why he wanted this and he played along, even though almost all his advisers told him not to get involved in an Israeli election campaign.'

Seeing my astonishment, he added that in the closing stages of the election, when it seemed that the coalition led by Peres had defeated Likud, the director of the Labour Party's foreign relations committee, Israel Gat, contacted Ghali and suggested that Sadat might like to send a congratulatory telegram to Peres. Sadat said to him, 'Tell Gat that you couldn't find me.' When he heard that Likud had won, he was relieved.

In 1991 Yair Hirschfeld and I set up the Economic Co-operation Foundation. We considered that part of the 'new world order' proclaimed by President Bush should also be a new regional order, and if we were going to make this work we would need to gain experience of co-operative living in many spheres of life in which there had been no previous attempts at co-operation between us and our Palestinian neighbours or the Arab states – from economic development to educational planning. We inaugurated the partnership in consultation with Max van der Stoll of Holland and with representatives of the European Community and the EC's ambassador to Israel, Gwynn Morgan. Together with Palestinian research units we began drawing up joint economic surveys. The partnership was a non-governmental organisation which was a useful preparation for the Oslo process, both because the economic appendices to the accords were the result of the research we had begun in 1991, and because it allowed Yair Hirschfeld and later his friend and acolyte Ron Pundak to devote all their time to the process. Subsequently, in the course of discussion of the permanent settlement in Stockholm, again the existence of the partnership made it possible to hold closed consultations on current issues, to institute research into problematical and sensitive topics and to devote a lot of time to the serious business of talking. This was the adoption of an American model of extra-governmental institutionalism which I operated until I was appointed a deputy minister and to which I returned at the end of my period in office as a cabinet minister, with the object of advancing the unofficial aspects of the political process.

Nineteen-ninety-one was my year of frenetic political activity. In May there was a conference of the Mashov caucus, the most important ever held. Many working groups had prepared for it: Avrum Burg concentrated on issues of religion and state, I focused on social issues, while discussion of the political agenda was a natural extension of our previous decisions. Burg called the conference 'the congress of the three separations': between Palestinians and Israel, religion and state, trade unions and the health service.

In a report entitled *The Peace Process* we called for exploitation of the propitious moment created in the wake of the ending of the Gulf War, to recognise the right to self-determination of the Palestinians and to talk with any Palestinian agency which recognised Israel's right to survive and eschewed terrorism, all this on the basis of Security Council Resolutions 242 and 338. In the absence of agreement, we called for the consideration of unilateral measures 'of which the objective is political separation between the peoples, given a preference for withdrawal from Gaza in the first instance'.

A month later, and following on from my previous conversation with Ghali, the sextet of MKs, plus Nissim Zvilli, received an invitation from the Egyptian government to visit Cairo and attend a series of political meetings. The visit took place on 12 June, arousing considerable interest as well as predictable and virulent criticism on the part of Likud, accusing us of jeopardising the government's efforts to achieve peace.

The visit had great significance over and above the meetings themselves, interesting as they were. It contributed to the cohesion of the group, to the crystallisation of its political approach and to the decision which we took to see the forthcoming party conference as an ideological crossroads, after which we would determine our future conduct. This was not a conventional episode, since the Egyptian government, our host, had invited our group specifically, rather than a delegation representing the various cliques and shades of opinion in the party. Again it was Dr Bar Zohar who was most critical of the project, even complaining to the Egyptian ambassador in Israel over the arbitrariness of the choice of the delegation.

Exactly a month later I travelled to Egypt again. The point at issue this time was the establishment of a committee to prepare the way for a conference which would supposedly take place under European sponsorship and address the prospects of peace in the aftermath of the Gulf War. The initiative for the conference had come from David and Simon Susskind, leading members of the Jewish community in Belgium and veteran peace campaigners, and from Israel the participants were MKs from Labour, Mapam and Ratz. André Azulai represented the King of Morocco in the discussions. Leader of the Egyptian group was Dr Elbaz, and he surprised us by including in his delegation Dr Nabil Shaath, a founding member of the PLO.

I had heard much about Shaath, who described himself as 'the Palestinian Abba Eban'. A specialist in business administration who had taught at the University of Beirut and in the USA, he owned a large computer firm in Cairo, was close to Arafat and believed in peace with Israel. He was born in Jaffa, his family was divided between Egypt and the USA, and a few years earlier he had suffered a personal tragedy when his wife was killed in a road accident.

This was not the first time that I had been obliged to avoid members of the PLO since the passing of that ridiculous law but this time, spurning his proffered handshake, I felt particularly disappointed: how can it be that Israeli law forbids me to talk peace with a Palestinian who wants peace and is in conflict with those who oppose it?

This was not a satisfactory debate from my point of view. Wrapped up in myself, unable to exchange a word with the Palestinians, unable to contribute, I felt utterly and unbearably helpless. I knew that if I was not allowed to talk with Dr Shaath, others would come and try to lead the Palestinian people, and I would be unable to talk to them since there would be nothing to discuss. After all, it is the 'who' that determines the 'what'.

I had a private meeting with Elbaz and he apologised for the embarrassment that he had caused me. He reckoned that, in the wake of the Gulf War and James Baker's efforts, an international conference would be convened before the end of 1991. He continued to criticise the leaders of the PLO for their conduct during the Gulf War, and he told me he had sent Arafat three draft statements, expressing a more measured response to Iraq's invasion of Kuwait, but he had declined to use any of them. Elbaz considered that many in the Palestinian camp were no friends of Iraq, but this did not mean that Arafat's leadership was in danger. As he had predicted before the war, now that it was over Arafat was still the only leader and there was no one who could take his place. Sooner or later Israel would have to talk to him directly.

Amr Moussa, whom I also met, told me that the first priority of the Egyptian Foreign Ministry was a solution of the Middle East dispute. He reckoned that Syria would agree to participate in the international conference, thereby making the conference viable. Abu Mazen had been visiting Cairo the same day, and from a conversation with him Moussa gained the impression that the PLO was prepared to accept a formula whereby it would not participate officially in the conference, but would have control of the Palestinian delegation. The PLO was also prepared to consider a permanent settlement which would include full demilitarisation of the West Bank, security for Israel and a Palestinian–Jordanian confederation.

The date of the fifth congress of the Labour Party was approaching with the anticipated hostility between Peres and Rabin casting a long shadow. While we were busy talking, Likud scored one of its most spectacular achievements with the setting up of the Madrid Conference, but the talking was in itself important. Members of the sextet decided to make an effort to broaden our power-base. Avrum Burg and I prepared a series of draft resolutions for the congress and obtained the support of ten key activists for this paper. When it had been agreed, we sent the material to all the participants in the congress, offering a genuine alternative to the institutionalised policies of the party. A number of our proposals were accepted.

In the political section we sketched the outline of a permanent settlement with the Palestinians: the basis for agreement would be Security Council Resolutions 242 and 338, recognition by the Arab states of Israel's right to exist in peace and security, an end to our domination of two million Palestinians and a solution to the problem of Palestinian refugees outside the borders of the State of Israel. Jerusalem would remain undivided and under Israeli control, with guarantees regarding the special status of sites sacred to Islam and Christianity, which would be self-administered. Economic agreements and joint projects would oil the wheels of the peace process. Israel would recognise the right to self-determination of the

Palestinians and would be prepared to deal with any Palestinian delegation acknowledging Israel's right to exist, accepting Security Council resolutions, opposing terror and eschewing violence. If there were no progress in talks with the Palestinians, Israel should inform the UN of its intention to pull out of the Gaza Strip, having made appropriate security arrangements.

My specific proposal regarding the Palestinian state was not accepted by the ten above-mentioned signatories. Although explicit terms like 'PLO' and 'Palestinian state' were not used, such was the only plausible interpretation of our proposals. As for the solution of the refugee problem, the emphasis on solving it outside the borders of Israel implied that we had no reservations about a solution to the problem in the context of a Palestinian state.

The Labour Party met for its most solemn session a few days after the opening of the Madrid Conference. Shamir, who had always ruled out any contact with the PLO, had found himself confronted in Madrid by Dr Haydar Abd el Shafi, one of the founders of the PLO and a vociferous critic of Arafat's moderation. To the public it seemed that the hawkish government had succeeded in holding its own and taking control of the conference. The gap in the polls was to Likud's advantage and we convened in a gloomy and pessimistic atmosphere. In fact this atmosphere encouraged engagement in real ideological debate, since the elections still seemed far away, and the major effort was directed inwards rather than out.

In the debate on social policy our group stirred up a storm, in particular on account of a very pungent speech by Haim Ramon on the subject of trade union anachronism. But in the voting we were trampled underfoot by the Old Guard and barely succeeded in getting any of our resolutions passed. On the other hand, Avrum Burg surprised us with his success in gaining a majority for his resolution calling for separation between religion and state, although in the end he acceded to Peres's request to hold a supplementary debate and accept a more moderate resolution. In political issues Peres put all his authority behind us and helped us to get our resolutions passed, either because they were close to his own viewpoint or because according to rumour we were contemplating defection, and he feared that rejection of our proposals might push us over the edge. In most of these political issues we found ourselves, directly or indirectly, opposing Yitzhak Rabin.

When the congress, one of the most fascinating and important in the history of the Labour Party, was over, we had the feeling that we had succeeded in raising the trade union issue to the top of the agenda for the first time in decades, and we had succeeded in passing the political resolutions that we considered most important: the refusal to consider the PLO as a negotiating partner had been revoked, a slim majority had voted in favour of territorial compromise on the Golan Heights, the decision had been taken to freeze settlements, irrespective of area, a resolution had been passed calling for repeal of the law banning contacts with the PLO, and in regard to Israeli Arabs there had been approval of my proposal to abolish the differential between Jews and Arabs in the level of child benefit allowances. Admittedly, the refusal to countenance a Palestinian state remained in force, but at the end of the congress we felt that we had covered a prodigious distance and changed the political face of the Labour Party. I attributed this to our advanced state of preparation, to the crystallisation of policy which had taken place at the conference of the Mashov caucus, and to the fact that most of the other factions were content with commenting on papers that we presented.

With the beginning of the Washington talks I resumed my meetings with Faisal Husseini and urged him to continue negotiating in spite of his bitterness and disillusion. He felt that the Palestinians had been forced to concede far more to Baker than they were entitled to concede. They had given up on representatives of the Palestinians outside of the West Bank and Gaza, given up on representatives from Jerusalem, and at the end of the day there had been no progress in the bilateral talks, while the multilateral talks were a premature expression of normalisation. He felt uncomfortable being hand in glove with the Jordanians and he believed that the Jordanians were also unhappy with the arrangement, and that the whole performance was just a ploy to persuade Shamir to attend the Madrid Conference.

At a meeting that we held on 5 May, he raised a series of complaints against Eliakim Rubinstein, sometimes angrily and sometimes with humour. Rubinstein, leader of the Israeli delegation in Washington, had suggested the holding of municipal elections in the occupied territories, to which the Palestinians had replied that this was no part of what had been agreed concerning the content of bilateral negotiations, just as elections to professional bodies are not a matter of government policy. Then Rubinstein suggested the transfer of medical services to Palestinian control. He was told that most of the apparatus was already, in fact, in the hands of the Palestinians, but if they were going to take over the entire operation, then they would need census records and a substantial budget. The offer was withdrawn.

Husseini told me that in a private policy meeting he had played the role of Rubinstein and asserted in his name that general elections in the territories were liable to lead to victory for Hamas, thus endangering the entire peace process. Therefore, it was better to take the smaller risk and hold local elections. The leader of the Palestinians in the delegation, Dr Haydar Abd el Shafi, laughed and said that Rubinstein was too smart to say something like this. When the talks were resumed Husseini received a call in the middle of the night from the Palestinian delegation in Washington. 'We want to talk to Mr Rubinstein,' said the voice on the line. For a moment he couldn't understand – but then he got it: Rubinstein had been presenting his arguments exactly as if he had heard Husseini's mimicry on the eve of the delegation's departure to Washington.

When the meeting was over we reckoned we would not meet again until after the elections. Neither of us knew that before then a third force would try to mediate between us and bring us together to set in motion the real breakthrough in the Israeli–Palestinian dispute.

The ten years between the formation of Mashov and the Madrid Conference were the years in which I developed my 'hobby' – trying to split the atom of the Israeli–Palestinian dispute, on the assumption that thereafter the attainment of comprehensive peace in our region would be far less difficult. My working hypothesis was that the dispute *could* be solved, there *was* somebody to talk to, namely the PLO, and there *was* something to discuss if both sides were prepared to be creative. The investment in talks with the Palestinian leadership in the territories and in Jerusalem had paid dividends in enabling me to gain a better understanding of the problems, the emotions, the 'other man's mind', and also the deep divisions among the Palestinians themselves. The many papers that we had prepared on three different levels – within Mashov in anticipation of Labour Party debates, confronting the PLO through the intermediary of a third party (Max van der Stoll), and in direct communication with Palestinians in this country – had identified and clarified the points which needed to be addressed and had gradually enlarged the common denominators. When I decided to take the risk of embarking on the Oslo process, we weren't like blind men stumbling around in the dark, fumbling for initial contact with the other side; we could immediately take the bull by the horns.

PART TWO

Oslo

NOON ON THAT Wednesday, 29 April 1992, was unusually hot and I regretted my decision to walk from my home to the Tandoori restaurant in Tel Aviv's Dizengoff Square. On the way I wondered what excuse I would use to account for ordering for myself only diet-cola, without causing embarrassment to the two men whom I was due to meet – Dov Randell, from the political department of the Trade Union Confederation, and a certain Terje Rod Larsen from Norway, director of the Fafo Research Institute. The spiciest food that I'm capable of eating is gefilte fish.

It is hard to reconstruct such occasions, even those not in the distant past. The events that have unfolded since then have imprinted their stamp on the original picture, but one thing is absolutely clear – it never occurred to me that a cordial meeting such as this was to engender a process which would influence Israel, the region and the world and that 'Oslo' would be the term applied to it, for good or for better.

I wasn't in the sunniest of moods. Admittedly, a few weeks earlier I had succeeded in gaining a prominent position in the 'primaries' and my close friends – Avrum Burg, Haim Ramon and Haggai Merom – were also highly placed in the running for the thirteenth Knesset, but the atmosphere surrounding the man alongside whom I had been working since 1977, Shimon Peres, was sombre. The Rabin faction, which for fifteen years had felt itself in a minority in the Labour Party, was gaining the upper hand and excluding most of Peres's people from the election campaign staff. My own personal relations with our new candidate for the premiership were decidedly unfavourable. For the first time in many years I had been allotted no official role in the election campaign and so I took upon myself a crowded and exhausting schedule of touring the country, paying special attention to the Arab sector. Peres suspected that Labour was going to lose on account of a policy of misleading propaganda and undue emphasis on personalities. In any case, there was certainly no confident expectation of victory.

When Randell called and invited me to a meeting in the middle of the election campaign I was inclined to turn the invitation down, but when he mentioned Fafo I said I would be there.

Terje Larsen radiated warmth, charm and a keen sense of practicality. Rather thin and in his late forties, he was unmistakably Norwegian and his English was very good and very Scandinavian.

I told him about the Economic Co-operation Foundation which I had been heading since its inception in 1991. This foundation, born in Holland and enjoying generous financial support from the EC, was still in its infancy; it had no office and its only address was the home of Dr Yair Hirschfeld, its executive director, in Ramat Yishai. The research that we were engaged in at that time dealt with the potential for developing economic links between Israel and the occupied territories. We called the research 'from dependence to inter-dependence' and we intended to point to those areas which could be developed in the future with projects that did not simply rely on the exploitation of cheap Palestinian labour. Terje was very interested, and did not query the prodigious quantities of diet-cola that I was pouring down my throat.

At this very first meeting we felt like old acquaintances, and he proceeded to tell me his story. He had set up the Fafo Research Institute in 1982 and had been running it ever since, dealing with political, social and economic issues. The initiative for founding the institute had come from Norwegian trade union interests, but its researches were taken seriously by the government and it had become a major organisation employing scores of workers.

In 1988 Larsen's wife, Mona Juul, a young diplomat in the Norwegian Foreign Office, was posted to her country's embassy in Egypt. Larsen went with her to Cairo. He knew nothing of the Arab–Israeli conflict and had no particular interest in the Middle East; his sole intention was to take an extended break after years of intensive work and play a lot of tennis, but he soon became bored and started looking for ways to occupy himself.

In the Egyptian capital he met, through Mona, with Fathi Arafat, brother of the PLO chairman, and from him he heard, for the first time, details of the Israeli–Palestinian dispute. In the course of these conversations it occurred to him that Fafo's expertise in researching standards of living in different places could be mobilised to the benefit of the Middle East, with the analysis of statistics comparing Israelis with Palestinians in the territories, in areas such as housing, health and employment. He felt that the very act of starting a survey and establishing a unified database could assuage some of the tension between the two sides.

Henceforward the essential problem was the formulation of a questionnaire for residents of the territories which could be endorsed by both the Palestinian leadership and the civil administration, and he had spent an exhausting year shuttling between the two sides and trying to obtain agreement on the form of such a questionnaire. In the course of this process he met people like Sari Nusseibeh and Faisal Husseini on the Palestinian side, and senior officials of the civil administration on the Israeli side, and his impression was that on both sides there were serious and responsible people who were capable of talking to their counterparts.

The project began to operate; it needed scores of interviewers and to supervise it Larsen appointed Marianne Heiberg, wife of the Norwegian Defence Minister Johan Jorgen Holst. The initial findings were very interesting. For example, through the replies to his questionnaire he learned of the high level of healthcare provision in the Gaza Strip. When we met, he was still deeply involved in the work and visiting the area frequently to check on the progress of the survey, although he was once again based in Oslo, whither he and his wife had returned. While Terje resumed his management of the institute, Mona was appointed office supervisor of the deputy Foreign Minister, Jan Egland.

Larsen told me that in January 1992 his wife had entertained a delegation of Palestinians from Tunis, led by a certain Muhammad Karia (Abu Ala), Arafat's most senior economic adviser and director of the important Sumud fund. Besides Fathi Arafat he had met none of the people from Tunis; he reckoned that they were no longer relevant and the leaders of the Palestinians were to be found within the territories, not outside them. Mona persuaded Terje to meet Abu Ala, and their conversation lasted several hours. Terje was much impressed by his Palestinian interlocutor and said he was convinced that Abu Ala could find a common tongue for contact with Israelis committed to peace. On his return home he told Mona that Fafo could constitute a perfect venue for a secret Israeli–Palestinian meeting, although he reckoned that the ideal candidate for such a meeting would be Faisal Husseini. Terje told me that the previous day he had met Husseini in Jerusalem and put the idea to him. Husseini reacted favourably and suggested he should examine, with me, the prospect of establishing a conduit for talks immediately after the elections.

'What do you say?' Larsen asked. I told him that if Shamir continued in office as Prime Minister, he would do everything in his power to scupper the peace process, not because he didn't want peace but because he didn't believe in peace. If Rabin were to be Prime Minister there was a chance that something might happen, in particular with the Palestinians, since he had committed himself to reaching agreement on autonomy within six to nine months. All the same, I was sceptical about the prospect of this commitment being honoured, both on account of the existence of a joint Jordanian–Palestinian delegation riven by mutual suspicion, and on account of the personality of Dr Haydar el Shafi, Shamir's mirror-image. If there were no secret track between us and the Palestinians, nothing would happen. If this could be a Norwegian track – so much the better; if not, I would try to find an alternative venue.

'We can provide you with a venue,' Larsen replied. 'At any time of your choosing, before the elections, after the elections, whether you remain in opposition or return to power. We'll provide a quiet place where you can work quietly, out of the way of the media.' I told him that I was already in contact with the Palestinians through the intermediary of Yair Hirschfeld and I suggested that the two of them should get together to discuss ways of ensuring the success of the enterprise. We parted on the friendliest of terms, with Larsen promising to get in touch next time he was in Israel. It was agreed that in the meantime no one else would be told of the proposed track.

A few weeks later I received a letter from Larsen, dated 26 May 1992. Apparently he had tried to contact me earlier, but without success. After our conversation, he wrote, he had become more optimistic about the prospect of getting progress with the Palestinians. He had met again with Faisal Husseini, who had expressed great interest in setting up an open-ended meeting in Oslo between me and a few Palestinians under his leadership. Larsen would be back in Israel in mid-June and would try to arrange a triangular meeting.

A week before the elections, when my calendar was already full to overflowing, Yair contacted me and told me Larsen had arrived and wanted to set up a joint meeting with Faisal Husseini and myself to establish the guidelines for future action. In the past week, the optimism of the Labour Party had been boosted, with people daring to speak openly of the prospect of victory. The meeting took place on 19 June, a Friday morning, so I would not need to cancel a political engagement. We met in the ornate surroundings of the American Colony Hotel in East Jerusalem – Faisal

Husseini, Terje Larsen, Yair Hirschfeld and myself. Husseini reviewed the state of the Washington talks as they currently stood, and it became clear that there had been no progress worth speaking of. He turned to the idea of the secret track proposed by Larsen, and commended it. He also expressed the hope that Rabin would indeed be the next Prime Minister and it would be possible to reach agreement with the minimum of delay, using a 'laboratory' to be located in Oslo. This was an excellent meeting, but it was one which led nowhere: these four participants, who had agreed to work together to support the official political process, were never to meet again in the same configuration. The eventual 'laboratory' was quite different from what was conceived in the Tandoori and designed in the American Colony.

But this I did not know at the time. My feeling then was that I had engaged in a process which could come to fruition after the elections if political circumstances permitted.

At that time commentators were saying that President Assad of Syria was looking forward to victory for Shamir, fearing that a moderate Israeli government would expose his own reluctance to make peace, while Arafat was rooting for Rabin as the only one with whom a deal could be struck. I don't know what Arafat and Assad were really thinking on the eve of the 1992 elections, but in hindsight it could be said that the commentators had it about right.

The taste of victory on 23 June was strange and unexpected. In the crowded and stifling banqueting hall of the Dan Hotel in Tel Aviv I had the feeling that the Rabin camp was celebrating victory over the Peres camp, as if the results proved that only with Rabin could the Labour Party win; the triumph was to his credit and Peres would have to show him due deference.

I travelled to Jerusalem to appear on British television's *News at Ten*, facing Ehud Olmert of the losing party. On the way I heard Rabin proclaiming his 'credo', and my flesh crawled. It sounded as if he was denouncing Shimon, denouncing me. We had waited so long for this victory, and when it came I felt a stranger in the winning camp. My inability to share in the jubilation was painful indeed.

The days that followed were occupied with putting together coalitions. The sense of alienation persisted, with the Peres faction seeming to be out of the running. I was glad that Haim Ramon was involved with this and I knew he was more experienced than the others, but I greatly regretted the exclusion of the United Torah Judaism Party from the coalition and I sensed that one day we would pay a heavy price for this. Rabin wanted no stand-in and no deputy. Many continued to refer to Peres as 'deputy Prime Minister', but from 1992 onward there was no such post, and it was not known whether Peres would even serve in Rabin's government. Would Rabin offer him Education? The Treasury? Defence or Foreign Affairs? Rabin kept his cards close to his chest until the two of them had held a private conversation.

The conversation delivered no simple answers. It was clear that Rabin was offering Peres the Foreign Affairs portfolio reluctantly, and intended to impose drastic restrictions on his freedom of action: Rabin would handle relations with the USA and would take overall charge of all the political negotiations in Washington, with Eliakim Rubinstein continuing to serve as chief negotiator. Peres would be in the picture and would be responsible for the multilateral talks which were a kind of supplement to the fundamental negotiations and were concerned with issues such as water, quality of the environment, refugees, arms control and economic co-operation. These talks were being conducted at sub-ministerial level. Months later Peres was still trying to raise the steering committee of the multilateral talks to ministerial level but without success, essentially on account of Saudi Arabian opposition.

On 13 July 1992 the Rabin government was inaugurated, with the appointment of deputy ministers deferred to a later date. Motta Gur, who was expecting demotion to the rank of deputy Defence Minister, was in a state of utter dejection during the weeks of limbo which followed, unable to understand the delay. He suggested we should both go to the Prime Minister and demand an end to prevarication, but I didn't think this a good idea. In the end we were both appointed on 5 August. At Rabin's request, Peres agreed to the appointment of Gad Yaacobi as ambassador to the UN, while Rabin agreed to appoint me deputy Foreign Minister.

Since the multilateral talks seemed at that time the principal concern of the Foreign Office, I took the thick files of the discussions which had been held in this forum since the first meeting in Moscow in December 1991, and with the aid of my political adviser and office manager Shlomo Gur I studied the material, the professional assessments and the options for exploiting the forum as a means of forging additional political contacts. Peres agreed to my request to take charge of the Israeli delegation to the higher steering committee of the multilateral talks, a committee which met twice a year under the sponsorship of the USA and Russia, appointing working groups in the various fields and giving them codes of conduct. The next meeting was to be held in December in London, and I intended to be thoroughly prepared for it.

A fresh round of talks with the Syrians, with the Jordanian–Palestinian delegation and with Lebanon began on 24 August. From the avalanche of documentation which I received from Rubinstein's delegation, I gained the impression that nothing much was happening. I hoped that the Prime Minister was getting additional information from other channels, reporting substantive developments in Washington, but I doubted this was the case. Admittedly, in the Syrian track, handled by Professor Itamar Rabinowitz, some new things were being said but there was no explicit reference to 'land for peace' and the talks very soon degenerated into the trading of tired old clichés. In the Lebanese track there was no progress and no expectation of progress; Uri Lubrani and Yossi Hadas went through the motions, knowing it was a futile exercise. Eli Rubinstein continued to negotiate with the Jordanian–Palestinian team, with good humour and a lot of Yiddish jokes, while by his own admission the establishment of a new government had had no discernible effect, so he was still standing firm on the issues on which the previous government had told him to stand firm.

This was a strange sensation. The peace industry was booming. With each round of talks Rubinstein was climbing aboard an Air Force jet with a dozen clerks and expert advisers, most of them Foreign Office personnel. It seemed everything was happening at once: Director-General Hadas handling Lebanon and Deputy Director-General Eitan Bentzur handling the Palestinians, the head of the political research centre, David Afek, dealing with Syria – along with diplomats, senior civil servants, clerks and typists. Half the department decamped to Washington and set up shop in the Mayflower Hotel. This had a serious effect on the day-to-day running of the office and added considerably to my own administrative workload, though when I read through the reports every evening I knew nothing was happening. The most we could expect would be detecting a Syrian reference to an agreement on peace in exchange for evacuation of the Golan, and having to search the archives to discover whether this was a first-time statement or some Syrian representative had said something similar in the past. Generally these were recurrent statements.

It was a dream government – Prime Minister Rabin and Foreign Minister

Peres, while people who for years had been considered extreme left-wingers were serving as senior ministers: Shulamit Aloni, Yair Tzaban, Haim Ramon, Uzi Baram. I myself was regularly present at cabinet sittings, I received copious quantities of important information and briefed the media on political developments, but no real upheaval had taken place, and high-ranking roles did not make us any more influential regarding the most vital issue of all: negotiating for peace with our neighbours.

On 9 September, in the course of a round of talks when I found myself in a particularly pessimistic mood, my first foreign colleague, Jan Egland, the Norwegian deputy Foreign Minister, arrived in the country on an official visit. In his mid-thirties, tall, blond and affable, he was deputy to Torvald Stoltenberg, whom I had known years before. Egland told me that the formal side of the visit was merely a pretext, and its real purpose was to implement the plan that had been mooted in a conversation between Larsen and myself back in April, regarding secret discussions in Oslo. He asked for a meeting at night, after dinner, to assess the practicalities. He had no idea just how timely his arrival was.

During the day we held standard political discussions. Egland met other members of the government, and in the evening I hosted a formal dinner in his honour at the Dan Hotel in Tel Aviv, attended by the Norwegian ambassador and other dignitaries. At about eleven p.m. we parted with complimentary speeches and exchanges of memorabilia, and a quarter of an hour later we squeezed into a room in the nearby Hilton, for the real talking.

Participating on the Norwegian side were Egland himself, his office chief Mona Juul and her husband, none other than Terje Larsen. On the Israeli side, besides me were Yair Hirschfeld and Shlomo Gur. Egland expressed his pleasure at the change that had taken place in Israel (he was himself a member of the Norwegian Labour Party, albeit an unelected appointee). He said that Stoltenberg knew of the agreement between Larsen, Faisal Husseini and myself, and had authorised him to confirm the promise that Oslo would host a secret session of talks. He added that the Norwegian Foreign Ministry was standing behind the Fafo Institute for the purposes of financing the project.

We spent some time analysing the options for continuing the 'Madrid process'. We all agreed that continuation of the existing apparatus was doomed to failure: talks of which all were aware and which were covered by the media, parallel talks with all the delegations following prior co-ordination between Arab foreign ministers in Damascus, the existence of a joint Jordanian–Palestinian delegation and the continuation of the ludicrous attempt to bypass the PLO and deal with 'residents of the territories', although everybody knew who they were taking their orders from. We all agreed on the need for a parallel track, in the form of a series of conversations between myself and Faisal Husseini, with the intention of dismantling the obstacles currently blocking progress in the Washington talks.

The original idea was to revive something which had been tried and had failed five years before in the London Agreement, of which I had been among the negotiators – to establish a secret track, solve the problems, conclude the process and, with the agreement of the leaderships on both sides, lay the completed work on the negotiating table without the existence of the track ever being known. To the world it would seem that all the problems had been solved by official negotiation, while the truth would be very different.

When we parted, this time for real, and had reached the handshaking stage, Egland asked me whether my bosses would support the project. I told him that Peres was the one whom I reported to, and very soon I would indeed inform him of the Norwegian offer and of the prospective interlocutor. We agreed that I would let him know when I could make the trip to Norway, and he would co-ordinate this with Husseini. After weeks of frustration, it seemed to me I could see a ray of light.

Two days later I had a private meeting with Peres. After so many long years of working together, since October 1977, we could refer to the jokes that we shared by numbers. Meetings between us were usually very economical. I would go up to his office on the second floor of the Foreign Ministry with a boxfile containing all the material requiring his attention or his ratification. On this occasion Shimon was in a gloomy mood; as usual, the look on his face betrayed his feelings unmistakably. 'Has something happened?' I asked him. 'No, nothing's happened,' Peres replied, 'and I don't believe there's anything that can be done. I had a meeting today with Yitzhak. I told him I wanted to meet Faisal Husseini and hear what he has to say about the Washington talks.' 'Well?' I pressed him. 'And he told me that for the time being we should avoid such contacts. In short, I've been refused permission to meet Faisal Husseini! What do you think of that?'

This bizarre state of affairs was something I could never have envisaged. I mumbled something, put aside the first paper in the file which was headed 'Meeting between Faisal and self, Oslo' and turned to other business. This conversation with Peres determined the final constitution of the Oslo process and radically altered the nature of the track. I had to rethink the entire business.

It was obvious to me that if the Prime Minister wouldn't let the Foreign Minister meet Husseini, I could hardly ask Peres to sanction such a meeting in Norway. It was equally obvious that to meet in Oslo without informing Peres, having been told of his unsuccessful attempt to meet Husseini, would have most unpleasant repercussions if it became known. I knew that I couldn't tell anyone the reason for cancelling the Oslo track, since this would expose the relationship between the Prime Minister and the Foreign Minister and the vulnerable status of my immediate superior.

On 24 September another round of Washington talks ended in an atmosphere of goodwill but without any results. The political process was expected to take a long holiday, until after the American presidential elections in November if Bush were to win, until some time after January 1993 should Clinton be elected. Rabin's promise during the electoral campaign to reach an agreement on autonomy in six to nine months seemed very difficult to achieve, and now the prospect of a secret track was ebbing away. Egland contacted me several times, and Terje Larsen was also in touch. They were trying to set up a meeting between me and Faisal and I put them off with various excuses, pleading pressure of parliamentary business and the like.

A few weeks later I spoke with Yair Hirschfeld. I told him I couldn't see myself going to Oslo and I would prefer him to go there instead and talk to the Palestinians. I would brief him on the principal obstacles in the negotiations and he should try to determine what could be solved and what seemed impossible. The question was whether Yair would meet with Faisal or with someone else. I left this for him to decide, although I reckoned Husseini would be perplexed, having agreed to meet me, to be confronted in the end by Yair, whom he had regularly entertained in his home in Jerusalem.

Husseini himself had constantly been urging us, every time we met him and long before the establishment of Rabin's government, to talk to members of the PLO. I explained to him that although I considered the Law of Association misguided and iniquitous I wasn't going to break it, but I would do everything in my power to have it repealed. Back in

1991 I had introduced a private member's bill to rescind the law, and it had fallen at the preliminary reading, with a sizeable proportion of Labour members voting against it. In the party congress the dovish faction had succeeded, as we have seen, in getting a resolution on the issue passed, but in the meantime the party chairman had been replaced, and after the upheaval in the election Rabin was in no hurry to press for repeal.

The Justice Minister, David Libai, wanted to revive the issue, but Rabin delayed this, his main fear being that repeal of the law would induce the USA under President Bush to renew negotiations with the PLO, negotiations which had been suspended since the abortive raid by Force 17 on the beach at Nitzanim on 30 May 1990. It was an attempted terrorist attack by the most loyal military group to Arafat. To Rabin it was important to maintain the distinction between the PLO and 'residents of Judaea, Samaria and the Gaza Strip'. If it is true (as is sometimes alleged) that on coming to power he had already made up his mind to talk to the PLO, then his attitude to the Law of Association concealed his intentions most effectively.

Here Meretz played an important role. It was easy for Rabin to ignore the demands of ministers and deputy ministers in the Labour Party; it was much more difficult to ignore the senior coalition partners, with whom he had agreed that within six months from the inauguration of the government the amendment to the Prevention of Terrorism Order, forbidding contact with the PLO, would be repealed and that, if it was not, Meretz could put forward draft legislation of their own. Meretz ministers urged and even threatened, and in the end a government-sponsored bill was introduced in the Knesset, passing its first reading on 2 December 1992. The bill was approved by a margin of one – 37 votes to 36, with no abstentions. Rabin himself was not present for the vote, and it was important to him to stress that repeal of the prohibition did not mean that the Israeli government was about to embark on negotiations with the PLO. Far from it. Private individuals would no longer be barred from participation in meetings and symposia, but the government had no intention of instituting negotiations. Even Libai stressed this in his speech to the Knesset when he introduced the bill. But there could be no doubt that the dam had been breached, and when we travelled to London for a meeting of the steering committee of the multilateral talks on 4 December, we knew that very soon it would be possible to speak to the PLO. The passing of the law rendered the London meeting vitally important as a prelude to the Oslo track.

The meeting of the steering committee constituted a unique opportunity to make progress in the bilateral talks. That Friday everyone was in London. I arrived at the head of a delegation composed of Foreign Ministry and Defence Ministry personnel; Terje Larsen was there (technically he was attending a trade conference elsewhere in the city, which just happened to coincide with our deliberations); Abu Ala (Muhammad Karia) arrived to represent the PLO at the multilateral talks but taking no direct part in negotiation, although in fact he was guiding the Palestinian delegation, which theoretically had no connection with the PLO. Yair Hirschfeld came to London, as he put it, to make contact with anyone who might turn up.

The American team was led by Ed Djerijian, assistant Secretary of State, the Russian team by Victor Pasavaliouk, head of the Middle East section of the foreign ministry. The Palestinian delegate was a representative of the Palestinian Diaspora, possibly a member of the PNC and possibly not, who at the very last moment had been declared 'kosher' by the research centre of our Foreign Ministry. He delivered an extreme and impassioned speech, as if there had been no major upheaval in Israel that year, and I responded to him with vigour and with uncharacteristic indignation. Leaders of the Arab delegations rallied to my defence – which was a pleasant surprise. He himself approached me afterwards and explained that the things he had said were not just repetitions of dated slogans, but rather an expression of protest at the way the Rabin government was persisting with the unworkable notion of a joint Palestinian–Jordanian delegation and was still pretending there was a distinction between the PLO and the residents of the territories. 'The time has come for you to sit down with our real leaders and stop closing your eyes to reality,' he said. He didn't know that at that very moment, not far from the Guildhall where we had convened, in London's Cavendish Hotel a senior member of the PLO was meeting Dr Yair Hirschfeld to prepare the way for the kind of contact that he recommended. At the time I wasn't aware of this either.

That evening I was visited in my hotel room by Ed Djerijian and his deputy Dan Kertzer, who had been my friend since he served in Israel in the early 1980s. Also present was Shlomo Gur. The Americans were famished, so we ordered a big tray of sandwiches and held a heart-to-heart discussion which lasted for hours. The questions hanging in the air were:

Clinton having won the US election, what would be his policy towards the Middle East; who would replace Baker as Secretary of State; would there be any role for Denis Ross in the peace team (after the period in which he left the State Department to work for Baker in the White House, helping Bush in his electoral campaign); would Rabin prefer to address the question of the Golan Heights before making a deal with the Palestinians? Djerijian asked me what I would advise Clinton to do, if consulted in an official capacity. I told him that an immediate contribution towards progress with the Palestinians would be resumption of negotiations between the USA and the PLO, the negotiations which had taken place between Bob Pelletreau, US ambassador to Tunis, and Yasser Abd Rabbo. I stressed however that this was not Israeli government policy and I reckoned Israel would anticipate the USA in this. Kertzer said he supposed it was better for the time being to carry on down the road mapped out in Madrid; the USA could not afford to be too hasty on the issue of negotiations with the PLO. I told him I understood the American position, and I also understood that the USA had time. Israel had no time. We had won power for a term of four years, and already half a year had passed with no progress towards peace; as long as we were in the driving seat we had to exploit every opportunity to advance the progress.

Later I was visited by Yair Hirschfeld, running as usual on high-octane fuel and claiming he had 'lots of news to report'. With even more exuberance than his norm, he told me that Hannan Ashrawi had suggested he use the steering committee meeting as an opportunity to meet Abu Ala.

The meeting had been set up in Terje Larsen's hotel room. Yair arrived five minutes before Abu Ala and Larsen himself did not participate. Yair told me that Abu Ala was fifty-five years old, tiny and bald-headed, with a good sense of humour, affable and warm. He was a resident of Tunis but his family lived in Jordan. He was Arafat's trusted adviser in financial and other matters.

Abu Ala spoke of the dire consequences of wasted opportunities and said that moderate elements in the Palestinian camp were in danger of losing ground to Hamas. In his view, the best way to make progress was to reach agreement on the principles governing the interim settlement, and to do this by means of American shuttle diplomacy between the Palestinians and Israel. He also presented Yair with a draft statement of the principles on which agreement was needed. I told Yair that the Americans were not prepared to play such a role, which meant shaking the

Madrid structure, and that Abu Ala's analysis was correct. It was essential to move quickly. The most effective solution would be a meeting between Yair and Abu Ala in Norway, where the various options could be debated intensively and the prospects for progress rapidly assessed. That same day it was agreed with Larsen that the next session would be held in Norway. We had a place, we had a host, we had negotiators, and from this moment on the new track was the most closely guarded secret of both Israelis and Palestinians.

We told Dan Kertzer, informally, of the existence of the track. He was the only American who was briefed by me personally, and in very general terms; he knew none of the details, and asked no questions. I didn't ask him if he was reporting to anyone, but the conversation between us was strictly off the record. Kertzer welcomed the establishment of the track, so long as it wasn't a substitute for the Washington talks and didn't impair them in any way.

Back in Israel, I decided not to share information on the existence of the track with anyone. I knew that if I passed this on to Peres he would be obliged to brief Rabin, and I feared that Rabin would demand an end to the process before it had even begun. If the process were to succeed, I reflected, it could be reported retrospectively, and if it led nowhere it would just be another episode in the long-running drama of Israeli–Palestinian relations. Since the track was a deniable exercise and since I wasn't personally involved, it was preferable not to report it and thereby compromise its prospects of success.

Various assessments of this decision were later made public. The Palestinians knew, from the very first phase of the talks, that I was standing behind them, and they assumed that Peres knew what was happening but preferred to keep his knowledge secret. This impression of theirs contributed to the success of the talks. It is possible that had they known I was the only government official aware of the negotiations they would not have invested as much as they did. At home there were some who alleged that I had informed Rabin about the talks and bypassed Peres, others who suggested I had told Peres and he had delayed reporting it to Rabin. The truth was much simpler: I had no idea that this track was going to lead whither it led. I saw it as a valuable experiment, something I did not want to jeopardise, and I knew that if I reported to my superiors it would not get off the ground at all. The price which I paid for this was my non-participation in the track, and the creation of deniability, according to which this was an extended seminar on regional development which just happened to be taking place in Norway.

December 1992 was a month of attacks by the Islamic fundamentalist group 'Hamas'. On the 7th, three Israeli soldiers were shot dead in Gaza. On the 12th, Hamas guerrillas fired on an army jeep in Hebron, killing one soldier and injuring two. The following day a staff sergeant of the Border Guard, Nissim Toledano, was kidnapped near his home in Lod and held hostage against the release of Sheikh Ahmed Yassin. Three days later the head of Toledano's body was found in the Judaean desert, his hands tied and his throat cut. The next day, 17 December, Rabin decided to expel 415 Hamas activists from the territories, a decision supported by the government.

The expulsion, which was soon revealed as one of the government's worst mistakes, dumping the deportees in the December cold on the Israel–Lebanon border and directing the world's television cameras towards them, also halted the official negotiations. In the more pragmatic sections of the Arab world no tears were shed for the deportees, but the moment that Israel takes action of this sort, the Arab world feels the need to express solidarity. The expulsion gave the strong impression that nothing had changed in Israel, despite the election of a Labour government.

The Palestinians, who theoretically should have rejoiced at the blow struck against Hamas, feared lest it intensify hatred and turn the Hamas deportees into heroes. In the end, the government was forced into an embarrassing climbdown, reducing the duration of the expulsion. We were anxious about the effects of the expulsion on the forthcoming meeting in Norway, but we soon understood the rules of the game: in a secret negotiating process life is not influenced by what is going on outside. We constructed for ourselves a bubble in which we were absolved from the obligations of official protests and official posturing, from meaningless oratory and the slamming of doors. In the world of Oslo we could simply search for common ground, firmly believing that it existed.

In my office, even before the first meeting, two cadres were rapidly constituted. In one I had advisers, aides and secretaries who formed a kind of partition insulating me from the world in which airline tickets and hotel rooms are booked and other technical services are handled. The other was effectively an Oslo team, consisting of Shlomo Gur, Orit Shani, my office manager, and myself. We wrote and typed, checked and cor-

rected, passed and received information, fretted over timetables and constituted the only link in this country to the two negotiators. Dr Yair
Hirschfeld was joined by Dr Ron Pundak, Yair's one-time pupil and the son of
the renowned Danish–Israeli journalist Nahum (Herbert) Pundak, an expert
on Jordanian affairs and a former member of the defence establishment.

Before the journey to Norway I told Yair that from my point of view the
most important thing was to make clear to Abu Ala that these talks were
not taking place in the conventional framework of pyramidal power, that
only I was aware of them and that the objective at this stage was to study
ways of overcoming obstacles in the Washington talks. It was essential to
take account of the lack of symmetry in this encounter: on our side two
academics of no formal status on a mission known only to me, on the
PLO side a senior official representative.

It was not until months later that I learned of the excitement in Tunis
at the prospect of the meeting, excitement which was no less than ours.
Abu Ala briefed Arafat on his meeting with Yair, and Arafat passed the
information to Abu Mazen, in charge of the Israeli desk. Abu Mazen had
reservations about embarking on negotiations with a certain branch of
the Israeli government regarded as more dovish than the Prime Minister
and his entourage, but decided not to miss the opportunity, especially as he
considered that the Norwegian venue raised the importance and prestige of
the meeting. The composition of the team was meticulously arranged and
it was decided that Abu Ala would be accompanied by Hasan Asfur,
secretary of the Israel negotiations committee, who was an expert in all
aspects of the Washington talks and was a member of the communist (as
opposed to Fatah) faction of the PLO, and Maher el Kurd, Abu Ala's
economic adviser. For Abu Ala himself, his first meeting with Israelis was
an exciting prospect; Yair was the first Israeli he had ever encountered face
to face. Asfur brought with him a wealth of information, and Maher el
Kurd his fluent English. Abu Ala prepared an Arabic draft of his statement,
which el Kurd would translate, and he also brought with him ten points
set out by Abu Mazen in relation to the permanent settlement. Abu
Mazen's agenda envisaged the establishment of self-government in the
territories occupied in the Six Day War, elections and discussions on the
permanent settlement two years after implementation of the interim
settlement.

In the township of Sarpsborg, less than 100 kilometres to the south of

Oslo, a seminar was convened, labelled 'Human Resources' and hosted by the Fafo Institute, which was reporting on the findings of its survey in Gaza, with the participation of two Israelis and three Palestinians. By the time this meeting took place on 20 January 1993, such camouflage was no longer necessary, because the previous day the law prohibiting contacts with the PLO had finally been repealed. There were many strongly held reservations about this measure, and I was afraid that a Likud filibuster could delay completion of the second and third readings by a further week, but to my relief we succeeded in concluding the voting in time; at the third reading, repeal of the law was supported by thirty-nine members, against twenty who favoured continued prohibition. Yair and Ron were the first to act in the new legal framework.

Marianne Heiberg, wife of Defence Minister Holst, delivered an address on the Fafo research and then the two sides held their opening rounds, with Terje Larsen and his wife Mona Juul serving as exemplary hosts, supplying all the needs of the delegations while taking care not to intervene in the discussions; throughout the course of the negotiations, until the summer, they would continue to provide this service.

Although the initiative for the track had come from us, it was Abu Ala who opened the proceedings with an outline of the issues important to the Palestinians. He expressed frustration over the lack of progress in negotiations and over the non-participation of the PLO. He said that if the problem of the deportees were not solved the multilateral talks would be suspended, and he referred to a long list of confidence-building steps such as the reunification of families which could, in his opinion, improve the atmosphere between Israel and the Palestinians. Abu Ala spoke at length about the multilateral conferences, expressing disappointment with the slow progress registered in them.

He did not disguise the parlous state of the PLO, especially following both the suspension of dialogue with the USA and the Gulf War, but he hoped that the situation would change as a result of Abu Mazen's forthcoming visit to the Gulf states.

The biggest surprise in Abu Ala's statement was his attitude to the Israeli idea of 'Gaza first'. For the first time a positive Palestinian response was heard regarding this notion, which had been proposed by Peres many years before. It was important to Abu Ala to stress that Israeli withdrawal from Gaza would not take place at the expense of withdrawal from the West Bank. The suggestion was that Israel should announce its intention

to move out of Gaza within two years and in the meantime some international agency would take responsibility for the Strip; international aid
and investment would be channelled towards the region in a kind of
miniature Marshall Plan, while vigorous co-operation between Israel and
the Palestinians would assist the rapid development of the sector.

Abu Ala also surprised Yair and Ron with the new ideas that he brought
with him, especially in the field of co-operation between Israel and the
Palestinians. The idea of a maritime canal linking the Mediterranean to
the Dead Sea, which had been mooted before and rejected as unfeasible,
was now being raised again. Abu Ala spoke of a free trade area between
Ashdod and Gaza and of co-ordination between a new port to be built in
Gaza and the existing one in Ashdod. He raised the idea of a gas pipeline
from Egypt, as a project which could be routed via the Gaza Strip to Israel.
He spoke of co-operation in the petrochemical industry and of an oil
pipeline from Mafrak in Jordan to Gaza, and other ideas such as joint
development in the region of the Dead Sea.

Yair contacted me several times in the course of that weekend, and after
a series of 'well nows' and 'I've got so much to tell yous', he managed to
deliver a succinct account: the partners were very serious and taking the
track with alarming and possibly excessive seriousness. Abu Mazen and
Arafat were standing behind the Palestinians, and they themselves had
come as a hierarchical delegation whereas the Israelis were neither delegation nor hierarchy, with only me standing behind them. I did my best
to calm the agitated Yair, and told him that on his return we would discuss
the whole business and in any case a further meeting would be arranged
as soon as possible; in the meantime we should content ourselves with
weighing our forthcoming moves and compiling orderly written proposals
in preparation for the next meeting.

The world's routine continued. The Hamas deportation was still over-
shadowing and impeding the peace process. The ironies of history: Rabin
now told Peres it was all right to meet Husseini, but Peres failed to persuade
Husseini to return to the negotiating table, the latter making a series of
demands which the Israeli government, in its smart new straitjacket, could
not concede. I devoted a lot of my time to the multilateral talks and
held briefings for leaders of delegations. There was the question of the
employment of Arab trainees in the Foreign Ministry. I handled the visit
to Israel of Amr Moussa, the Egyptian Foreign Minister, and arranged a
series of discussions aimed at changing the map of our respective spheres

of influence. Negotiations on establishing diplomatic relations with the Vatican demanded my attention, and the choice of senior diplomats to represent us was my responsibility too. The daily routine of the Foreign Ministry was not uninteresting, but it was hard to concentrate on it when my thoughts were constantly turning to the new track.

Yair and Ron returned to 'team headquarters' and the four of us – they, Shlomo Gur and myself – sat down and attempted to analyse what had happened. They told us of the meticulous security arrangements and of the prodigious efforts invested by the Norwegians in the preservation of secrecy, although by then there were a number of them who knew what was happening, including Foreign Minister Stoltenberg and possibly also Prime Minister Gro Harlem Brundtland. Their impression of the Palestinian delegation was that these were men who had come to do business and who assumed that senior echelons in the Israeli government must be aware of the existence of the track. The Gaza initiative was a surprise, the detail of the economic proposals was a surprise, but the greatest surprise was the seriousness of these men and their sincere commitment to peace.

It was clear that the PLO was feeling pressure, that it couldn't reconcile itself to the fact that it was playing no part in the bilateral or the multi-lateral talks, that it was in danger of losing its primacy over Hamas. A settlement with Israel in which PLO-Tunis had a major role to play, including a foothold in Gaza, could constitute a lifeline and, specifically, a way of bypassing some of the obstacles that had emerged in Washington.

The Palestinians were afraid of an interim settlement turning into a permanent settlement, in which case they would be thrown back into a state of perpetual autonomy and nothing more, the outcome envisaged in his time by the late Menahem Begin. Before agreeing to five years of interim settlement, they demanded to know from the outset what the form of the permanent settlement would be, but this Israel could not give them. Questions regarding the interim settlement were complex and mostly involved issues that would not be covered by autonomy: what would be the future of the Jewish settlements, of army camps, of Jerusalem? What would be the limits of autonomous authority, and would the Palestinians be empowered to legislate? What would be the size of the Council of the Palestinian Authority? (Israel favoured an executive body, of twenty to thirty members, whereas the Palestinians wanted numbers appropriate to a legislative assembly, 150 or thereabouts.) To circumvent these questions Israel suggested early transfer of limited powers as an initial stage, without waiting for the solution of all the complex problems on the agenda. The Palestinians had rejected this in Washington. The notion of 'Gaza first' could be a short cut, circumventing some substantive problems by deferring decision on them until after implementation of this very significant step.

At this stage it was understood by Yair and Ron as well as by Abu Ala that if we reached agreement in Oslo we should immediately inform the Americans and they – if they accepted it – would send Warren Christopher, Clinton's Secretary of State, to the region for the formal presentation of the agreement to Faisal Husseini and to Rabin and Peres. We never envisaged anything more than this emerging from the track. In months to come the question of marketing the product was to turn into a central issue, often being repressed, only to pop up again.

We decided to prepare a methodical paper, a statement of principles which could serve as a draft agreement at the very next meeting and which would not be in the nature of an Israeli statement of position as a basis for negotiation, but a document taking account of the Palestinian proposals and our reactions to them. Our guiding principle throughout the talks was to try to avoid conventional negotiating tactics, where the parties begin with speeches intended to mark out the distance between them and then move towards compromise. We tried to locate the limits beyond which the other side could not go, to understand what our own limits were, and to strive towards the construction of broader options in which both sides would have room to manoeuvre.

The question which bothered us most was whether to tell Peres. On the one hand we felt that something much more serious than we had initially envisaged was happening here; on the other we feared that if this was reported to Rabin and Rabin took steps to abort the track before anything had been agreed, we would never forgive ourselves for the lost opportunity. We decided it was preferable to retain the option of deniability, and set about preparing the draft agreement.

Terje Larsen contacted me and then Jan Egland did so. They were both very happy with developments and both told me that the Palestinians felt something significant was set to emerge from the track. Terje Larsen added that Abu Ala wanted to be sure there was serious political backing behind this pair of academics, and asked if I would be prepared to participate in the next round. I told him that I preferred to carry on with the existing apparatus. He promised to see to all the complex technical arrangements and to set up the next meeting. Neither Larsen nor Egland knew of the content of the discussions, and neither had been informed of the 'Gaza first' option. They asked no questions.

In setting out the draft statement of principles we raised a number of central points: implementation of 'Gaza first' would be separated from elections to the Palestinian Authority. My main worry, based on protocols that I had seen from the Washington talks, was that we might fail to agree on the form of the elections, or the Palestinian leadership might boycott the elections, with the result that the implementation of self-government would be deferred indefinitely. To me, 'Gaza first' simply meant Gaza before the elections. A further anxiety was that delaying the elections would in itself delay the beginning of talks on the permanent settlement and the completion date. It had been set out in the Camp David accords that negotiations on the permanent settlement would commence two years after the elections and be concluded within five. I preferred to have the five-year period written into the interim agreement, so that the Begin ploy, of postponing the permanent settlement indefinitely, would not be repeated.

On the issue of Jerusalem we set out the Labour Party position, which had not been raised in Washington (Palestinian residents of Jerusalem would vote in a separate category, as resident aliens, and could be elected only if they had an additional address outside Jerusalem). As to the issues on the agenda of the permanent settlement, we considered that if we transferred certain problematical questions – refugees and Jerusalem for example – to this agenda, we could avoid a situation in which these issues could jeopardise the interim process. Naturally, we did not guarantee our willingness to compromise on these issues, any more than on those of frontiers and Jewish settlements and other questions, but the very fact that these issues were now on the agenda was enough to solve a series of problems which had prevented agreement on autonomy since discussions on the subject had begun following the 1979 peace treaty with Egypt.

With our own eyes we witnessed the spectacle of Gaza, this cramped and poverty-stricken place, which in September 1992 Rabin had wanted to dump in the sea, changing from a proverbial eyesore to a part of the solution. It was a little hard to understand the motives of Abu Ala and his sponsors in recommending this. When the idea was raised in the 1980s it had not been worked out in detail and the Palestinians had tended to dismiss it, explaining to the media that 'Gaza first' was just a ploy on the part of Israel; the intention was to convert it into 'Gaza last' and thereby conclude the Israeli withdrawal.

In November 1992 Peres had suggested to the Egyptian leadership that the notion of 'Gaza first' should be supplemented by Jericho or Jenin, to prove to the Palestinians that the Israelis were not confining themselves to withdrawal from Gaza. The proposal was rejected by the PLO. And now, at the beginning of 1993, here were the leaders of the PLO putting forward the Gaza option as a solution and making no reference whatsoever to Jericho! Was this a sign of weakness? Failure of internal co-ordination? Or was this just an experimental probe, to discover if there was anyone standing behind Yair and Ron?

The second round of talks, convened on 11 and 12 February 1993, showed us that this was not an experimental probe. This time it was Yair and Ron who took the initiative and made proposals and the Palestinians who reacted. The draft we had prepared, which was accepted as the basis for negotiation, comprised three sections: fourteen principles which were intended to guide both sides towards signing the intermediate agreement, a supplement dealing with Israeli–Palestinian co-operation in such areas as water, agronomics and human resources, and a supplement outlining a Marshall Plan for Gaza and district, involving training of personnel, energy, tourism, transport and small businesses.

The location was the same, the township of Sarpsborg, the participants were the same. The Norwegians took the same cautious steps as before but were now more involved in, and more aware of, the talks and their outcome. This was a very practical session in which we came to the conclusion that all the potential for informally exploring ideas had been exhausted. It was in fact the unexpected success of the second round that persuaded us that our approach to the third round could not be the same, that following the moment of truth for the Palestinians, our own moment of truth was not far away.

Abu Ala quoted Rabin as saying that negotiations with the Palestinians could take from five to ten years. He pressed Yair to reveal just how official this track was, adding that if the leaderships on both sides were not fully aware of the Sarpsborg talks, there was no point in carrying on. Yair avoided a direct answer and spoke of the need to reach an understanding which could be presented to the leaderships, and such an understanding was indeed moulded in the course of that long weekend.

I sat at home with the text of the draft agreement, and over the weekend Yair called me five or six times during intervals in the talks, usually late at night. When my wife Helena gently drew my attention to the eccentric hours at which the phone was ringing, I told her that Yair was involved in a sacred duty. 'Oh, you mean you're making peace with somebody?' she asked – and said nothing more. No one at home knew what was happening in Norway until the public announcement at the end of August.

The framework that emerged was as follows: the document, comprising principles and supplements, would be approved in the secret track and the Americans would be informed. This would be the signal for Warren Christopher to arrive on the scene and conduct shuttle diplomacy between Husseini and Rabin, leading rapidly to agreement between the two and subsequently to public signing of the documents. This would mark the start of the five-year period within which negotiations on the permanent settlement must be concluded.

On the eve of the signing of the statement of principles, Israel would begin transferring a wide range of powers, covering all aspects of self-government, to the Palestinian councils. A few months after this, elections would be held for a temporary Palestinian Assembly which would sign an interim agreement with Israel. By the end of the second year of the interim agreement, Israel would implement full withdrawal from Gaza, to be replaced by Egyptian or international trusteeship, and simultaneously talks on the permanent settlement would begin.

A few points remained unresolved: we had not reached a satisfactory solution to the issue of the voting rights of residents of East Jerusalem, we had not yet agreed on the official and legislative prerogatives of the temporary Assembly and we couldn't accept Abu Ala's suggestion of arbitration in the event of failure to agree on implementation of the deal. The Palestinians gave us to understand that these positions were not to be regarded as non-negotiable, and that they needed to return to Tunis and confer with Arafat and Abu Mazen.

Two days after the conclusion of the round we received a message from Terje Larsen: the leadership in Tunis had approved the three-section document in principle and was ready to move towards compromise on the issues as yet unresolved, if we too were prepared to make concessions. This was the stage at which we had no choice but to involve the Foreign Minister and the Prime Minister. For the time being no further meetings in Norway had been scheduled, and it was clear that, without a proper mandate to continue the process, nothing could be done. The four-sided forum convened once more. Our assessment was that the agreement was reasonable, surprisingly so, and it should be possible to settle the unresolved issues. We prepared a paper in which we referred to the measures we expected on the part of the Prime Minister and the Foreign Minister in advance of Warren Christopher's anticipated shuttle diplomacy – including detailed analyses of the proposed transfer of authority in the fields of taxation, education, health and leisure, suggested procedures for the Palestinian elections, alternatives to the notion of arbitration, close scrutiny of proposals for economic co-operation, and consultation with the Americans at the highest level.

I took the document with its three sections and showed it to Peres in the course of a private meeting. I didn't present it as a turning point in the Israeli–Arab dispute, nor as a historic milestone. I told him that Yair and Ron had held two meetings in Norway with Palestinians from Tunis and that between them they had come up with something which could form the basis for more American shuttle diplomacy. Peres asked who the Palestinians were and I told him. He had never heard of them previously, which added to the non-specific nature of the business. 'Right, I'll go through this and see if there's anything interesting. Is there anything else?' There was nothing else, and with that the conversation was over.

I went down the stairs, reflecting that the Palestinian and Norwegian leaderships must now be chewing their nails in their impatience to hear whether there was support in Israel for a document which just might – conceivably – put an end to Israeli–Palestinian confrontation. I had handed Peres a paper, one of many, not giving it any dramatic twist, not urging it on him, and he didn't ask why I hadn't informed him of the meetings earlier.

In the circumstances, I couldn't have acted otherwise, while Shimon doesn't ask questions like that anyway. At the very most you might detect a hint of unease in his tone of voice.

I didn't press him to hurry, and he certainly had a lot of material to read. In 'Oslo headquarters' we felt very tense as we awaited his verdict. The days lengthened and eventually a meeting was convened, also attended by Yair, Ron, Shlomo Gur and Peres's office manager, Avi Gil. This was subsequently to be the new, regular forum of those-in-the-know about Oslo. Peres had read the document thoroughly; he made no comment on the two supplements but he wasn't happy with the statement of principles, especially in regard to the voting rights of the Arabs of East Jerusalem. He asked a number of questions about the trusteeship arrangements which were supposed to control Gaza in the interim period. We discussed the issue at length, each of us contributing his conception of the function and scope of trusteeship, but Peres remained unconvinced.

But we already knew that the point at issue was the legitimisation of the process. He asked no questions about the actual meetings, about the negotiating procedures. I told him of our concern that he himself and the Prime Minister should be aware of the existence of the track and should guide us through the next phase. Ideally, Yair and Ron could state at the next meeting that Rabin and Peres were aware of the track. Alternatively, they could keep that secret, but they themselves could act in the knowledge that from now on the game was real.

Rabin and Peres set up a private meeting. Such meetings usually dealt with internal party matters, appointments and more general political issues. There was no written record and usually they were conducted in a cordial and constructive spirit, in spite of the intense animosity between the two men, animosity which had not abated even when their working relationship was institutionalised and became more formal. Peres used to prepare himself for these meetings and also summarise them after the event, but the fact that the meetings were tête-à-tête meant that, though they provided the opportunity for frank and sincere exchange of opinions, there was anxiety – at least on Peres's part – that Rabin would forget having endorsed one or other proposal put forward by Peres, and would afterwards accuse him of contravening the understanding between them. Rabin was a man who preferred tête-à-tête sessions, and in an intimate forum he was much more open and affable than he was in larger gatherings, but political discussions in such a restricted forum and without minutes represented a high-risk strategy. My experience led me to the conclusion that three-cornered meetings were preferable and should invariably be minuted.

Peres went to see Rabin with a copy of the document. For the reasons stated above, it is impossible to reconstruct the conversation, but on his return the following became clear: Rabin was not enthusiastic but he was not calling for cessation of the talks; he didn't want to give the impression that he was behind them; the talks should continue but in the spirit of private academic discussions; he didn't want the track to jeopardise resumption of the Washington talks, although he wasn't optimistic about those either. The feeling in the expanded 'Oslo headquarters' was that

Rabin didn't want to alienate Peres at this stage by preventing his involvement in the Norwegian process, but he was personally unimpressed by what, if anything, had been achieved so far.

Our relief was tempered by anxiety: we had received a green light to continue the talks, but we wondered how long we could maintain the framework that had been evolved without confirming that the track was known to Rabin and Peres or without sending an accredited official representative. Our function now would be to try to obtain changes in the documentation while convincing the Palestinians that the track was still a valid and worthwhile project.

It was clear that from my point of view a chapter had ended. From now on this was no longer a process of which I was in effective charge, capable of terminating it or joining it as I saw fit. I had become part of the team steering the process and this was a very complex feeling. I had no doubt that more gridlocks were to be expected – some of them perhaps capable of halting the entire enterprise – and that decision-making would be a much slower and more cumbersome process. On the other hand I was greatly relieved: the fear that Rabin and Peres might demand immediate termination of the game had faded, and responsibility for future steps would now be shared with my superiors.

The first meeting in Sarpsborg was a birth, the admission of Peres to the secret of the track was a birth, as was the briefing of Rabin. We were convinced however that this was not the Prime Minister's perception of things. Peres briefed him, he listened and placed no obstacles in his path. Perhaps he even thought it would do Peres good to have something outside the normal routine to concern himself with.

Now we could ask Terje Larsen to schedule the third round, and in the expanded 'Oslo headquarters' we added our comments to the papers which Yair and Ron had brought with them. Peres got himself involved, as only he knew how to get himself involved, either because nothing was happening in official channels against the background of the Hamas deportations or because this was the only opportunity to deal with Palestinians that Rabin would allow him.

The issue of the Arab franchise in East Jerusalem was especially difficult for Peres and he wanted to go back and redefine it. As for Gaza, we discussed the significance of trusteeship and began to look for alternatives, including transfer of all responsibilities to the Palestinian Authority in Gaza before the transfer of responsibilities in Judaea and Samaria. Peres was surprised that in Norway the Palestinians had not raised the issue of Jericho. It was true that when he had raised it with Mubarak he had received a negative response, but in a subsequent meeting between Mubarak and Rabin the Egyptian President had said that Arafat was amenable to the Gaza–Jericho concept (although he also wanted control of the Jordan bridges, an obviously impossible demand because it meant much more land). The question was: had the Palestinians given up on the idea, or were their envoys unaware that such an offer had been made, in which case they were not as senior as we had been led to believe?

Rabin wanted to salvage the Washington talks – not because he believed in their efficacy but rather because of his acute embarrassment at the way that the fiasco of the Hamas deportations had led to the suspension of the political process, just as a new President was moving into the White House. Through Peres, he asked us to use the opportunity of the next session in Norway to urge resumption of the Washington talks.

This was the background to the third meeting: Yair and Ron arrived, their unofficial status apparently unchanged, without the authority to reveal to the Palestinians that, besides mine, they had the support of Rabin and Peres. It was Terje Larsen who got the hint and who told Abu Ala that this time there was support at the highest level, and it was up to Abu Ala to believe this or not. The amendments which we demanded to the draft were significant, suggesting, perhaps, that new actors had arrived on the stage. The demand to resume the Washington talks was a further hint. The Palestinians, for their part, were afraid we were simply using the Oslo track as a key to unlock the Washington process, and they persisted in their attempts to discover whether Yair and Ron were simply negotiating on their own behalf. The pressure was mounting. Later we were informed that Abu Mazen and his staff were aware of the existence of other tracks – envoys apparently sent by Rabin to conduct indirect dialogue with representatives of the PLO – and the question that concerned them was: is Rabin really conducting a united orchestra, in which various elements are making contact with the PLO with his knowledge and under his supervision and reporting back to him, or are these just private initiatives of which he may or not be aware?

It was not until 20 March that the meeting got under way. Same place, same personnel. We began by asking for the return of the Palestinians to the Washington talks, and Abu Ala said this could not easily be arranged.

On the other hand, it was clear from what he said that the PLO considered the Norwegian track the most important negotiating channel. The Egyptians had been informed both of the existence of the track and of the papers exchanged there, knowledge which was confined to the triumvirate of Mubarak, Foreign Minister Amr Moussa and the President's political adviser, Osama Elbaz. The Norwegians had informed the Americans; Foreign Minister Stoltenberg had briefed Warren Christopher but had shown him no documents. The PLO leadership had decided at this stage to isolate the members of their Washington delegation, confining knowledge of the existence of the track to a group consisting of Arafat, Abu Mazen and the participants themselves.

It was in the interests of the Palestinian delegation to accelerate and conclude the process, and for this reason they expressed willingness to make certain concessions in the formula, especially on the issue of elections – location of polling stations and entitlement to vote. In return, they asked for earlier withdrawal of Israeli forces from Gaza. We stressed our determined opposition to international supervision of the elections, which the Palestinians insisted they needed for internal reasons, so that the Islamist opposition could not deny the importance and the relevance of the elections.

By the end of the third meeting on 21 March there was an understanding that the Washington talks would be resumed; there was also an agreement, accepted by both delegations and supposedly ready for submission to the leaderships on both sides for ratification. This time there were three appendices, two of them dealing with economics and identical to those in the previous version, and a third addressing electoral procedures for the temporary Palestinian Council. It was agreed that Palestinian voting in Jerusalem would be conducted in the places sacred to Islam and to Christianity, that the legislative powers of the Council would be subject to future accords between Israel and the Palestinians, and that the concept of arbitration would be confined to specific issues and would be invoked only when all other means had been exhausted.

The picture that was emerging was as follows: if the PLO leadership and the Israeli government were to approve the draft agreement, by means of American shuttle diplomacy or some other expedient, it would then be for the delegations in Washington to sign the statement of principles with its three appendices, and with this the clock would start ticking: Israeli withdrawal from Gaza and establishment of trusteeship there within two years, and, after two years, beginning negotiations on the permanent settlement, to be concluded at the latest within three years.

After the signing in Washington certain responsibilities would be immediately transferred to local Palestinian councils, negotiation would be concluded on the procedure for elections to the official Palestinian Assembly in accordance with the principles agreed, and these elections would take place within three months from the date of signing. On inauguration, the Council would have legislative powers to be agreed with Israel, and would have a police force at its disposal. The central effort was to be economic, focused on Gaza but also involving the West Bank, aimed at persuading Europe, the USA, Saudi Arabia and the Gulf states to contribute massive aid to the Palestinians, acting in partnership with Israel.

To the Norwegians the American involvement was very important, both at Foreign Minister level and in contacts with Dan Kertzer. To the Palestinians Egyptian involvement was vital and we regarded the involvement of both parties as positive. The agreement was that the Norwegian track would continue to function as a secret channel, to which all issues requiring clarification would be referred. In Norway we would continue to work on problems associated with the various official negotiating channels – bilateral and multilateral – and proceed with the development of plans for the revitalisation of Gaza and for co-operation in major projects. In the course of his visit to the White House, about a week before, Rabin had endorsed the participation of Faisal Husseini in the Washington talks. Abu Ala saw the agreement to include Husseini in the talks as real progress; he didn't demand participation by the official PLO in the official talks, but it was important to him to stress that, even after signing of the agreement, the Norwegian, or PLO–Israeli track, would remain the decisive channel of negotiation.

At the end of the day, this wasn't quite the way things turned out. Although the agreement of 21 March 1993 was broadly similar to the final statement of principles, it was not the same document and some of the things which we had taken for granted in March, such as trusteeship for Gaza, were not even mentioned in September. The Americans did not take up the role which we had envisaged for them, the Norwegian track was exposed and ceased to exist and even the official Israeli–Palestinian track did not continue to operate after the signing of the statement of principles which took place six months later.

In the meantime, the most sensitive political issue – the status of the PLO – was not mentioned at all and, stranger still, the idea of Jericho as an adjunct to Gaza was not yet on the agenda. It seemed that the end was in sight! On parting, it was agreed that we should try to schedule the next round to coincide with the resumption of the official talks in Washington, and so it was no accident that the fourth round of the Oslo track was convened just three days after the resumption of talks in the USA.

During March we began to hear reports that the Norwegian Foreign Minister, Torvald Stoltenberg, was about to relinquish his post and take up a UN appointment in former Yugoslavia. Stoltenberg was one of the more modest heroes of the business, but without his enthusiastic support the Norwegian track would never have got off the ground at all. It is always worth remembering that one of the prosaic reasons for Oslo's hosting of the secret track was its willingness to meet all the logistical expenses of the project. Financial considerations were never mentioned as grounds for restrictions on flights, accommodation, preparation of materials, and this was of great importance to us, especially when the track was operating without official backing; the PLO, in financial straits ever since the Gulf War, was also enabled to operate without financial limitations. The cost of maintaining secrecy and security was a heavy burden on the Norwegians, to say nothing of the direct expenses incurred by the participants, and Stoltenberg was the man who endorsed this, who monitored the talks, reported on them to Warren Christopher and saw their success as a political goal of the highest order. Would his replacement be equally committed? Might he say that this was no concern of his, and that if the Palestinians wanted to make deals with Israel they should do so elsewhere and stop spending the budget of the Norwegian Foreign Ministry? Would Jan Egland remain in his post?

On 2 April the official appointment was announced – Johan Jorgan Holst was to be Foreign Minister. I sighed with relief. Never before had I taken such an interest in the appointment of foreign ministers, except in neighbouring countries or in major powers. Besides our encounter in Oslo we had also met in Israel, when as Defence Minister he had been a guest of Yitzhak Rabin, in December 1987, and I liked the man. I called Egland and he promised me a 'smooth transition' to his new boss as far as our business was concerned. I urged him to be nice to the new minister and be sure to keep his own job, as I couldn't cope with a new minister and a new deputy while the talks were in progress. He promised to bear this in mind.

On the telephone, Holst sounded very excited about this secret project of ours. He said he had understood something was going on but hadn't known the details. Now he was studying the business and intended to be very much a part of it. I commended the efforts of his colleagues – Stoltenberg, Terje, Egland and Mona – and said that continued involvement on the part of the Norwegian government would be greatly appreciated. He assured me there was no question over Norway's continuing involvement; he saw this as the 'jewel in the crown' of his foreign policy. This seemed to me somewhat hyperbolic, an excess of courtesy on his part, but I was relieved to know that changes in the cast were not going to impair the production. It even occurred to me that Holst's acquaintance with Rabin and the fact that both of them were former Defence Ministers might induce our Prime Minister to take the talks more seriously. Today, with both men dead, I have no way of verifying this hypothesis.

As a prelude to the resumption of the Washington talks at the end of April, we held a series of meetings with American and Palestinian representatives. From the Americans we heard of their dissatisfaction with progress thus far and with the Israeli position – insofar as we were standing firm on the same issues as before, issues which to them seemed unimportant. Although Clinton had told Rabin that he wanted to see a lot more progress on the part of Israel, he preferred not to make his strictures public. Moreover, when Egland applied to travel to the USA to brief the State Department on the progress of the Norwegian track, he was asked not to go. He had to content himself with regular telephone conversations with Dan Kertzer, using the secure lines of the American embassy in Oslo. The American government was still bound by its own ban on talking to the PLO and so was prepared to listen with only half an ear to what had been going on in Sarpsborg, but it expressed appreciation of the joint document and the hope that in Washington too it would be possible to adopt its principles. My guess was that the government was reluctant to present to the two sides a document which it had had no hand in preparing.

The Palestinians in the territories were looking forward to the resumption of the Washington talks. We met with Hannan Ashrawi and with Faisal Husseini – no longer a problem. I reflected on the vicissitudes and reversals of the past five months: the Oslo track had been conceived as a means of enabling Faisal and myself to hold secret discussions, and it was

Hannan Ashrawi who had initiated secret contacts between Yair and Abu Ala. Now, in April 1993, Faisal and Hannan were delegates to the official talks in Washington which we were circumventing in Norway, and we couldn't tell them what was going on there because of the PLO leadership's insistence on secrecy...

Faisal and Hannan both complained vehemently about the blockading of the territories and were also worried by the continuing presence of the deportees on the Lebanese border – not least for fear that members of Hamas would return to Gaza as heroes. They appealed for the repatriation of Fatah exiles so that extremists would not be the only ones who had cause to celebrate. Faisal expressed particular concern about the economic situation in the territories and stressed the need to supplement the political talks with economic agreements. He suggested the establishment of a Palestinian development agency which could accept funds from around the world, especially from Saudi Arabia and the World Bank, for the financing of major industrial projects in Gaza and the West Bank and the alleviation of high levels of unemployment. He also underlined the need for Israel to support the leadership of the territories in the Washington talks by making substantial improvements in conditions in the territories, bringing in Palestinian experts from abroad to assist in development, and negotiating on the return of deportees.

In a conversation between Rabin and Peres it was agreed that the next round in Norway would take place only after the Washington talks had begun. It was also decided to reopen the issues of voting in East Jerusalem, arbitration and legislative powers. We held an extended meeting at Peres's home to prepare ourselves for the forthcoming meeting, and the decision was taken that the PLO would be told not to embarrass us at the multi-lateral talks by sending along members of the Palestinian National Council. We would consult Abu Ala and agree on a list of topics to be discussed at the forthcoming meeting of the multilateral conference on economic issues, to be convened in Rome.

At the meeting in Peres's home all members of the 'Oslo planning staff' were present, and it was clear that the Israeli Foreign Minister was sold on the idea, was well acquainted with the material and was interested in a rapid and successful conclusion. In his mind's eye he was already there, at the talks, from now on the success of the talks would be his success, ideologically and personally. No longer a foreign minister of multilateral conferences and cocktail parties, he was personally supervising what he now perceived to be the best possible opportunity for kick-starting the stalled negotiations. The meeting itself focused more on analysis of options than on conclusions. Peres was not yet ready to put forward final positions regarding the draft agreement, and as a result of this Yair and Ron would be obliged at the next meeting to focus discussion on the link between the Norwegian track, the formal talks in Washington and the multilateral talks. This was a very tough assignment. So long as the track remained secret and informal, the other side's scepticism as to the authority of Yair and Ron had been persistent and sometimes tiresome, but the intensity of the work and the opportunity to make rapid progress towards a respectable agreement seemed ample compensation. Now, with the conversion of the secret track into something endorsed by Rabin and Peres, the two academics had lost the extensive room for manoeuvre which they had previously enjoyed, and on the other hand they were still on their own, not allowed to reveal who was standing behind them. I never saw those two less enthusiastic than in the run-up to this round of talks.

But their gloom lifted when they arrived at the new venue. This was a small hotel in the suburbs of Oslo, the Holmankolen Park, cleared of its residents for their benefit. In this ambience of stoical tranquillity, facing the forests, with the delegates forced into one another's company all day, in the evening, at meals and in intermissions, it was possible to devote time both to the important political issues and to the development of the personal relationships that are so important in talks such as these.

It was evident that the Palestinians felt time was running against them, and that they feared the growing power of Hamas. The meeting was convened on 30 April, three days after resumption of the Washington talks, and Abu Ala said that Arafat had decided the talks should continue in spite of inter-Arab difficulties and the problem of the Hamas deportees, to convince us of the importance which he attached to the Norwegian track. He had needed to coerce the delegation into travelling to Washington, in spite of fears of the reaction in the Palestinian bazaars and elsewhere, because he reckoned that in Oslo it would be possible to reach rapid agreement on all the political and economic issues on the agenda. Without such agreement no progress could be made; with such agreement all kinds of new opportunities would be opened up. He pointed out that the Palestinian Communist Party had abandoned the Washington talks, and said this was a loss from the point of view of the PLO leadership.

Abu Ala expressed regret that this meeting had not taken place before the resumption of the Washington talks. Had this been the case, it would have been possible to co-ordinate the opening speeches; as it was, he said, Eli Rubinstein had delivered a tough and uncompromising tirade which had alienated the Palestinian delegation and not done Israel any favours either.

He was firm in his commitment to progress. He promised that members of the PNC, Yusuf Siah and Elias Sanbar, would *not* participate in the economic negotiations in Rome, to avoid embarrassing Israel, and that in the negotiations the Palestinians would support the establishment of a World Bank fund and the supply of electricity to all parts of the region. We co-ordinated arguments against the establishment of a permanent economic secretariat, in deference to Palestinian fears of a hostile Syrian reaction.

Yair was asked if he had with him definitive Israeli positions regarding the trusteeship formula agreed at the previous session – a question which caused him acute anxiety. He was forced to admit that deliberations in Israel were not complete and he had no official answer; he hoped that firm proposals could be worked out and presented to the Palestinians within a week.

At this stage, and for the first time in the course of the four extended meetings between the two sides, the Jericho idea was thrown into the ring. Abu Ala said that after much deliberation the PLO leadership had come to the conclusion that the residents of the West Bank would refuse to believe in the prospect of Israeli troop withdrawals from this sector as well if at this stage the only perceived withdrawals were those from Gaza. To restore confidence in the West Bank, a symbolic exit from the sector should be considered, and the most convenient place for both Israeli and Palestinian purposes was Jericho. He made no reference to the fact that this was actually a 'circular deal' – originating in a suggestion from Peres to Mubarak, referred by Mubarak to Arafat and now brought back to us. Abu Ala did not repeat what Mubarak had told Rabin, that the Jordan bridges should be controlled by the Palestinian Authority, but he stressed the need for tight co-operation in this area between Israel and the Palestinian police. At the same time, he was at pains to point out that consideration of the Jericho idea should not impede agreement; it was not a condition for agreement, only a private proposal. Then he launched into an account of his vision for the future.

He spoke of the need for a joint plan whereby both sides would seek to educate for peace; of his belief in the prospect of inducing Saudi Arabia to finance development projects in Gaza and the West Bank, with emphasis on housing, sanitation, hotels and a new port (as it later proved, his optimism was misplaced); of the transference of the PLO leadership to Gaza in gradual stages, probably to be concluded with the arrival of Arafat himself, and of very close co-operation with Israel on issues of security and economics. His dream, he said, was to establish a Jordanian–Palestinian confederation and a tripartite Israeli–Jordanian–Palestinian economic union. He proposed, as a matter of urgency, the creation of ten small working groups to address issues such as joint action against terrorism, environmental quality, energy and communications; the Norwegians immediately undertook to finance the activities of all these groups. The question was: when could we sign the statement of principles and start making real progress? The next meeting was scheduled for the following weekend.

How long could we delay our response? In Israel we hadn't even got as far as discussing it with the Prime Minister and the Foreign Minister. As usual, current issues were taking precedence – the inconclusive paper-shuffling in Washington and the continuing hermetic blockade of the territories. On the other hand, in the multilateral context there actually was some positive progress, proving the efficacy of the Oslo track: besides the fact that the PNC was not represented at the Rome talks, there was a high degree of harmony between the Israeli and Palestinian delegations regarding all the draft resolutions, much to the astonishment of the various Arab delegations. When asked to explain, the Palestinians could only shrug and say: 'We have our instructions.'

'Oslo Command' had no choice but to instruct Yair and Ron to attend the next session and not to address the statement of principles; to apologise, explain that deliberations were not yet complete and move on to other issues. Other issues discussed at the next meeting included the latest offer regarding Jericho, the forthcoming session of the working committee on refugee affairs in the context of the multilateral talks, and the Washington talks. Abu Ala said that the PLO was in an awkward position because nothing was really happening in Washington, and to admit this fact publicly would be playing into the hands of the extremists. Against this background they considered it vital that Israel engage in some confidence-building measures such as unification of families and release of detainees. Yair and Ron promised to look into this.

This meeting, the fifth in all, was convened in Oslo itself, in the government guesthouse near the royal palace. The biggest surprise of this round of talks was the ministerial involvement: the new Norwegian Foreign Minister, who was well aware of the potential of the talks taking place in his country, participated in two sessions over the weekend of 8–9 May, devoting most of his efforts towards ensuring Israeli–Palestinian co-ordination in the refugee affairs committee. The latter, in which very little of a practical nature had been achieved, was one of the most sensitive committees, with a lot of wrangling over definitions (particularly relating to the precise scope of the 'family', for the purposes of unification of families). It was a natural area for emotional and hard-hitting speeches.

The fifth round was the last in this phase of the talks. On their return Yair and Ron told me of their conviction that they could proceed no further with the apparatus as it then was. No way could they go back to the Palestinians without referring to the draft agreement, and no way could they pass the time chattering about the importance of the Washington talks, when everybody knew nothing was happening there. Too many parties were involved in the Oslo track; it was all getting too serious. If it was decided to kill it off, it would be a mistake, but a logical one; if the decision was to continue, we had to make up our minds on the statement of principles.

On 13 May the weekly meeting between Rabin and Peres took place. Peres told the Prime Minister the latest news from Oslo and said he felt this was the time to take the bull by the horns and make the negotiations official, reaching agreement on the statement of principles and getting it signed. This meeting was held exactly ten months after the government's inauguration, so Rabin's promise to complete negotiations on the interim settlement within six to nine months was already void. Rabin always considered himself a man of his word, and there can be no doubt that he deeply regretted his failure to fulfil one of his most important election pledges.

He asked Peres what he proposed, and Peres proposed himself: he would personally head the Israeli delegation, travelling secretly to Oslo and taking charge of the negotiations. Predictably, Rabin vetoed the proposal. In his opinion, involvement by senior politicians would have far-reaching and possibly dangerous consequences in a situation where Israel had not recognised the PLO and the American government was still prohibiting contacts with it. If an extra team member was required, a senior civil servant was preferable. Shimon suggested the ranking civil servant closest to him, Uri Savir. Rabin ratified the proposal the following day.

I had known Uri since Peres's first visit to the USA as Prime Minister in October 1984. After seven long years of serving as Labour Party spokesman, I had been appointed government secretary and Shimon was looking for a new spokesman, somebody young and professional with acute political antennae. Among those he consulted was his spokesman in the Defence Ministry, Naftali Levi, and Naftali warmly recommended a young man, a second-generation Foreign Ministry diplomat named Uri Savir currently serving as press attaché at the consulate in New York.

After meeting with President Reagan and Secretary of State Shultz in Washington, we spent a weekend in New York. Uri was responsible for organising the Prime Minister's interviews in the city, and he knew he was 'being watched'. Shimon asked me and his policy adviser, Nimrod Novik, to check whether this young man was fit for such an important and sensitive post. We watched him during that weekend at the Regency Hotel and judged him eminently suitable for inclusion in the team that was being constructed around Shimon, nicknamed 'The Blazers'. Uri came across as a shrewd operator with a fine sense of humour, a versatile linguist and media expert whose political heart was definitely in the right place. We shared our impressions with Peres and he accepted our recommendation. Before our return to Israel I invited Uri to my hotel room, dealt with some requests on his part for press interviews and concluded by saying, as if it was an afterthought, 'You'd better start packing, you're coming home with us!' We had worked together ever since.

Uri was a genuine asset. As the Prime Minister's spokesman he soon became his confidant and one of the people closest to him. He was part of the team which I set up to work in close support of the Prime Minister for the twenty-five months of his term; and at the end of that period when I was appointed political director of the Foreign Ministry, he took over as the Minister's office chief. After two more years of working with him very closely, I appointed him consul-general in New York. This was without doubt a meteoric rise for a diplomat who had left New York as a press attaché and was now returning four years later as head of the consulate – which is incidentally Israel's biggest diplomatic mission anywhere in the world.

Uri served in New York for a further four years, while Labour was in the unity government and then in opposition. This was a highly successful tour of duty and his skilful handling of his Jewish and non-Jewish clientele and of the media was impressive, so much so that Foreign Minister David Levy summoned him home and appointed him deputy director of the European desk in the Foreign Ministry. In practical terms, Uri played a much more central role than that of the conventional deputy director and when we returned to power – Shimon as Minister and I as his deputy – he participated in the most important and sensitive meetings.

The director-general of the Ministry, Yossi Hadas, was about to retire, and in early 1993 Peres was looking for candidates to replace him. When Uri's name was mentioned in discussion of the appointment, anxiety was raised as to whether veteran employees might see this as unduly rapid promotion; would men twenty or twenty-five years his senior have difficulty following his instructions? Other names were suggested and dropped; some of these were serious and trustworthy people but none was close to Peres, who did not want to waste time 'breaking in' a new director-general. I advised Shimon to follow his instinct – if he was happy to have Uri appointed, he should do it and stop worrying. After all, this would not be an outside appointment but someone from the very heart of the Ministry and one of the most talented men around. In the end the appointment went ahead and, although initially a few eyebrows were raised, before long it was clear to all that the job fitted him like a glove. A few weeks after being appointed he became, without knowing it, the first senior official Israeli negotiator to face the PLO.

The business hit Uri like a bolt from the blue. He had barely had time to get into the director-general's shoes, to study the issues and the agenda and set his priorities, and already he had been 'volunteered' for a job that was way outside his purview. He knew the USA well, had also served in Canada and had grown up in Finland, but had no experience of Middle East negotiations. He wasn't familiar with the issues under discussion, nor had he been following the Washington talks.

His jaw dropped still further when I invited him into my office and introduced him to the members of 'Oslo Command', before letting him into the secret of the Norwegian track. We were all there: Yair and Ron, Avi Gil, Shlomo Gur and myself. For six months or so the process had been operating, with only a wall separating his office from mine, and he had had no idea that anything like this was afoot. We showed him the material, explained the dilemmas facing him, described some of the personalities involved – Norwegian and Palestinian – and prepared him thoroughly for the next meeting, scheduled for 21 May.

The next three weeks were a period of crisis with many upheavals. On the one hand we had lifted the status of the talks to official level, on the other doubts were being raised about the very continuation of the track. At the end of this period it became clear that the talks would continue to be held, and held with increasing frequency, until a conclusion was reached.

For the meeting at the Holmankolen Park, Savir arrived with clear instructions to get changes in the statement of principles, not to agree to it, and to stress the importance of the continuation of official talks in Washington. So in his opening speech he underlined the importance of the Washington talks and Abu Ala followed suit. Although it was clear to all that Oslo was far more significant than the official talks, due lip-service was paid. There could be no doubt that Oslo would remain the real laboratory for months and possibly years to come, but the bilateral and multilateral debates would always be conducted elsewhere. The notion of perpetual secrecy was still maintained.

When Savir and Abu Ala shook hands, Israel effectively recognised the PLO. This was a boost for the PLO, one which it did not seek to exploit. The discussions between the heads of the delegations proceeded remarkably well, easing Uri into his new and demanding role. They addressed the statement of principles, deleted the appendix concerning electoral arrangements, made the issue of arbitration hypothetical, changed the proposal regarding elections in Jerusalem, added a codicil on security and drafted a clause facilitating the inclusion of Jericho.

Abu Ala asked for humanitarian gestures on the part of Israel to mark the Muslim festival of Eid el-Adha, due to begin on 1 June: gestures including the release of prisoners and detainees and the repatriation of long-standing exiles. He painted a gloomy picture of morale on the Palestinian side; there was widespread disappointment at the stalemate in Washington, while the progress being made in the Norwegian track could not, of course, be divulged. The continuing blockade was making life in the territories unbearable, funds from the Gulf were no longer coming through, and without an injection of hope there would be intensifying demands for suspension of the Washington talks.

Uri was impressed by Abu Ala's emphasis on economic issues. His opposite number hung great hopes on Palestinian–Israeli co-operation in economics and infrastructure, and even expressed his appreciation of

Israel's striking achievements in these areas. He suggested the marketing of peace by means of a special educational project, an idea which, regrettably was never to be realised.

The meeting concluded with the Palestinians again stressing the importance of rapid agreement on the statement of principles, so that it could be presented to the Americans in readiness for signing by the delegates in Washington, whereas we knew that we wouldn't meet again before resumption of the Washington talks, resumption that had not yet been scheduled.

Immediately after the end of this round, Holst set out for his first visit to the USA as Foreign Minister. He was eager to brief Warren Christopher on the progress of the negotiations, explaining that now, with the inclusion of Uri Savir in the team, they were quasi-official. On Friday evening he called me at home from his hotel in Washington. 'In an hour from now I'm meeting the Secretary of State,' he told me. 'What can I tell him?' I laughed. 'What's the joke?' he asked, clearly bemused by my response. 'It's rather comical when the Norwegian Foreign Minister asks the Israeli deputy Foreign Minister what to say to the American Foreign Minister about the Middle East peace process,' I explained. Holst saw the funny side but still wanted an answer. I suggested he say there was progress in the Oslo track and Israel had upgraded the status of the talks. 'If he doesn't press you, don't volunteer the fact that Savir is involved,' I added.

Later that night, after his meeting with Christopher, Holst called me again. 'I told him. He didn't press me, and my impression is he thinks Oslo is just a talking-shop. He doesn't know about Uri.'

The trio returned from Oslo, Uri in euphoric mood. It took some time before he calmed down sufficiently to give us his more objective impressions. He was convinced of the importance of the track, firmly believing 'there's someone to talk to'. But he said that a lawyer should go over the text before any further negotiations on the statement of principles took place. At a meeting of the extended forum of Oslo-watchers we shared out among ourselves the many assignments set before us – revision of the electoral appendix, draft proposals for the marketing of peace, preparation of an appendix on security and decisions on projects in the economic sphere. We also decided to invite Yoel Singer to give his opinion of the draft statement of principles. Yoel asked few questions, and within two days he had flown in from America.

I had first met Yoel in the course of the interminable wrangling over the future of Taba, in 1985–6. Shimon was then serving as Prime Minister, and the business of locating border posts in the region of Taba and the question of resorting to arbitration were a long-running preoccupation, until in January 1986, after a protracted night session, the cabinet decided in favour of arbitration and as a result the Egyptian ambassador returned to Israel. (What actually happened was that the current chargé d'affaires of the embassy, Mohamed Bassiouny, was promoted to the rank of ambassador.)

Yoel was then a colonel, head of the international law section of the Israel Defence Forces (IDF). He impressed me with his logical analyses, his pragmatism, his professionalism and, especially, his willingness to speak his mind even when at odds with his superiors – Chief of Staff, Defence Minister or Prime Minister. Apart from this, he was the son of Gideon Singer, a well-known cabaret star of the 1950s and 1960s.

In one of my first conversations with Shlomo Gur, on my entry into office, I told him I would have liked to have someone like Yoel working with me on the peace process – someone open, professional and trustworthy. Shlomo told me Yoel wasn't in Israel; he had been discharged from the army and had joined the law firm of Sidley & Austin in Washington. It wasn't likely he would want to come back and work in the Foreign Ministry.

I asked Shlomo Gur to check this out for me. I also told him that I couldn't commit myself to employing him, since the appointment of a legal adviser from outside was likely to be very problematical in the Foreign Ministry, where virtually all appointments were internal.

Yoel's wife Naomi was working as secretary to the ambassador in Washington, so it was easy to contact him. Shlomo came back to me and said: 'Yoel promises that if he's offered a job as legal adviser to the Foreign Ministry, he'll drop everything and come.' The rest was down to me: finding a suitable post for the current legal adviser, a veteran employee of the department, an eminent professional who had held the job for many years, and protracted arguments with representatives of the workers' council who were not impressed by my revolutionary proposal, not least because – if the post needed filling at all, which they disputed – there was no shortage of internal candidates. Peres supported me in my efforts, and it seemed to me the business was well in hand, but in early June the appointment had yet to be confirmed and Yoel was still working for his law firm in Washington. When we reached the point where we needed a

discreet legal adviser, it seemed natural that the three of us – Peres, Uri
and I – should turn to Yoel. So Yoel came.

Singer was the veteran peacemonger among us: in his twenties he had
been a member of the autonomy team to the talks with the Egyptians
headed by the Interior Minister of the day, Yosef Burg, then he was
a partner in brokering a peace treaty with Lebanon which was never
implemented, and later still he represented the army in the negotiations
over Taba, which was how we met. As we had done for Uri we arranged
an 'initiation ceremony', and in the space of three hours he was a party
to the whole secret. He was astonished by the Oslo story and very curious,
taking the draft statement of principles and settling down to read it.

For a long time he scanned the paper, continually making notes. We
suspected he was going to tear us apart, and sure enough he didn't spare
us the lash of his criticism. Yoel didn't like the notion of trusteeship in
Gaza, especially as this trusteeship was not adequately defined. He feared
any kind of trusteeship in which the UN was involved alongside states
such as Jordan, Egypt or Tunisia, either out of traditional Israeli distrust
of UN involvement or because such trusteeship in Gaza was likely to
lead to Palestinian demands for similar arrangements in the West Bank.
Another idea, of turning Gaza into part of a Jordanian–Palestinian confederation, didn't appeal to him either, since it would imply the existence
of a Palestinian state in Gaza.

He preferred full autonomy in the Strip, as against partial autonomy
(which means autonomy only in a few spheres) in the West Bank. It was
very important to him that the formal authority for awarding autonomy
should be in the hands of Israel, even if this was understood and not
stated explicitly. But the most surprising thing, tossed into the ring with
typical Singer nonchalance, was the idea of agreeing mutual recognition
with the PLO, so that both sides would know who was signing the
agreement.

The logic that guided him was very clear: sooner or later news of the
negotiations between Israel and the PLO would leak out and it would
emerge that the PLO itself had promised Israel nothing other than an
agreement on principles between the two delegations. If, on the other
hand, there were to be mutual recognition, the PLO could promise an
end to the *intifada* and the cessation of all acts of terror on its part, the
disarming of other groups – on its arrival in Gaza – and so forth. The PLO
was an address while the Palestinian Delegation in the Washington talks

was only a delegation. In these circumstances, Israel would agree to allow the PLO leadership to move to Gaza, at a later stage, and to operate there.

Yoel drew up a draft agreement on mutual recognition between Israel and the PLO. It contained a dozen clauses and he wrote it out by hand, on notepaper from the Hilton Hotel where he was staying. I was so alarmed by the heading, fearing that unfriendly eyes might see it prematurely, that I erased it with Tipp-Ex and replaced it with something slightly more innocuous, substituting 'Palestinian representatives' for 'PLO'. Yoel laughed and asked what I was so worried about. I told him that I reckoned Oslo was quite enough to be going on with; if we proposed an agreement with the PLO, Rabin and Peres would probably throw us down the stairs. 'At least let's call it something else.' As it turned out, my prediction was less than accurate.

We went up to Shimon's office for a meeting convened to tie up loose ends from the previous round, to discuss Yoel's observations and to prepare for the next day's meeting between the Foreign Minister and the Prime Minister. The full team of those privy to the talks was present, the team which was to remain unchanged until the signing of the accord: Peres, Savir, Singer, Gil, Gur, Hirschfeld, Pundak and myself. Singer expressed warm appreciation of the statement of principles and raised a series of points, some of them substantial, others less so, and two in particular on which he dwelt at length: withdrawal from Gaza in place of trusteeship and mutual recognition with the PLO.

Peres didn't fall off his chair; he didn't jump for joy either. He seemed very relaxed and in control of the situation after a period of months during which he had felt unease and even frustration at Rabin's manifest intention to run all the shows himself. He analysed the status of the talks in all tracks, and as usual this was a thorough and judicious analysis, observing developments from an elevated perspective and making connections that were not superficially evident. Regarding trusteeship, its advantage in his opinion was that it enabled Egypt, Jordan and possibly Tunisia as well to become involved in the process and work towards eventual confederation. He was utterly averse to mutual recognition with the PLO. He preferred relations with the PLO to be kept vague and he felt that recognition of the PLO was too precious an asset, for which Israel would require compensation not only from the Palestinians themselves but also from other agencies such as the European Community, which had been demanding this of us for years. At this early stage recognition was a card to be kept in the hand.

A dispute of a very intense and speculative nature developed between us. I said that I agreed with Yoel: we were conducting negotiations without admitting even to ourselves who we were talking to; we had already effectively recognised the PLO and yet we were still trying to deceive ourselves and not securing even a cessation of violence in return for our efforts.

Peres did not veto the proposal to allow the PLO leadership to travel to Gaza but he decided, at the end of a meeting which had dealt with many other issues relating to the statement of principles, that there would be no agreement with the PLO and the mechanism would remain as it had been envisaged from the start – agreement between the delegations in Washington. As we left the Minister's office Yoel told me that we must not neglect the issue of mutual recognition; it was up to us to convince Peres and Rabin of the need for it. Neither of us knew that what seemed to us that evening to have been solid progress was in fact rather less substantial than the air in Shimon's office. We were just a few hours away from the worst internal crisis of the Oslo track.

The next day, 6 June 1993, Rabin and Peres met in private. Peres was supposed to be briefing the Prime Minister on the latest meeting under Uri's leadership and showing him the ten principles thrashed out for the interim agreement. He returned after the conversation looking gloomy; I know no face that betrays inner feelings more clearly than does Shimon's. 'How was the meeting?' I asked him. 'Okay,' he replied. 'Yitzhak isn't too happy about some points and in the meantime he wants nothing done, no more trips to Oslo, before resumption of the talks in Washington.'

This was not all. At noon the next day, a sealed envelope bearing the stamp of the Prime Minister's office, delivered by hand, arrived on the Foreign Minister's desk. In the letter, spread over two pages, Rabin described the 'Oslo contacts' as a threat to the peace process, and expressed the suspicion that the extremists of PLO-Tunis were intent on under-mining the Washington negotiations between ourselves and the moderate Palestinians. The fact that the Palestinian delegation in Washington had refused to meet representatives of the US State Department in the last round was evidence, he suggested, of extremist instructions emanating from the PLO.

There was more: Rabin suspected that the PLO was trying, with hypocritical blandishments, to sabotage negotiations in all the tracks – Syrian, Lebanese and Jordanian. The declaration of principles, which he had now seen for the first time, was unacceptable, especially in view of the fact that it had been put together without prior consultation with him. In conclusion, Rabin demanded a suspension of contacts pending the resumption of negotiations in Washington or at least until the next meeting between him and Peres.

I invited the 'war council' to meet me in Jerusalem. We felt our world was growing dark; we couldn't understand the turnabout in Rabin's thinking, considering that only two weeks before he had been prepared to endorse Uri's participation, and yet now he saw the process as a threat. What had happened in the meantime? Even today I have no answer to this question, a question which I suppose will never now be answered. One possibility is that when Rabin heard of the refusal of the Palestinians in Washington to meet members of the peace task-force led by Dennis Ross, he drew the conclusion that there was a connection with Oslo. The reason could be something else entirely. One fact did become clear later: the letter did not arise out of consultation between the Prime Minister and one of his aides, since none of them knew of the existence of the Oslo track.

Within a few hours Yair and Ron had drawn up an orderly and detailed report, setting out the advantages of Oslo. The declaration of principles was presented as an agreement on Palestinian self-government in exchange for cessation of terrorism, co-operation with Israel and establishment of a basis for joint economic ventures; Israel would retain the core authority over the five years of the interim period, would relinquish control of Gaza and would remain responsible for the security of Israelis in the settlements. PLO involvement in the process would lend greater legitimacy to the pragmatic elements which would represent the Palestinian cause in the territories and would no doubt have to contend with extremists who opposed the agreement.

At the forthcoming meeting in Oslo, the two of them would press for agreement on the declaration of principles, to facilitate the transfer of partial powers to the Palestinians, the restoration of support for the process from American, European and Arab quarters, the construction of economic aid for the Palestinians and plans for the marketing of peace. At the end of the exercise the paper would be signed in Washington by the two delegations and the interim period would begin. Certain powers would be transferred immediately to the Palestinians, a Palestinian police force would be established and would confiscate arms held illegally by Palestinian citizens, and discussions would begin on arrangements for elections to the Palestinian Council. Within a few months the elections would be held and the Palestinians would establish their own institutions, while Israel would pull out of Jericho and enable the Palestinians to use this city as their centre of operations. Within two years Israel would also withdraw from Gaza, and two years after the signing of the statement of principles negotiations would begin on the permanent settlement.

On the basis of this paper and the conclusions reached in our discussions, Peres composed his reply to Rabin. He noted with satisfaction that the Palestinians had told us in Oslo that the Washington talks would be resumed on 15 June, meaning that the PLO understood the importance to us of the official talks and was maintaining them primarily as a means of keeping Oslo afloat. He stressed the fact that the PLO's positions in Oslo were considerably more moderate than those of the Palestinians in the official talks, both in terms of the authority to make agreements and in relation to early implementation of withdrawal from Gaza, without waiting for finalisation of details of the interim solution. Issues such as the Jewish settlements and Jerusalem would be deferred to the agenda of the final settlement and did not constitute an obstacle to the interim settlement, while the moderating influence of the Oslo track on the multilateral talks had been demonstrated on several occasions. As for the ten points: they did not bind Israel and were definitely negotiable.

The day after the sending of Shimon's reply, 10 June 1993, we were invited to the Prime Minister's office – Peres, Singer and myself. From this time until the signing of the deal, three months later, this forum met on a regular basis, at least once a week, to oversee the Oslo talks. Rabin was very pleased to have Singer as a member of the club. This was another of Yoel's assets, one which I had not taken into account. Rabin had encountered the young legal officer in various circumstances and appreciated his professionalism and integrity. Gaining Rabin's trust was a particularly precious acquisition, and Yoel had it. I was always expecting the quartet to be joined by a fifth member – the Prime Minister's military secretary or his office chief – but our meetings took place without any additional participants. Rabin insisted on maintaining absolute secrecy; in his office only he was aware of the existence of the track, and he feared that any exposure was liable to destroy it. He was relaxed and affable, *au fait* with the details and interested in the continuation of the process. It was as if that bullying letter had never existed. What had happened? Yet another reversal that would never be understood.

Rabin opened the meeting with emphasis on the importance of the official channels. His priority was the effort to persuade our opposite numbers to accept the compromises suggested by the Americans and sign the declaration of principles in Washington. We told him that the greatest advantage to Israel of the Oslo draft agreement was the specification that powers would be transferred to the Palestinians on a gradual basis and that in the meantime civil administration and military government would remain in place. Rabin appeared to be convinced. He wanted this point expressed more explicitly in the agreement, to make it clear that external security would remain in our hands throughout the period of the interim settlement, with only internal security transferred to the Palestinians in the territories, and that all violence against us on their part must cease.

Yoel took up the last point, saying that guaranteeing this would require official agreement with the PLO. I feared that Rabin was going to boot us all out of the room at that juncture. But he didn't fall off his chair either. He looked at Shimon, and Shimon said: 'I don't see any need to recognise the PLO at this time.' 'I agree with Shimon,' said Rabin, with a hint of relief. But Yoel was not deterred. With indomitable courage in the face of this invincible duo, he asked: 'What if I propose this in Oslo in a private capacity, in my own name?'

'In your own name you can propose whatever you like,' Rabin replied, dismissing him as casually as if letting him out of school early to go home and collect his cinema tickets. From this moment, Oslo ceased to be a secret track underwriting the Washington talks, and became the track establishing recognition between the government of Israel and the Palestine Liberation Organisation.

Yoel was supposed to be the last addition to our delegation in Oslo. His status was bizarre: an attorney in an office in Washington, unconfirmed candidate for the post of legal adviser to the Israeli Foreign Ministry, working for no financial incentive and, as meetings became more frequent, the busiest of us all. A few days in the week in his Washington office; towards the weekend, the four-sided forum in the Prime Minister's presence; at the weekend, Oslo; at the start of the week, reporting to Peres and to me on the talks; and as the week progressed, back to Washington. Privately, I likened him to the lover of Irma La Douce who works by day in the Paris meat market and by night is his loved one's rich and elderly suitor. No one in his ornate Washington office, with its 700 employees, could have imagined what this attorney got up to at weekends.

From Rabin's point of view, Yoel's first mission was like that of the dove dispatched by Noah, to see if the waters had receded. If Yoel returned with negative impressions, the track would almost certainly be shut down. Yoel knew this, and he prepared himself meticulously. During the three days remaining before the next Oslo meeting he compiled a list of forty questions requiring clarification from the Palestinians. Most of them were in the form 'what happens if ...?', and they addressed topics such as the scope of the elections, the precise status of Gaza after withdrawal of Israeli forces, external security during the interim period, the roles of Jordan and Egypt, identifying the future signers of the agreement in Washington (leaders of the joint Jordanian–Palestinian delegation? The Palestinians alone? Which Palestinians?), the cessation of the *intifada* and all other violence, eligibility for election to the temporary Assembly, the situation likely to arise in the territories in the event of no agreement on elections, the benefits of trusteeship in Gaza from the perspective of the Palestinians, the nature of the link between Gaza and the West Bank, the chances of producing a memorandum of understanding alongside the statement of principles and so on and so on.

At the end of this round I flew to the USA. In Washington, after the sensitive discussions with the peace team, I was visited in my hotel room by Dan Kertzer. In conversations with the team Oslo had not been mentioned, but Dan knew of the information given by Holst to Warren Christopher, and even before sitting down he fired the question: 'Who did you send to Oslo aside from Yair and Ron?' I told him I was no longer the one doing the sending, this was all being handled at the very highest level, and the person concerned was Yoel Singer. For some reason I was reluctant to reveal the fact that the director-general of the Israeli Foreign Ministry was negotiating with the leadership of the PLO.

The Mayflower Hotel, where as usual we were accommodated, was a hive of activity, swarming with Israelis: members of various committees, representatives of the Prime Minister's office, the army, and the Defence and Foreign Ministries, communications experts, security personnel, clerks and secretaries. Eli Rubinstein, friendly and good-natured as ever, ruled this empire with a firm hand and a felicitous turn of phrase, and in the evening I attended a daily briefing session for heads of delegations on the state of the negotiations. In none of the tracks had progress been made, although in the Palestinian track there had at least been some straight talking. I felt as if I had stepped through a time-warp and returned to an earlier period, meeting people whose futures I could reveal were I not forbidden to do so. Three or four people, currently sitting in Oslo, were destined within less than three months to close the gaps which in Washington seemed unbridgeable.

The seventh round in Norway was convened on 13 June 1993. The first session took place in the private apartment of Terje and Mona in Oslo, the second in a villa belonging to the Norwegian Foreign Ministry. The Palestinian trio was unchanged, but the Israeli side had now become a quartet. While at the sixth session it had been Uri who held the stage, this time it was Yoel's show. He asked the questions and gave the answers.

The Palestinians were uneasy about this. Every week a new Israeli was turning up and apparently calling the shots, until the next one appeared and took over. On the other hand, they treated Yoel's participation as further proof of the importance of the talks and assumed that it pointed to increasing involvement on the part of Rabin, whose name cropped up frequently in Yoel's speeches. However, his forty questions drove them to the conclusion that all their efforts so far had been in vain, and that they would have to start again from zero just when it had seemed to them that all that remained was getting the Prime Minister's final assent to the declaration of principles. So sure were they that the end was near that Abu Mazen was standing by in Tunis, waiting for a call from Oslo to tell him all was in order and he could instruct the delegation in Washington to sign the declaration of principles. Then again, the new difficulties put forward by Yoel were in themselves an indication to them of Israel's determination to get down to some serious talking.

Because of the need to use every minute of the weekend, the meeting began at one o'clock in the morning and at this stage Yoel set out his questions regarding each of the clauses of the draft agreement. The next day, at 10 a.m., Abu Ala began his series of answers. This was, without doubt, the most intensive and practical session of talks so far.

Singer criticised the pace of the talks proceeding in Washington, but left no room for doubt that that was where the important negotiations were taking place; Oslo performed only an auxiliary role. Towards the end of his speech, in an emphatically undramatic tone of voice, he asked about changes to the Palestinian Covenant, about the PLO's undertaking to call a halt to the *intifada* and acts of terror, about agreement with the PLO regarding Gaza. He stressed that these were his personal questions and he had no mandate from Rabin, Peres or me. The Palestinians recorded the questions but made no immediate response.

Abu Ala expressed the discontent of the PLO leadership over the lack of progress in Washington and the continuing closure of the territories. He said that vagueness in the declaration of principles was not necessarily negative, but a means whereby the two sides could interpret the agreements in the manner best suited to their respective domestic requirements, opening the door to negotiation, whereas insistence on premature clarification of all points was liable to prolong the negotiations and delay implementation of the interim settlement. The PLO regarded haste as essential, and it was clear to Abu Ala that by revealing his tactics he was enabling the Israeli delegation to stand more firmly on the issues most important to them.

He spoke with optimism of the future, of the progressive steps which would give both sides faith in each other and of the economic development which would convince the residents of the territories that peace was worthwhile. He was determined to convince Singer of the importance of the track, which he had only just joined. He told how not long ago Arafat had been interviewed on Radio Monte Carlo and had expressed himself in a manner very critical of Israel and its government. As soon as Yair and Ron drew Abu Ala's attention to this, he contacted Arafat who promptly gave another interview, speaking in a rather more conciliatory tone. He also expressed approval of the interview Rabin had given to the East Jerusalem paper *El-Kuds* in which he didn't rule out the possibility of setting up a Palestinian television channel before the elections to the self-governing Assembly.

They both returned to the subject of the mechanics of signing: Israel and the Palestinians, possibly through the intermediary of the Norwegians, would turn to the Americans and present them with the agreed document. The Americans would announce that this was a bridging document, drawn up on the basis of the positions of both sides. Naturally, both delegations would initially express misgivings, declaring that they would have to consult their superiors. Israel and the PLO would instruct the delegations to sign the paper without changes, whatever the personal feelings of the delegates.

'And what happens now?' Abu Ala asked as the meeting ended. Yoel didn't betray his personal feelings. Everything was open, he explained. Our superiors might instruct us to break off the Oslo talks, or they might tell us to carry on and make changes to certain clauses; they might ratify the agreement as it stood. Speaking for himself, he had been more impressed by the explanations he had heard than by certain vague clauses, but the decision would not be his.

Had the waters receded? Did the dove of peace, in the form of Yoel Singer, return with an olive branch? The answer to this is a cautious yes. In a meeting with the Prime Minister he reported his impressions in a precise and dry manner. It was very important to him that the corrected declaration of principles should be accompanied by a secret memorandum of understanding, to be signed separately and to constitute a detailed commentary on the economic principles. He reckoned that this would be obtainable. He noted that the Palestinians were not insisting on the establishment of trusteeship in Gaza, but would prefer the replacement of the departing Israelis by a third party for the duration of the transitional period. He did not detect among the Palestinians any great enthusiasm for elections, an impression which was confirmed when they requested implementation of the evacuation of Gaza before the elections to their self-governing Assembly. He reckoned that the intention regarding Jericho was for a symbolic withdrawal only, and the Palestinians understood that self-government would not apply to East Jerusalem, Jewish settlements and security locations. However, there was Palestinian insistence on their demand that self-government should consist of two bodies, one legislative and the other executive, whereas Israel's position was that there should be only one body, an executive with limited legislative powers.

And as for mutual recognition with the PLO? At this stage his assessment was that, if Israel agreed to recognise the PLO, the PLO would sign a series of undertakings guaranteeing cessation of violence and changing of the Palestinian Covenant. If not, there would be no Palestinian demand for such mutual recognition.

Finally, Yoel recommended continuation of the Norwegian process, suggesting that Israel prepare a new version of the agreement and, in tandem with it, a series of signed understandings. After prolonged debate Rabin accepted his advice, and once more we set to work drafting the new protocols. Yoel took the material with him when he returned to Washington, intending to prepare a new declaration of principles, as well as a nine-point programme for mutual recognition with the PLO – a project which he still described as his 'personal hobby'. Rabin ratified the statement of principles, which now looked a little different: trusteeship in Gaza had disappeared; withdrawal from Gaza would precede the elections; alongside the Gaza withdrawal there would also be withdrawal from Jericho – this too before the elections; in five specific contexts authority would be transferred to the Palestinians, and after the elections a process of phased redeployment would begin, in parallel with discussion of the permanent settlement.

Usually these conversations in the Prime Minister's office were relaxed and friendly. Sometimes they took place on a Friday, late in the afternoon when most employees of the Defence Ministry had gone home, in his favourite Tel Aviv office. Meetings were also occasionally held in Rabin's Jerusalem office, others at his official residence in Jerusalem or at the Accadia Hotel, where he and Leah were staying in the summer of 1993 while their private apartment was being renovated. Meetings at the Accadia he attended in his tennis gear. Usually the full foursome was present; when one or other of us was abroad, the reduced forum would go ahead, and sometimes these sessions came down to private meetings between Rabin and myself.

Previously I had spent hundreds of hours in Rabin's company – at Labour Party meetings, in government, in cabinet, in the foreign affairs and security committee of the Knesset – but in the course of this summer I finally had the opportunity to get to know him intimately, and for the first time ever I felt some sympathy for him. The weight of the world was on his shoulders. He had created this situation and he was paying the price: the economy, security, the coalition – everything landed on his desk. He was a desperately lonely man, perhaps because he was suspicious to the point of paranoia, perhaps for some other reason – certainly not because there was any shortage of people wanting to be close to him.

We could not understand his determination to keep the four-sided forum insulated from any involvement by personnel from his office or his department. Later, when the whole business became public knowledge, he explained that he hadn't wanted to involve the army in politics, but this was not the real reason. He was simply afraid of the possibility of leakage and felt that he needed no one's advice, or that no one's advice was so indispensable that it was worth risking leakage to obtain it.

Every time he would take the new draft of the declaration of principles, fold it and put it in his briefcase. Usually he was very focused, remembering the questions left open from the previous session and attentive to details. But not always. At one meeting we presented him with a new draft and he went through it and approved it. I asked him if he had noticed a small but significant change that we had made to a certain clause. He read it again, said that he really hadn't noticed it – and that the change was unacceptable. This was a change which had seemed to me very important and very positive, and somebody or other asked me why I had drawn his attention to it when he had already ratified the draft. I felt it was my duty to draw his attention to it, since there just wasn't anyone else doing this for him.

It was hard to work in such a fashion. There was no contact-person in the Prime Minister's office, and whenever a problem arose we had to contact Rabin directly, knowing that he had a thousand things on his agenda and we were distracting him with an issue which wasn't all that vital, which would never have existed at all if we hadn't invented it. Sometimes we regretted the absence of an adviser or a secretary at the Prime Minister's side. At one of the Friday meetings in the Defence Ministry Yoel set out some understandings which had been reached in Oslo, one of which referred to the powers to be devolved to the elected Assembly of the temporary government. Rabin saw the clause and went ballistic.

I had seen him angry before, but never in such a state as this – incandescent with rage and yelling at the top of his voice, demanding to know why his explicit instructions were being flouted. The three of us – Peres, Singer and myself – remembering how he had approved this clause at the previous meeting, tried to get this across to him in as polite and tactful a manner as possible, but he was not mollified. Finally Yoel said to him: 'Yitzhak, look at your papers.' With obvious reluctance he opened his briefcase, took out a file, found the comments that he had written in the margins of the previous draft and said simply: 'You're right.' But it was he, of course, who had established the *modus operandi* and we had no choice but to abide by it.

The positive mood of the negotiations in Oslo, the evident interest of the Palestinians in reaching agreement and the mandate given by Rabin to the delegation boosted our optimism regarding continuation of the process. Peres said, in one of the interviews that he gave at this time, that talks with the Palestinians were making more progress than was generally supposed – and almost simultaneously Arafat declared in an interview that nothing was happening in Washington. Within the Palestinian leadership eyebrows were raised and questions asked concerning the possible existence of a secret track. Abu Mazen said later that he had passed a message to Peres suggesting it was preferable to lower the level of optimism, but Peres replied that public opinion had to be prepared. In retrospect it has to be admitted that public opinion was not prepared, and Abu Ala's excellent idea of a joint peace-marketing exercise was never implemented.

Rabin delayed Yoel's next trip to Oslo pending further discussion among ourselves of the declaration of principles and the protocol of understanding. Since the meeting had been scheduled for 25 June, Yair and Ron, the two 'freelancers', decided to go on ahead, not wanting to offend the trio of Palestinians who had already arrived in Norway. Uri did not participate in this round of the talks.

Abu Ala was very agitated. When he was informed about talks between Labour Member of Knesset Ephraim Sneh and the PLO representative in Egypt, Nabil Shaath he suspected that Rabin was intent on 'stitching up' the Palestinians, keeping the Oslo talks going only as a means of guaranteeing survival of the Washington talks; that his aim was to get a quick and superficial agreement in Washington and use this as a basis for accelerated progress towards deals with Jordan and Syria, leaving the Palestinians out in the cold. Sneh had also asked for a meeting with Abu Mazen, but Abu Mazen had refused, reckoning that there was only one secret track and it had to be kept exclusive. Yair and Ron tried to reassure the Palestinians, telling them not to read any political significance into Yoel's delayed arrival.

Singer arrived two days later (explaining that, each time, he had to invent another dying grandmother to persuade his American employers to allow him leave of absence), and got straight down to business. He explained that he had held extensive talks with Rabin and had brought a list of the Prime Minister's remarks. Abu Ala also had a list of remarks, in red ink and in Arafat's handwriting, in the margins of the draft declaration of principles. Hasan Asfur smiled and said the best idea would be for the two 'Ra'ises' (leaders in Arabic) to meet and sort everything out between them. Everyone laughed at this, as if nothing could be more remote and inconceivable. If they had known that the distance between impossibility and realisation was precisely two and a half months, they would no doubt have gaped in disbelief.

Yoel apologised for the plethora of questions raised at the previous session, and expressed his appreciation of the sincere answers received. He explained that the business was sufficiently urgent to require continuous objective scrutiny by Rabin, Peres and myself. Abu Ala asked again whether Rabin was behind the talks between Ephraim Sneh and Nabil Shaath, and Yoel said Rabin had made it clear to him that Oslo was the only authorised track and that any other tracks were binding on nobody. Oslo would also determine what was to happen in Washington, but the Washington talks ought not to be allowed to collapse. He suggested that the Palestinians draw up a number of amendments to the draft declaration of principles, which should be accompanied by a signed and agreed protocol providing a more detailed commentary on every clause; with the signing of these two documents it would be possible to begin the process which was supposed to be completed over the next five years.

Abu Ala was perturbed by what he saw as unnecessary wasting of time; he had come ready to sign that day, and it seemed a new phase was beginning. The longer the delay, the greater the risk of leakage and collapse of the talks. But then he presented a series of questions in Arafat's name: how would Israel view the transfer of Arafat himself from Tunis to Gaza? What would become of the Palestinian institutions already existing in Jerusalem on implementation of the settlement? What was the significance of Rabin's distinction between political and security settlements? How many police personnel could be stationed in Gaza? What would be the status of the agreed protocol? What did Israel think of the idea of joint Palestinian–Israeli patrols? How could an executive arm also be a legislative arm and why was Israel opposed to separation between the two functions?

Yoel answered some of these questions, asked for time to refer the rest to higher authority, and set out an unequivocal line of argument which echoed the preference of Abu Ala: better a short and general agreement on principles reached within a limited space of time than quibbling over details which would only delay the start of implementation of the interim settlement.

'At the last meeting,' Abu Ala said to Yoel, 'you put forward your private proposal regarding mutual recognition with the PLO. Is this still relevant? If so, we will agree to it.' Yoel smiled and said that the proposal was still a private one, but he produced his new nine-point programme and handed it to Abu Ala for his perusal. There was not yet any connection between the declaration of principles and this programme of Yoel's. It was agreed that the next meeting would be held on 4 July. Yoel promised to bring to this meeting his proposals regarding the declaration of principles, the protocol of understanding and all appendices.

In the course of the following week there was a series of meetings with Rabin in which we ratified Yoel's new draft in all particulars. The basic difficulties remained unresolved: legislative powers of the elected Assembly, references to Jerusalem in the interim settlement, the issues to be discussed in the context of the permanent settlement, the status of Gaza and Jericho and the geographical limits of the region of Jericho, regulation of crossing-points and entitlement to vote in elections to the Palestinian Council. We reckoned that the combination of declaration of principles and protocol of understanding responded to our needs, but we couldn't agree even among ourselves on the difference in status between the two documents, who would sign what and would the protocol be kept secret, as Abu Ala wanted. As for the question of recognising the PLO, this was not touched on at all.

The ninth round of Norwegian talks was held in the hamlet of Grasheim, about 100 kilometres to the north of Oslo. Singer presented the completed document that he had prepared and made it clear that willingness to sign it would open the way to immediate implementation of the interim settlement. There was also discussion of the possibility that the document could be signed by the Palestinian element of the Jordanian–Palestinian delegation and by the Israeli delegation in Washington, or – alternatively – by Faisal Husseini and Shimon Peres.

Both sides criticised the way that the Americans were handling the Washington talks, and the bridging proposals which they had presented. The Palestinians expressed their anxiety that once more, as had happened in the time of Shultz and the London Agreement of 1987, the Americans might torpedo the deal as soon as they got their hands on it. The Israelis could not guarantee that such an outcome would not be repeated, but they hoped that since the Americans were aware of what was happening in Oslo, they would have no reason to be surprised or offended.

It was clear that Yoel's text would not be the final one, but our representatives reckoned that the Palestinians would insist on a few amendments and then the deal could go forward. Abu Ala commented on the need to equalise the status of Jericho and of Gaza following the withdrawal of Israeli forces, the need to refer to the Palestinian residents of Jerusalem in connection with elections and the vital necessity – from his point of view – of including some element of arbitration in the deal. He promised to bring detailed comments to the next session.

This meeting, held on 11 July in the Halvarsobel Hotel in Oslo, was the lowest point of the entire negotiating process and the one moment when it seemed that the talks were doomed. The telephone in my home never stopped ringing. From Tel Aviv it seemed more like tactical negotiating than anything else; in Oslo it was crisis-point. Abu Ala had brought with him no fewer than *twenty-six* amendments to the document which Yoel Singer had presented in Grasheim, the 'Grasheim document' as it was henceforward to be called. Later, Abu Mazen admitted that the PLO's demands emanated to some extent from lack of self-confidence. Their impression at this stage was that the Israeli negotiators were a lot more experienced and professional than they. Among the inner circle of those privy to the secret, there was not a single practising lawyer; he himself had tried to make use of his own legal training at the University of Damascus, but to no avail.

Yair told the Palestinian delegates that the amendments they were demanding had turned this meeting into the darkest hour of the conference; Uri said that this was an obstacle liable to send the process back to the beginning. He also declined to sign any protocol because if this protocol was read at home, the talks would be halted immediately. No one in the leadership would accept the Palestinians demands. In any case, he added, there was no prospect of completing this phase of the negotiations in the two to three weeks originally envisaged.

Abu Ala pointed out that the previous week Israel had done something similar; Singer too had put the talks into reverse and they hadn't seen this as the end of the world. The demands were tough: according to the Palestinians, Jericho was supposed to be a substantial region and not just a point on the map for the purposes of Israeli withdrawal. Abu Ala passed on a personal message from Arafat, asking us to make it clear that the Arabs of East Jerusalem would vote in the elections for the self-governing Assembly and not be fobbed off with the assurance that it would be debated in negotiations over the interim settlement. Another demand was that the passage between Gaza and the West Bank should be one of the existing roads or something new (a tunnel or an uplifted road) or an extra-territorial corridor. Sensing that he had perhaps gone a little too far in the points he had raised, Abu Ala added: 'But all of this is open to negotiation.'

It was clear that the inevitable had finally happened: the greater the involvement of senior leaderships in the process, the greater the volume of questions, speculations and demands. On the one hand this was evidence of serious and businesslike attitudes; on the other the road before us seemed longer than ever.

One ray of light on an otherwise gloomy day was Holst's visit to Tunisia. He met President Ben Ali, but his most important encounter was with Arafat. Before the meeting he was briefed by us on the crisis in the talks, so the conversation was focused on certain issues raised by Abu Ala in Oslo. Holst was impressed by Arafat's familiarity with the details of the negotiations and by the importance which he clearly attached to the Oslo track. For this very reason the Norwegian Foreign Minister stressed the danger of the talks collapsing under the weight of the Palestinians' new demands, addressing in particular the issue of the link between Gaza and the West Bank. It was his view that Israel would under no circumstances agree to an extra-territorial corridor, and after prolonged discussion Arafat was persuaded to drop this demand and settle for 'safe passage' – meaning the use of existing roads without hindrance on the part of Israeli security forces.

Terje Larsen and Mona Juul accompanied Holst during his conversations in Tunis, and when the talks were concluded they were asked by the Minister to come to Israel and report to us. Arafat – according to their report – was very proud of the PLO's success in keeping the Oslo track secret, diverting all rumours towards the meeting between Ephraim Sneh and Nabil Shaath. He was excited by the prospect of the Gaza–Jericho handover preceding elections and the establishment of an elected council, since this would boost his credibility in the eyes of the residents of the West Bank and in particular the Palestinians living in those specific sectors. He made it clear to his guests that it wasn't his intention to turn Jericho into a substantial chunk of territory, and that he understood the importance of security to the Israelis; in the future he saw close co-operation between Israel and the Palestinians. For some reason he made no mention of his own intended transfer to Gaza, perhaps assuming that this was a matter of course. All the same, there remained some unresolved points requiring further negotiation, such as the powers of the elected Assembly and the voting rights of the Arabs of East Jerusalem.

On 18 July, after another meeting between Larsen and Arafat, Terje and Mona joined us for a working lunch in Jerusalem, hosted by Peres and also attended by Savir, Gil, Gur, Hirschfeld, Pundak and myself. At this stage, a month before the signing, it still seemed to us that the date for finalisation of the agreement was receding, but the notion of linking the declaration of principles with mutual recognition was very much alive. It could be that we were all eager to tighten this connection, but we always seemed to be returning to the (apparently) marginal issue of the handling of the agreement after signing. Sometimes it seemed that the real points at issue were less problematical than the question of how to deliver the agreement into the public domain.

This lunch at the Laromme Hotel was important for us, in particular because of the opportunity it gave us to hear what Peres was thinking about the future of the process. Yet another paradox: in more than one instance what the host had to say (which we were supposed to know about) came as more of a surprise to us than the information conveyed by our guests. He said that he saw advantages in the winding up of PLO headquarters in Tunis and the installation of Arafat and his colleagues in Gaza, where they could take over the day-to-day running of the place – this on condition that he didn't claim the title of president. (In the end the controversy over titles in the interim settlement, signed in September 1995, was solved by the use in all the texts – English, Arabic and Hebrew – of the Arabic term *rais*, which can mean either 'chairman' or 'president'.)

Peres wasn't too optimistic about the prospect of holding elections for the Palestinian self-rule Council, so any discussion of voting rights and the status of East Jerusalem in this context seemed to him hypothetical. He wanted to wrap up the negotiations and not – as he put it – return to the quagmire of the Washington talks. He also feared that protracted negotiations would endanger the status of the PLO, and when we looked at him, blinking in disbelief, he added: 'I'm not in love with them, but when I think of the alternative, i.e. Hamas – then I become a romantic.' For Terje and Mona there could have been no clearer signal of what was brewing in the Israeli government than this remarkable utterance from its Foreign Minister.

Peres spoke at length about the economic packaging of the political agreement, viz. massive economic aid to the Gaza Strip amounting to millions of dollars, courtesy of the European Community, the World Bank and other international agencies. He compared the dimensions of Gaza with those of Singapore, and said that if the aid was generous enough Gaza could, with the help of its more talented and professionally experienced citizens, become the Singapore of the Middle East. I was not the only one at that table to feel a mild sense of scepticism.

As for the signing of the agreement, we discussed two possibilities: the first, signature in Oslo, binding on both sides but enacted in secret, followed by delivery of the completed document to the Americans, who then offer it back to the two sides in the manner envisaged from the outset; and the second option, a full-dress and emotional public ceremony, in the course of which Peres and Faisal Husseini sign the statement of principles. The credit in any event should be given to the USA, Peres insisted, but he feared that injudicious handling of the exposure of the agreement could lead to a fiasco similar to that of the London experiment, when the two sides (Jordan and Israel) concluded an agreement on principles with the intention of having it returned to them through American mediation; the US Secretary of State decided he wasn't going to play since he was afraid that his involvement might be seen as supporting Peres against Shamir, and the entire process collapsed.

Larsen suggested to Shimon that he should meet Arafat and try, secretly and face to face, to remove the obstacles currently blocking the way. Shimon demurred. Such a secret meeting, if revealed, was liable to cause unnecessary damage. However, for the first time he didn't rule out the possibility of such a meeting *after* the signing of the statement of principles, when it was all out in the open.

On parting, Peres gave the Larsens a letter for the Norwegian Foreign Minister in which he thanked Holst for the efforts he had invested in the negotiations and summarised Israeli positions at this stage of the process.

Holst replied in a letter mailed from Paris and dated 21 July 1993, written the day after he and the Larsens had held another prolonged conversation with Arafat and Abu Ala. In this conversation the Minister made it clear to Arafat that Norway was not a mediator, just the host. Norway had no direct interest in the Middle East conflict, nor in promoting any particular solution; it was motivated solely by the desire to advance the cause of peace everywhere in the world, and here there was a rare window of opportunity which should not be wasted. The present government in Israel was prepared to take a bold step and he, the undisputed leader of the Palestinian people, also had a historic choice to make – whether to follow the road towards consensus or head in another direction.

For Israel, Holst maintained, security was the primary concern. If the *intifada* were to be revived, or terrorist acts committed, the agreement was bound to fail. The Palestinians stood to gain self-rule, which could be converted at a later stage to full independence, as well as economic development in co-operation with Israel and the whole world. Holding up the process, endangering it for the sake of arguing over a formula, was likely to be a fateful mistake. The whole world, he guaranteed, would be overjoyed to discover that against all the gloomy predictions of continuing jealousy, prejudice and extremism in the Middle East, against all the odds, pragmatic elements, yesterday's enemies, had come together and were working quietly towards peace. He appealed to Arafat to do his utmost to ensure that the next round of talks in Norway, scheduled for 24 July, would see signatures on documents.

Arafat agreed that this was a time of historic breakthrough, but he also expressed the fear that Israel would present its departure from the Gaza Strip as a generous gift to the Palestinians, when in fact it would be ridding itself of an intractable mess and an infernal nuisance, and would be only too glad to leave the Strip behind. He wanted it clearly understood that without Jericho there would be no agreement and that there must be access between Gaza and Jericho, though the precise nature of this was open to discussion. He repeated his suspicion that in the declaration of principles the Palestinians would receive a few symbolic concessions which would give Israel a clear run to pursue peace with Jordan, Syria and Lebanon. These states would consider themselves absolved of any obligation towards the Palestinians, who, excluded from the Washington talks, would be left to themselves, unable to influence the permanent settlement, faced with the formidable problems of Gaza and ignored by the rest of the Arab world.

Arafat said he was aware of Israeli sensitivity on the security issue, but he would have difficulty signing such a historic document if it contained no mention of Jerusalem. There should be some reference: perhaps in relation to the rights of Jerusalem's Palestinians to participate in elections, or perhaps referring to the city's importance to members of all religious persuasions. He promised a flexible Palestinian stance in the next round of the Oslo track, said that he knew the destinies of the Palestinians and Israelis were intertwined and that it was essential to work together for the shared future. At the end of the meeting he suggested that, if there were problems signing a declaration of principles, it should at least be possible to sign a joint statement. Here Abu Ala intervened, saying that nothing less than a declaration of principles could be considered, after all these long months of negotiation.

In his letter to Peres, Holst was clearly optimistic about the prospects of success in the next round and progress towards the signing of a deal. Three months after his appointment, the new Norwegian Foreign Minister obviously regarded the Oslo track as the leading item on his political agenda; as far as he was concerned, success in the talks would be his own success.

Among ourselves we responded with a smile, surprised and gratified to find that 'our' track had become such a family affair at the summit of Norwegian politics. Two families had adopted the process – Johan Jorgen Holst and his wife Marianne, who had also entertained the delegates in their home and whose little boy had made his own contribution to the progress of the track, sitting on the knees of both Abu Ala and Uri Savir. The other family of course was the Larsens. For the sake of these people alone we could not fail.

The talks of 25 July began, for our part, with the hope that the Holst–Arafat discussions had changed the atmosphere and that the delegation headed by Abu Ala would arrive in a new spirit, ready to move towards signing. In both delegations the pressure of time was felt, whether on account of the increasing involvement of the higher political echelons of Israel, the PLO and Norway, or leaks that had reached the press, or new American attempts to put forward a bridging deal, which reassured neither side and were a response to the threats of Faisal Husseini, Hannan Ashrawi and Saeb Erakat to resign from the delegation in protest at the lack of progress in Washington.

Premature exposure of the track seemed to us the most serious issue at this time. First, we didn't yet know if the Oslo connection would be revealed officially before the elapse of the thirty-year period had permitted the release of the protocols from the state archives. We still reckoned that the deal would be an American deal, with Oslo continuing to function as a behind-the-scenes forum. Second, such exposure would place both sides in a very awkward situation, bringing the world's press to Oslo and spoiling the informal atmosphere in which the talks had hitherto proceeded.

I was being regularly contacted by journalists, and I was very careful not to lie to them. Since their information was usually inaccurate, I had no difficulty denying the stories put to me. Thus, for example, when there was a rumour of contacts between representatives of Israel and the PLO in Sweden, I could state categorically that no such thing was happening, that Sweden was not a venue for talks. But I knew that I couldn't keep these acrobatics going for much longer.

At the Oslo meeting it soon emerged that there had been no real change. Abu Ala said he had come ready to sign the agreement, but at the same time he presented a fresh list of demands for amendments. Although the guarantees given by Arafat to Holst had been upheld, in reference to the 'safe passage' and the abandonment of the demand that the Arabs of Jerusalem vote in the Holy Places, many questions were left open. The Palestinians expressed the fear that our sole intention was to defer as much as we could to the debate over the permanent settlement, leaving them with a murky and emasculated interim settlement and giving no guarantee at this stage that the permanent settlement would ever be agreed.

Both sides had harsh things to say to the other. Uri told Abu Ala it was time he stopped fretting and started leading. Abu Ala was not impressed. He made an emotional speech, his eyes moistening as he announced his intention to ask Arafat to replace him. Incidentally, in a conversation which took place in Tunis that very day between Ahmed Tibi and Abu Mazen, the latter said that he didn't believe in the possibility of reaching agreement with Israel and that he intended to resign from overall control of the talks.

Uri did not let Abu Ala's peroration go unanswered. He too was emotional as he spoke of the dangers of lost opportunities, of the tremendous efforts already invested in the Oslo track, declaring that we would never forgive ourselves if we failed to seize this rare moment, when Israel was offered the chance of peace and the Palestinians the chance of real self-government. He suggested a review of the document clause by clause and a reassessment of what had been agreed and what had not; on this basis it could be decided whether further discussion was worth while. The Palestinians agreed to this. But Uri and Yoel themselves raised two new topics, relating to the powers of the Palestinian Council and to security issues, and these demands soured the atmosphere of the talks.

From a distance of several years it can be said that some of the disagreements were of little significance, hardly justifying the length of time spent debating them. For example, the Palestinians insisted that the declaration of principles would include a pledge to insert Security Council

Resolutions 242 and 338 in the permanent settlement, intact and undiluted; Israel's contention was that the Resolutions should be inserted in a
manner to be agreed by the parties. After interminable debate it was
decided that the permanent settlement would include Resolutions 242
and 338 – without any reference to 'manner to be agreed' or 'intact and
undiluted'. In fact, what was being discussed was a general principle which
could not be taken to any court of law, a compromise of no practical
significance, then or in the future. On the other hand, the voting rights
of the Arabs of East Jerusalem *did* constitute an issue of great significance;
the decision that the manner of their participation in elections would be
determined at a later date was actually an incentive to them to participate
in elections.

The points of disagreement were well defined, and the Israeli delegation
decided not to schedule another meeting but to wait for an announcement
from the PLO, via the Norwegians, that the Palestinians were prepared to
modify their positions. Meanwhile, in a private meeting Uri gave Abu Ala
a document specifying seven conditions for mutual recognition between
Israel and the PLO, and proposed a solution whereby the two sides would
compromise on eight points apiece, so that recognition of the PLO could
become part of the overall agreement. In making this offer, Uri was
following the instructions of Rabin's steering committee; even at this late
stage, Rabin was determined that the question of mutual recognition
would not be raised in the official talks. This was the first time that an
Israeli participant in the talks tied the two agreements together. The
meeting ended on an emotional but negative note, with a sense that
perhaps this was the end. No more dates were fixed.

Holst was under pressure. It had seemed to him that everything was
going so well and now, suddenly, there was deadlock and an air of dejection. He contacted me, sounding sombre, and begged me not to let my
enterprise sink into the mud. I told him I didn't believe the Palestinians
could afford to forgo an agreement at this stage, and I saw this as the
darkness before the dawn. He accepted this assessment, and told me of a
conversation between Abu Ala and himself after the end of the round, in
which Abu Ala told him that the new Palestinian demands were a response
to the demands raised by Singer. On their side too, he said, lawyers had
been let in on the secret, and the involvement of lawyers in negotiations
always meant extra complications. The declaration of principles needed to
be a political, not a legal document. He added something which astonished

Holst, stating his opinion that the Israeli demands were backed not only by Rabin, but also by American elements determined to stiffen Israeli resolve. I told Holst that conspiracy theories were nothing new in the Middle East: we used to see Russians behind every tree, and the Arabs still saw Americans everywhere. Holst said that he had offered to change roles, from host to mediator, if both sides agreed to this, and had told Abu Ala that the Palestinians had to be led towards tough and painful decisions and this was the moment to do it. Abu Ala told the Minister of Uri's offer of a 'package deal' and expressed the hope that Arafat would agree to it. 'That depends on you,' Holst told him.

I asked the Norwegian Foreign Minister to share with Peres his impressions in the wake of the eleventh round, and sure enough he sent him a long and somewhat anxious letter. Peres sent him a courteous and very cordial reply in which he expressed his concern at the Palestinians' aspiration to determine elements of the permanent settlement at this early stage, something liable to jeopardise the entire process. His expression of personal appreciation for Holst was no doubt gratifying to the Norwegian Minister, who was henceforward prepared to do everything in his power to prevent collapse of the talks.

At a meeting of the 'team of four' in Rabin's office, something happened which I had not at all expected and which led me once more to reconsider my opinion of the Prime Minister. At the outset of the talks, I had insisted that the five-year period of the interim settlement would begin on signing of the declaration of principles, without waiting for the elections to the Council, and this had been agreed by both sides. In the course of the eleventh round of talks, the Palestinians had asked that the transfer of powers begin not with signing of the agreement, but with the pull-out from Gaza and Jericho and the arrival there of PLO personnel. This request reflected the unwillingness of the Tunis officials to see powers transferred to the residents of the territories, before they had had the opportunity to go in and take control themselves. Although there was apparently nothing in this request that should bother us, Yoel asked for something in exchange: 'If you're postponing transfer of powers, let's say that the five-year interim period also begins with the pull-out from Gaza and Jericho.' Abu Ala did not object to this. Now, sitting in Rabin's Tel Aviv office, Yoel boasted of his recent achievement, only to have Rabin say: 'Why do you need that? I see no reason why the five years shouldn't begin with signing.' I was glad to hear his response, and to be assured that the permanent settlement was something he took seriously and did not want to delay unnecessarily.

What worried me was the way both Rabin and Peres insisted on total separation between declaration of principles and mutual recognition. Yoel and I knew they could not be separated, and we feared that our bosses would have great difficulty accepting this in weeks to come. There was a general feeling that the moment of truth was approaching. We didn't believe the whole thing was going to blow up in our faces, but nor did we suspect that within a month this would be the world's biggest news story. We were still a small team veering between hope and despondency and Rabin was still sharing nothing with his entourage; at the end of each meeting with us he would fold the relevant papers and tuck them away in his briefcase for further, private perusal.

This was a very busy summer for the Israeli government. Secretary of State Warren Christopher and the peace team headed by Dennis Ross arrived for a round of shuttle diplomacy between Damascus and Jerusalem, and for the first time there was a feeling that things were moving. Rabin himself was changing his priorities at an alarming rate: having initially promised agreement on autonomy within six to nine months, and having discovered just how problematical this was likely to be, he now said he preferred to reach accommodation with the Syrians, seeing that at least they had a state and a leader with whom binding agreements could be made. In this context he came up with a number of surprising statements which appeared to contradict his pledge never to abandon the Golan Heights. He announced that the extent of withdrawal from the Golan would be equivalent to the extent of peace, and accepted that in the interests of gaining peace with Syria it would be necessary to dismantle Israeli settlements on the Heights. In the summer of 1993 it seemed that the Syrians too felt that differences over the timescale and scope of an agreement were narrowing. Accidentally or otherwise, there was a degree of competition between the Palestinian and the Syrian tracks. I saw no contradiction between the two, believing that a comprehensive deal would receive overwhelming public support, but Rabin said he couldn't handle both fronts simultaneously.

In a tête-à-tête between Christopher and Rabin, the Secretary of State asked how the talks with the Palestinians in Oslo were progressing. Rabin fobbed him off with one of his famous hand gestures, his substitute for a remark such as 'It's not worth talking about.' Later, when the Americans analysed the conversation, they wondered what that gesture at the beginning of August had meant: did Rabin think that nothing real could be achieved in Oslo, or was he reluctant at this stage to involve the Americans further by telling them more than he believed they already knew? When I asked Rabin about this months later, he responded with precisely the same gesture and said: 'What does it matter now?'

But just when it seemed that the Syrian track was making good progress, Christopher held a poll among members of his team in Jerusalem's King David Hotel, and in a thoroughly democratic manner asked them whether they preferred to take their holidays at this time or to continue with shuttle diplomacy until the white smoke appeared. Most members of the team said they had promised their spouses a vacation; reservations had been made (especially on the West Coast) and, anyway, nothing ever happens in August. Only a few dissenters warned Christopher against breaking the momentum of the talks. Some of those who voted for holidays told me later that they would never forgive themselves for this shortsighted decision. Speculation about this is clearly futile, but if it had been possible to reach agreement on principles with the Syrians in August 1993, it is almost certain that the Oslo track would have dragged on much longer and possibly ground to a halt. As it turned out, the agreement reached with the Palestinians swung Syrian opinion against the idea of negotiating with Israel.

At the beginning of the month there was an exchange of unaddressed letters between Rabin and Arafat, via the link established between Ahmed Tibi and Haim Ramon. The letters did not deal directly with the Oslo track, being more concerned with the need to keep the Washington talks on course, but the assurances conveyed in them facilitated further progress in the secret track, dealing as they did with the issue of greatest concern to our late Prime Minister – defining Israel's security powers and responsibilities during the period of the interim settlement. Rabin found Arafat's response largely satisfactory.

There were also political developments. An indictment was shortly to be served against the Minister and leader of Shas, Arye Deri, and under these circumstances he was obliged to resign from participation in the government. We knew that Shas would not stay on board without Deri, and we would soon become a minority administration with fifty-six coalition members (Labour–Meretz) and outside support from Hadash and the Arab Democratic Party. Obviously we were going to try to broaden the coalition, but we preferred to make deals with the Palestinians – or the Syrians – when the government could depend on a solid majority.

Norwegian politics were also a factor. An election was looming, and while the current government had some impressive domestic achievements to its credit, a major foreign policy success would do it no harm at all. Holst's efforts and the pressure he exerted on both negotiating parties were not entirely unrelated to these considerations.

In the four-sided forum, Rabin agreed to initiate formal discussion of mutual recognition between the PLO and Israel. It was evident from his remarks that he was prepared to give the Oslo track another chance – but not for long. The dominant sensation was that of time running out.

The signals emanating from Tunis via Oslo made it possible to convene the twelfth round of talks on 13 August. Some of the Palestinian demands had been withdrawn or – more accurately – deferred to the detailed negotiations over the Gaza–Jericho arrangements and negotiations over the interim settlement. These included, for example, the question of the extent of the Jericho enclave and the issue of Palestinian–Israeli co-ordination at the crossing-points between Gaza and Egypt and between Jericho and Jordan.

The principal effort of this round was the attempt to erase some of the qualifications and parentheses which characterised the different versions favoured by both sides and arrive at an acceptable compromise. This time, one of the central questions was the location of the institutions of the Palestinian governing Council. To us it was very important to stress that the effective capital would be Jericho, while the Palestinians insisted on the right to hold debates in any location of their choosing. The compromise that was eventually concluded (that, until the elections, these institutions could operate only in the sectors ceded to the Council's authority) was not reached at this meeting. Nor was there any progress on mutual recognition. We parted with a sense of continuing crisis. True, Abu Ala had not resigned, as he had threatened, and the ending of the previous round, in July, had been unnecessarily dramatic, but there had been no real progress and it seemed that in spite of pressures of time there was no choice but to carry on at this new and irksome pace for many months to come. Such were our conclusions at the end of this round.

A few months before, and without any reference to the Oslo process, arrangements had been made for an official visit by Peres to Norway and

Sweden. We wanted to exploit this visit as a means of nudging the secret negotiations forward and perhaps even concluding them. Peres was due to set off for Sweden on 17 August. The morning of that day there was a meeting in Peres's office, attended by Uri Savir, Shlomo Gur, Avi Gil and myself, to discuss the best way to proceed. I suggested to Peres that he co-ordinate his moves with Holst in dealing with the PLO leadership, as a means of settling the issues which remained unresolved. Shimon agreed at once.

I had difficulty locating Holst. At this early hour of the morning he wasn't at home or in his office. It turned out he was visiting Iceland, and eventually I got through to his hotel room. The time in Iceland was earlier still, and even in Jerusalem it was only mid-morning. I told him Shimon would be in Sweden later that day, and asked if he could meet him for talks before he moved on to Norway. 'No problem,' he told me, stifling a yawn. I suggested a rendezvous at the royal guesthouse in Stockholm, where he could meet Peres after the evening's official banquet. 'Okay,' he said, 'I'll be there.' 'Just a moment!' I persisted. 'You know exactly where to find him? You don't need to clear it with the Swedes?' 'It'll be all right, I'll be there on time,' he assured me. 'You know we have excellent relations with the Swedes, even if we did split from them in 1905 . . .'

He arrived on time, and this was a night of long phone calls between Stockholm and Tunis. Nine calls were logged that night between the two capitals in the space of seven hours; in Sweden Holst, with Peres prompting, was talking to Arafat, while in Tunis the entire negotiating team was on hand – Abu Mazen, Abu Ala and Hasan Asfur. I was in Jerusalem keeping Rabin up to date, through the evening and the morning after.

It can't be helped. You conduct negotiations for years, months or days. At the end there comes a night when everyone is hurrying and everyone is under pressure – and compromises take shape. This was the night that the decision was taken over the insertion of Resolution 242; there was also agreement, at last, on which subjects would be on the agenda of the permanent settlement (we abandoned the proposal whereby each side would put forward its own topics for discussion), and on the status of military government in the sectors which we were to evacuate. As for the border-crossings with Jordan and Egypt, a formula was agreed leaving technical details to the negotiation over Gaza and Jericho, and agreement was reached on international monitoring of the elections. The final point unresolved was the question of the location of the central institutions of the Palestinian Authority. In the morning I went to see the Prime Minister with a number of options; we decided which of these should be supported and in the course of that day I updated him several times as news of the final stages of discussion filtered through from Sweden and later on, from Norway.

Rabin was in a somewhat agitated state. It was clear to him that the business was to have a positive outcome and this was putting us face to face with the PLO. This wasn't easy for him, but the decision had been made. He was tense, but not angry, and to some extent the conclusion had freed him from a dilemma. I felt comfortable working with him now; it was hard to believe how far we had come in the course of this year.

The PLO leadership reached the conclusion that the agreement was ready for signing, and asked the legal adviser Taher Shash, who was based in Cairo and had accompanied the Palestinian delegation in Washington, to come to Oslo and read the updated text. Shash came to Oslo, read through the document and pronounced it legally satisfactory from a Palestinian point of view. We insisted that the declaration of principles (which eventually became one integrated document) should be signed in both parts – the document and the protocol – and both parts published. The PLO's demand to administer autonomy from Jerusalem was rejected, but Holst was assured that, following ratification of the entire agreement by the Knesset, a letter would be sent to him guaranteeing that existing Palestinian institutions in Jerusalem would not be impaired as a result of the agreement.

On the night of 19 August, after conclusion of the formalities, the signing ceremony was held. That morning seven Israeli soldiers had been killed in Lebanon and there was little appetite for celebration, but it was still an emotional occasion. I was at home in Tel Aviv and I didn't go to bed until the long-awaited call came through from Oslo: 'All's well. We have an agreement on principles. Uri and Abu Ala have signed. Although you weren't with us, your presence was felt.' Several participants in the meeting sent me emotional tributes, separately or in the margins of the agreement. Yair passed on to me a message from someone I had never met, written in English in the margins of his address at the signing ceremony: 'Dear Yossi, We missed you on this historic occasion but your spirit, your thoughts and your belief in peace were with us. Regards and best wishes, Abu Ala, 19.8.93.'

And now? No chance of retiring now. Who will sign the agreement which has been signed only in initials? Who is our Palestinian counterpart? What will be the role of the Americans? Will they accept the part that we have scripted for them in this play, without their knowledge, or will the débâcle of the London Agreement be repeated?

The Norwegians were excelling themselves. Holst was devoting all his time to the implementation of the deal, travelling with Peres to California to present the fruits of our labours to the Secretary of State, and immediately thereafter playing a central role in the negotiations over mutual recognition with the PLO.

This was a most peculiar time. We had in our hands an agreement signed jointly by the director-general of the Israeli Foreign Ministry and one of the most senior officials, effectively the Finance Minister, of the PLO. But we didn't recognise one another. The world knew nothing of the agreement. The American peace team was away on its holidays, and even the Israeli government had not yet been informed of these startling developments. The talks in Washington were dormant, and no one could say definitely what the connection was to be between the document that we had signed and an agreement on mutual recognition. Was one dependent on the other, or would we sign an agreement in Washington with the Palestinian element of the Jordanian–Palestinian delegation and then settle down to leisurely and longwinded negotiations over a historic act of recognition between ourselves and those who for a quarter of a century had been reckoned our most implacable foes?

Expressive of the confusion of those days was a call which I received on 22 August from the Prime Minister. He told me that the head of military intelligence, Uri Sheuy, was aware that in Oslo intensive negotiations were proceeding with the PLO; following his conversation with Sheuy, Rabin wanted to know whether the agreement contained any reference to cessation of terrorism. I told him that the preamble to the agreement constituted mutual commitment to peace, but a guarantee on the part of the PLO to refrain from terrorism existed only in the mutual recognition agreement, the seven-point plan which hadn't yet been signed. I sensed unease at the other end of the line. 'Yossi, for me terrorism is the central issue. Even the *intifada* is less serious because the agreement will put a stop to it. But there's no way we can sign an agreement with the Palestinians without a commitment from the PLO to halt terrorism. Talk to Holst and see what can be done.'

I talked to Holst, but it was clear he too thought it impossible to obtain a commitment to cessation of violence from someone we didn't recognise. Almost until the moment of the historic signing on the White House lawn, Rabin was torn between his aversion towards recognition of the PLO and his hankering after a definitive commitment to cessation of PLO terrorism, a commitment which only the PLO could give. In days to come, the need for a commitment to refrain from terrorism proved more powerful than his dislike of the PLO.

The briefing of the Americans proved straightforward enough. The plane which was henceforward to be made available to Holst on a regular basis was a tremendous boon, whisking Peres and Holst, accompanied by Avi Gil, Yoel Singer and the Larsens, from Norway via stopover in Israel to California and a meeting with Warren Christopher and Dennis Ross, who were both (separately) spending their vacations there. The contrast between the frenetic activity of the Oslo–Tunis–Jerusalem axis and the tranquillity of California on 27 August 1993 was positively surreal.

At this stage and against a background of rumours and leaks it was clear that the idea of presenting the agreement as an American document would not be acceptable since it was very far from reality. In a three-cornered meeting with Christopher and Ross, Peres did suggest this, but both immediately said it was out of the question. At the most the Americans would thank the Norwegians for their contribution to the process and announce that negotiations would continue in the USA.

The question of how much the Americans knew and how much they needed to know was something which Peres felt he ought to clarify. In fact, Denis Ross had received a quantity of reliable information from the Egyptians, Dan Kertzer had received information from me, from Yair Hirschfeld and from Larsen, and Christopher had been briefed by Stoltenberg and Holst; however, the Israeli government had never, officially or systematically, updated the US government on the process of events. Christopher showed neither anger nor disappointment. On the contrary, it seemed that a traditional American aspiration was being fulfilled here: the USA would not impose peace, but would assist parties seeking peace to reach their objective. In this case the two sides had come to terms and now sought American patronage and American hospitality; these would be gladly given.

Peres revived the trauma of Shultz's refusal to visit the region after the London Agreement. The Secretary of State and the leader of the peace team reassured him. They well understood the potential involved in such a historic reconciliation on the White House lawn, a hundred years after the outbreak of the conflict and two years after the Madrid Conference and the start of sterile talks in Washington. The fact that the marathon negotiating weekends had taken place in Oslo and not in Washington was not a problem for them.

Warren Christopher had not made a great impact as deputy to Cyrus Vance in Carter's administration, but as a prominent attorney, personal friend and experienced diplomat he was a natural choice for appointment as Bill Clinton's Secretary of State, a role in which he acquired a reputation for integrity and for fostering team-work. But the biggest surprise was his appointment of Dennis Ross as head of the Middle East peace team. Although initially a Democrat, Ross had joined the Reagan administration and in the Bush years worked closely with Secretary of State James Baker. He played an important role in setting up the Madrid Conference and in Baker's shuttling between Damascus and Jerusalem, believing that the best hope for the peace process lay in Bush's re-election. His role as a state employee was changed to that of a political appointee and on the eve of the elections he left the State Department along with Baker to work in the presidential re-election campaign. When I met him in the White House a month before the elections, there was already a perceived possibility that Ross Perot would gobble up the Republican majority, and Dennis told me that without Baker at the State Department the Israeli–Syrian track would be doomed to failure. After the elections, when everyone assumed he would be returning to his academic activities, he bounced back as leader of the peace team.

This was a team decidedly dominated by Jews, proving that Bill Clinton was not afraid of making such appointments, which twenty years earlier would have been unthinkable. Dennis Ross, his assistant Aaron Miller, deputy Assistant Secretary Dan Kertzer and the White House's Middle East specialist Martin Indyk constituted the peace team alongside Edward Djerijian, the only non-Jew in the team, later to be US ambassador to Israel. This was the original composition of the team, although it was to change. I don't know if the composition of the team was a cause of concern to our Arab counterparts; I must admit that we found it reassuring, although we were aware that the positions taken would not automatically be pro-Israeli.

The group was broadened to admit the remainder of the Israeli contingent, now including Ambassador Itamar Rabinowitz, who had been aware for some time that something was afoot in Scandinavia but had been told few of the details. After exchanges of mutual compliments on the roles played by all parties in advancing the process in recent months, the unavoidable and deeply problematical question arose: with whom was this agreement to be signed two weeks from now? Was Israel proposing to reach political agreement with the PLO on American soil – in a land where contacts with the PLO were still forbidden?

It was only in the course of this conversation that the Americans were told who had signed the deal in Oslo; they now wanted to know who would be signing it in Washington. Peres and Holst told them that the matter had not been resolved and that the following Sunday negotiations would begin with the PLO on the seven-point recognition plan; it was anticipated that this would be conveyed to Israel in a letter signed by Arafat, whereupon Rabin would confirm its receipt. If agreement were not reached, the signing would probably be done at delegate level.

Peres read the text of the seven-point recognition plan to Christopher and Ross, saying that in his opinion, if agreed, it should meet the conditions imposed by the Americans and enable the signing to go ahead on American soil. Christopher said that consultation would be required between the White House and Congress if PLO representatives were to be admitted to the White House without breaking the law.

Peres asked Christopher if the USA would help in the realisation of two important objectives: for the Palestinians, concentrating world efforts on economic aid; for Israel, urging the Arab states, especially those of the Gulf and North Africa, to recognise Israel once the agreement had been signed and establish diplomatic relations.

Ross was anxious to know just how far Peres trusted Arafat. Shimon replied by drawing attention to the crisis in Palestinian fortunes which had brought the PLO to the negotiating table; an agreement was essential for both sides, particularly so for the PLO, and neither side would benefit from breaching it.

After a separate conversation between Christopher and Holst, a broader meeting was held with Americans, Israelis and Norwegians participating. Christopher said that he had taken the opportunity to brief President Clinton (also on vacation) on the agreement, although he hadn't yet mentioned the possibility of mutual recognition, or of participation by a PLO representative at the signing ceremony. He believed that the President would give his backing to the wrapping up of the Washington process, and next week he intended to give him full details of the Oslo story. The Secretary of State expressed his support for the seven-point plan. He understood that despite Peres's insistence that the declaration of principles should be separated from mutual recognition, this was a separation that could not be maintained once mutual recognition had become a live issue.

Peres asked Christopher to brief the European leaders Mitterrand, Kohl and Major, suggesting that invitations be issued to the signing ceremony in Washington. He also proposed that consideration be given to a special fund to assist the economic development of the Middle East. Holst was convinced that the 'cold fish' (Christopher) was enthusiastic, and at the conclusion of this lengthy meeting, for which he had interrupted his vacation, the Secretary of State extended a bony hand to each of the participants and said with a smile: 'This has been one hell of a working day!'

The world's only remaining superpower could rub its hands together in satisfaction at the prospect of the ending of a prolonged international conflict, to the resolution of which it had contributed so much in terms of money, manpower and diplomacy. The fact that the final breakthrough had not been achieved by American pressure but was descending from the heavens in the shape of a Norwegian executive jet – well, so much the better!

On Shimon's return to Israel, a special government session was held at which the declaration of principles was presented for ratification. Besides the ministers, those present included Motta Gur and me, regular invitees to cabinet meetings, also the Chief of Staff and senior officers, security service chiefs, Yoel Singer and Uri Savir. For the ministers this was not a total surprise. In recent weeks the number of leaks had amounted to a veritable flood, and in the previous day's papers almost all the details of the agreement had been published.

Eli Rubinstein sat in the government secretary's chair, looking mortified. This honest and talented fellow, the consummate non-political civil servant, always capable of defusing tension with a joke, who had led the negotiations with the Palestinians and the Jordanians and endeared himself to both these groups, who had served the Shamir government, when his instructions were to spin the talks out for as long as possible, and the Rabin government, which wanted to wrap them up with all possible speed – the man was stunned. Eli had taken my place as government secretary; I had known and liked him for many years, and it was painful to see the look on his face. He obviously felt betrayed, insulted and humiliated. Not that I needed to apologise to anyone, but I approached him and for once he didn't conceal his disappointment with a joke. 'If Rabin had given me as much rope as he gave you, I'd have got a deal with the Palestinians in just two days,' he complained. He suspected that Rabin had deliberately cramped his style, constantly denying his requests for more latitude, while in Oslo we had been enjoying an unlimited diet.

Ehud Barak, the chief of staff, was still reading the final pages of the agreement. I took my seat beside him at the end of the table and he smiled at me as if to say: 'You bastard, couldn't you have given me just a hint all these months? Call yourself a friend?' When he finished reading, I asked for his opinion of the agreement. He said that the prospect of friction worried him, and he was especially concerned about the safety of Jewish settlers. I pressed him, asking him what he would do if called upon to vote rather than to single out problems. Ehud thought for a moment and said: 'You've achieved something historic. I'd vote in favour, but I admit – not with an easy heart.'

Before the meeting opened, Motta Gur the deputy defence minister approached me. He looked very agitated and had only one question to ask: who had participated in Rabin's steering-group consultations before each round? I reckoned there was no reason to hide it from him now and I told him: 'Peres, Singer and myself.' He seemed reassured by my answer. The fact that Rabin had acted alone, not even consulting his military secretary, apparently soothed his resentment at the way that he, his deputy, had been kept unaware of the existence of the track and denied any opportunity to contribute.

I looked around me. The deal was 'sold'. It was clear that we would finish the session with a majority of ministers supporting the statement of principles which Rabin was about to introduce officially. There was a general air of excitement. Some were already familiar with the material, others seemed to have guessed what was in the wind. All were reading through the agreement page by page and I was wondering, How can you just read a document like this and think you've understood it? After all, behind every word lies a whole history of arguments, conflicts and sleepless nights. How are you to know for example that behind 'implementation of 242' there lurks the cancellation of 'implementation in a manner to be agreed', to say nothing of 'full and unqualified implementation'; what do you know of the sweat expended over the voting rights of East Jerusalem's Arabs, or the distinction between 'external security' and 'overall security'? Reading a document such as this is like glancing at the cover of a book and claiming to understand its contents. And yet at the end of the session they would support it as if it were just another proposal put forward by the Prime Minister which it would be impolite to oppose: a review of the road-building programme, perhaps.

Since 1975, I had clashed with a number of my government colleagues over the Palestinian issue. For example, Micha Harish had published in *Traffic Light*, the periodical of the Labour Party's Young Guard, a detailed article in which he compared the PLO with the Nazis and insisted that we could never talk to them. Later, in 1990, as mentioned previously, he sent me a letter criticising me for my 'Palestinian obsession'. A few years earlier, at a meeting of the Mashov caucus, Rabin had dubbed me and Avrum Burg 'PLO-ists' – not in anger but as if pointing out a fact. How times had changed! The doves were enthusiastic – Uzi Baram, Moshe Shahal, Ora Namir and of course Haim Ramon, who had set up a conduit of his own between Rabin and Arafat. And the Meretz ministers, naturally. All of them were now members of cabinet.

Yoel Singer introduced the document. Ehud Barak offered his comments and Eli Rubinstein registered twenty-one reservations. The ministers had their say and almost all of them were in favour. Arye Deri contributed a glowing analysis of the document and extolled the Oslo enterprise, although this was his swansong as a government minister. He was on the point of resignation on account of the charges filed against him; Shas was about to leave the coalition and he said he could not take on himself the responsibility of voting for the agreement when his party would soon be no longer part of the coalition.

I didn't participate in the debate. It seemed to me that everything had been said and further comment was superfluous. The result of the vote in the government session was a surprise – the Oslo Accord was approved unanimously. Only two ministers Shimon Shitrit and Arye Deri abstained.

That night I went home feeling free, for the first time since the launch of the Oslo track, to tell Helena the whole story. 'You must be pleased with the way the vote went tonight,' she said. 'Not at all,' I replied. 'I don't like what happened in the Cabinet today. Exercises in "collective consciousness" don't appeal to me. Until yesterday, even after repeal of the Law of Association, the PLO was seen as utterly reprehensible. It couldn't be mentioned in any official communication, there was virtually no dis-agreement, and anyone defying the consensus was seen as a PLO supporter rather than someone who understood there was no better alternative. And today – there's no problem, the taboo has been lifted! We have a nego-tiating partner, we have an agreement, the Prime Minister's in favour, all the ministers support it, and if there's one minister like Shitrit who finds it easy to conceal his jubilation, he has to abstain because opposing it would mean breaking the new consensus.' It was controversy that I had missed that day. Rather than unanimity, I would have preferred a respect-able majority after tough questions and mordant criticism. The consensus was created by the fact that the agreement could not now be changed, and a vote against it would be tantamount to a vote of no-confidence in the Prime Minister. All the same...

'Some people are never satisfied,' Helena told me. 'You should be marking this on the calendar as the second most important day of your life.'

Few of the ministers present at the government session knew that, while they were approving the statement of principles, tough and vigorous negotiation was in progress on the issue of mutual recognition between Israel and the PLO. In fact, when someone asked the Prime Minister whether this agreement constituted recognition of the PLO, he denied it, insisting that this was a deal between us and the Palestinian delegation; recognition of the PLO was a different and completely unrelated issue.

When he said this, Rabin still believed it would be possible to go to Washington and sign the agreement even if the negotiations on mutual recognition were to fail. In this, he was clearly mistaken. At the stage we had reached, I could not believe that the PLO would allow the Palestinian delegation to sign on its behalf. Just two weeks before the event that would have the world holding its breath we still had no idea who exactly the groom was to be – nor had the bride been chosen; but the parents had started inviting guests.

Arafat wanted an agreement on mutual recognition in which both sides would commit themselves to ending violence. We suggested an exchange of letters in which Arafat would sign the famous seven principles and Rabin would reply, confirming receipt of the document. We appealed to the PLO to promise an end to all violence and terrorism, and Arafat replied that at this stage he could guarantee an end to PLO terrorism but couldn't speak for other organisations. He also said that he reckoned the *intifada* would come to an end, but since it had not been the PLO that started it, he could not guarantee an end to the *intifada* as an automatic consequence of the signing of the agreement.

Holst, who had long since forgotten that he wasn't supposed to be a mediator, threw the full weight of his energy and expertise into the issue of mutual recognition, and the phone lines to Tunis and Jerusalem were hot. In the first week of September it seemed that agreement was impossible, and therefore signing of the statement of principles was itself in doubt. The climax of activity came on 4 September, in a marathon negotiating session in Paris: Uri and Yoel versus Abu Ala with Holst as referee. Secrecy was a thing of the past; the press had even located their hotel, and to negotiators used to the freedom of manoeuvre of recent months, such intrusion was most unwelcome.

Over the next few days the compromises emerged; there would be no agreement as such. The PLO would commit itself in a letter to be signed by Arafat. Israel's right to exist in peace and security (not just to exist) was acknowledged, the PLO would renounce all forms of terrorism and violence, but could make such pledges only on its own behalf. The *intifada* would not be mentioned, but would be dealt with separately in a letter to Holst, in his new role as international accommodation address. Arafat would agree in his letter to change the Palestinian Covenant but couldn't commit himself to a specific date, not knowing when he would gain the necessary two-thirds majority in the Palestinian National Council. Rabin would then write a brief reply to Arafat declaring that, in the light of the PLO chairman's guarantees, the government of Israel had decided to recognise the PLO as a representative (*not* the sole or exclusive representative) of the Palestinian people and to begin negotiations with it.

Arafat convened a meeting of the PLO's steering committee to obtain approval for the sending of the letter. Holst was supposed to fly to Tunis, receive the letter signed by Arafat on Thursday, 9 September, take the letter to Jerusalem, arriving the same afternoon, and get Rabin's signature on the reply. The most important political reversal for decades, official Israeli recognition of the PLO, was approved that Thursday afternoon at a cabinet meeting lasting less than an hour, and without debate. We had decided that even in the age of faxes there was a role for the messenger – but in this case the messenger was delayed. A modest ceremony had been arranged to mark Rabin's signature of the letter; personnel from the Foreign Ministry and the Prime Minister's office had been alerted, as well as Israeli journalists and foreign correspondents, but Holst was still in his hotel in Tunis, waiting to get his letter from Arafat. The meeting of the PLO's steering-committee dragged on for hours, the opposition of Faruk Qaddoumi and some of his colleagues proving genuine and problematical; others declined to attend the meeting in the (vain) hope that there would not be a quorum. So, as it turned out, there was no ceremony in Jerusalem that Thursday. The PLO's steering committee approved the text of the letter late that night, and Holst landed at Ben-Gurion airport the following morning. He met Rabin briefly and showed him Arafat's letter, and then the trio – Rabin, Peres and Holst – strode from the Prime Minister's private office to the press-briefing room near by.

Rabin appeared red-faced, with an expression that seemed to say he had no idea what was expected of him. Shimon was very agitated and Holst was as nervous as a groom on his wedding-day. The room was awash with jostling journalists and popping flash-bulbs, and the September heat soon had the measure of the inadequate air-conditioning. On either side of the stage sat representatives of Israel and Norway: on the Norwegian side, the Larsens and Marianne, the Foreign Minister's wife; on the Israeli side, Motta Gur, Yoel Singer, Uri Savir, Shimon Sheves, the director general of the prime minister's office Avi Gil, Shlomo Gur and myself. The three ministers took their seats at a table on the stage draped in blue and white and said what they had to say, and Rabin, not having a more sophisticated pen about his person, took out his felt-tip and signed the first letter he had ever addressed to 'Mr Chairman' – that is, Yasser Arafat.

This modest ceremony was the really important one. Mutual recognition between the erstwhile 'Gang of murderers' and the erstwhile 'Zionist cabal, stooge of world imperialism' was signed and became an irreversible fact. Whatever might happen in future, whatever disagreements and disappointments might lie ahead, there were now two sides, which would no longer leave the room the moment the other rose to speak. The same day, the USA announced the resumption of negotiations with the PLO.

At midday the Israeli 'Oslo' team led by Peres and the Norwegian contingent led by Holst went out for lunch in Mishkenot Shaananim. Holst told us of his experiences in Tunis and of the tension which had continued to the very last moment: would the steering committee endorse the letter and would Arafat sign it? We also discussed what lay in store for us the following week in Washington. The ceremony would be on Monday, and we still didn't know who would be there and who would sign! Holst would definitely be there, and he would sign. The Americans would sign, the Russians would sign. But who was to sign for the Palestinians? Who for the Israelis?

This was the question that had obsessed Rabin since the previous Thursday. Clinton called him and suggested he attend in person and sign alongside Yasser Arafat. Rabin wasn't thrilled by the idea but was reluctant to give Clinton a negative answer. Friday evening Christopher was on the line, saying that Arafat would be there and, on behalf of the President, he very much wanted Rabin to be there too. Rabin wrestled with himself and with his closest advisers – excluding Peres and myself on this occasion. Saturday morning I was summoned to Peres's home. Also present were Uri Savir and Avi Gil. Shimon told us that Rabin had called him, saying he was going to Washington to sign the agreement and he was inviting Peres to sign as well.

Peres had received this information with distinct lack of enthusiasm, to say the least. He claimed that Rabin was making a mistake, giving the PLO too much too soon. I disagreed. I told him that in my opinion a handshake between Rabin and Arafat would be a gesture of great symbolic importance, heralding the beginning of the end of the Israeli–Palestinian conflict and showing the Prime Minister assuming full responsibility for the Oslo process. Peres was far from convinced, saying he had decided not to travel to the USA at all. We all argued against his assessment of the situation, reminding him of the mistake David Levy had made in declining to attend the Madrid Conference.

He felt, unfairly I believe, that he had been sidelined. After several months in which he had invested considerable effort in the success of the process, it would be the Prime Minister – who had almost caused the abandonment of the process – who would shake Arafat's hand, while the press would focus on the roles of the negotiators, Hirschfeld, Pundak and the other members of the team; his own quite genuine contribution would not receive due credit. When he drew up his very short guest-list, he omitted Yair and Ron; these two came to Washington as guests of the Norwegians.

On the flight to the USA, the atmosphere was relaxed enough. We sat in the central cabin, dozing or chatting – the Rabins, Motta and Rita Gur,

Peres and I. Rabin went through his speech. Peres went through his. But when we arrived in Washington it turned out that the negotiating was not yet over. The morning before the ceremony was due to take place, we had an urgent call from Dr Ahmed Tibi at the hotel where the Palestinians were staying, asking to meet us. When he arrived, he explained that Arafat was packing his bags and about to leave, having discovered that, according to the preamble, the agreement was to be signed by the Palestinian delegation and not by the PLO. Apparently we didn't acknowledge that we were dealing with the PLO...

All were furious at the prospect of yet more tiresome arguments, at this, the very last moment. Rabin was livid. He wanted to leave the wording as it was, but in the end a compromise was reached: this was to be a declaration of principles signed jointly by a PLO team (although the expression 'Palestinian delegation' remained, in brackets) and by the government of Israel. Thus the negotiations which had begun on 20 January were concluded on the morning of 13 September 1993.

It was very hot in Washington, and humid as well. On the big White House lawn a stage had been erected, and all the world's press had managed to get there, in spite of the short notice. The world had got there too. I shook hands with the many Foreign Ministers whom I knew and embraced Boutros Boutros Ghali, who was moved to tears, whispering in my ear: 'I knew all the time you were up to something.'

In the course of the ceremony I sat, watching the three First Ladies, watching Peres and Abu Mazen, and finally the three leaders – Clinton, Rabin and Arafat – and for the first time in my life I had to pinch myself to be sure this was real. If I hadn't turned up for that meeting at the Tandoori, sixteen months before, would this have happened anyway? Was the need for secret talks with the PLO so self-evident that the same result would have transpired sooner or later, whoever the participants might have been? How much should be attributed to chance and how much to the natural momentum of political development?

After the ceremony the Israeli team was invited to meet President Clinton. Antony Lake, the President's National Security Adviser, whom I had met a number of times, introduced me to him. 'Now this one's over, got any more negotiations in mind?' Clinton joked, not realising just how far from a joke this was. Then, in more serious mood, he asked what was expected of him. I told him there was no alternative to the provision of American economic aid to the Palestinians, but negotiations with the

Palestinians and the Jordanians we could handle ourselves. On the other hand, if there were to be progress in negotiations with Syria, American involvement would be required. Clinton confirmed America's willingness to contribute to such a track, adding that this accorded with American interests, since Israeli–Syrian peace would signal an end to the era of Middle East wars.

I was impressed by the President, a young man of intelligence and sensitivity, obviously delighted by the signing of the agreement that had just been witnessed, convinced that in this, the Rabin era, investment in Middle Eastern peace was worth while. One of the reasons that convinced me later of the reluctance of President Assad to make peace with Israel, on the basis of any proposed compromise, was the adamant American commitment expressed in that brief conversation with Clinton on 13 September. I reflected that if Israel were prepared to go so far, and the USA likewise, the conclusion could only be that there was no real will from the third party. Our hands were clean, and if there is still no peace with Syria, this is without doubt the responsibility of Syria alone.

The rest of the day passed at dizzying speed. In the afternoon, in Peres's suite, we met with the PLO delegation to the Oslo talks, accompanied by Abu Mazen. I had never seen any of these people before, but they seemed to regard me as an old acquaintance. 'The man who started it all is the last to be met,' Abu Ala said to me. He wasn't quite the way I had pictured him in my imagination, in spite of Yair's detailed description.

This was an amicable conversation. There was nothing pressing on the agenda, no more compromises to be fought over. For a moment I felt as if I was in the army again, at the end of basic training when the sergeants stop being monsters and turn into human beings, staging stretcher-races or clowning around on the assault-course. The agreement was supposed to come into force within a month, and in the meantime it would be up to us to present it to our parliamentary institutions. We exchanged our assessments of the reception to be expected, for ourselves and for the Palestinians. We all hoped that the shock-waves from this extraordinary and positive event would also move Israeli and Palestinian public opinion, that people on both sides would realise a new page was being turned and that this was an agreement not to be judged on a narrow, partisan basis. We assured one another we would continue to meet, although it wasn't clear how and under what circumstances; nor were we sure with whom we would be negotiating over the interim settlement and Gaza and Jericho.

Would all these people, living comfortably in Tunis, really be prepared to shift their domicile to the slums of Gaza?

This, incidentally, was a question often repeated in the countless television interviews I gave that day between meetings. 'Will Mr Arafat be permitted to live in Jericho?' 'Will the PLO close its headquarters in Tunis and transfer it to Gaza?' My answers were evasive – not the kind of answers I like giving. The truth is that, at that stage, I simply didn't know how quickly things would develop, or if Arafat's arrival in the territories could be regarded as imminent. In spite of the handshake, and although Arafat had ceased to be a concept and become a human being, I too still had difficulty imagining him as a neighbour.

'How did you feel when the Prime Minister shook hands with Mr Arafat?' (*Mr* Arafat? This was a combination that had not been heard before that day. Hitherto, if mentioned at all, he had just been plain Arafat.) I said that I had been very excited, and that I felt this heralded the end of a chapter I had feared might never be ended. But the truth is that I watched the real event some days later, at home on video. There, in the stifling heat, drowning in a dark suit not designed to withstand humidity, in one of the back rows, it was hard to hear a word through the crackling loudspeakers or to see what was happening on the stage. With events like this, you can't beat sitting at home in front of the box. All the subsequent ceremonies – Gaza, Jericho, interim settlement – I watched from Jerusalem.

After that, it was the turn of the Jews. New York came to Washington and the entire Jewish establishment crammed into a giant marquee in the grounds of the Israeli embassy. Rabin spoke. Peres spoke. Senior rabbis spoke. Many were unable to conceal their pride that Uri, their former consul-general, had become one of the heroes of the peace process.

Some were solemn, others emotional. For some this was a very difficult experience; after years of campaigning against any American recognition of the PLO, of demanding an end to negotiations with the PLO in Tunis, they saw Israel's Prime Minister coming to Washington and conferring legitimacy on Yasser Arafat.

But no criticism was expressed. Surprise, the very impact of the event on the lawn, President Clinton's enthusiasm, the way the business had been accepted in Israel – all these factors combined to induce either silence or consent. Again, I faced the phenomenon of collective consciousness. I knew most of the people there, I knew what most of them would be thinking, and I was amazed that amid all the polite exchanges so few questions were asked. A stranger, straying into the marquee, would be trying to pick out the bar-mitzvah candidate; all were holding plates or glasses, shaking hands and exchanging felicitations.

This joyful Jewish consensus, against the background of a deal with the PLO, in a tent offering little protection from the heat and humidity of Washington, resembled nothing so much as a scene from one of Fellini's more lurid films.

On the way home we made a stopover in Morocco. It was no surprise that Morocco, the friendliest of the Arab states, would be the first to welcome us after the signing of the historic agreement. Twice before, in 1978 and 1981, I had travelled to Morocco with Shimon for secret talks, both of us incognito, and this was the first ever official visit. The King was delighted by recent developments, of which he had heard partial accounts from Arafat. I had a long conversation with his two sons, who foresaw a rosy future for the Middle East following events in Washington and expressed confidence that relations between Morocco and Israel would now be rapidly developed.

At home we got an enthusiastic welcome from senior Labour Party members – and from others too. This extraordinary combination of firm and radical leadership by Rabin, exemplary co-operation between the two veteran rivals, Rabin and Peres, an achievement to make the world clap its hands, the silence of opponents, reluctant to spoil the party – all this was immensely gratifying to Labour activists. As for me, I went home happy but exhausted and collapsed on a mountain of Rosh Hashanah newspaper supplements. The year 5754 was getting off to an auspicious start.

What was the breakthrough in Oslo? In fact it was twofold: there was the historic mutual recognition between Israel and the PLO; but this was made possible only by the other breakthrough, separation between interim and permanent settlement and the implementation of some interim measures on the ground even before elections to the Palestinian self-governing Council. For years the Palestinians had been saying – whenever asked to consider the five-year interim period – that they would agree to an interim period before the permanent settlement only if the terms of the permanent settlement were guaranteed to them from the start. They had demands of their own: a Palestinian state with the 1967 borders and Jerusalem as its

capital, eradication of the Jewish settlements and repatriation of Palestinian refugees. Israel, they conceded, would of course have other positions. So there should be negotiation to determine the principles of the
permanent settlement, and then the Palestinians would agree to an interim
period, knowing in advance how it would end.

Israel would not agree to this demand, having insisted – since 1978 –
that the interim period should be fixed without either side having any
preconceptions as to the form of the permanent settlement; the interim
period would in itself influence the content of the permanent settlement,
as well as providing the two sides with useful experience of collaboration.
In Washington the Palestinians had rejected this concept; in Oslo they
accepted it, in that they agreed – at variance with their positions in
Washington – that Jerusalem, the settlements and Israel's military security
zones would be left outside the scope of autonomy.

Something else also happened in Oslo. Since the start of negotiations
over autonomy with Egypt, it had been understood that the period of self-
rule would begin only after elections to the Palestinian Council. When it
emerged in Washington just how hard it was going to be to reach agreement on procedures for the election – international supervision, voting
rights of East Jerusalem's Arabs, the number of deputies to be elected, the
question whether this was to be a legislative or executive body – and
when it seemed that negotiations over electoral issues might continue
indefinitely, the idea was raised of transferring powers to the Palestinians
before the elections, including the establishment of a Palestinian police
force. Even in Oslo the central questions of electoral procedure were not
solved, leading us to wonder whether the Palestinians were as interested
in elections as they claimed, but we created a scenario in which the
interim settlement was no longer dependent on elections; so that, whether
elections were held or not, negotiations on the permanent settlement had
to begin no later than two years after the implementation of 'Gaza–
Jericho'. The moment that elections ceased to be a condition for determining the permanent settlement, negotiating on them, which began at
a later stage, actually became much easier.

The story of the Oslo track is a story of historical paradoxes. The
discussions that were supposed to be absolutely secret, to be revealed to
the world only with the opening of the archives, long after peace had
become a fact, did – it is true – maintain their secrecy for a period of eight
months; but, once agreement was reached, not only were they exposed,

they became known to every television viewer and newspaper reader in the world – and entered the language of political terminology. When someone says he is putting his trust in 'Oslo', no one imagines he is referring to the Norwegian capital.

The track which was supposed to facilitate conversations between Faisal Husseini and me became a track which bypassed Faisal Husseini altogether, while Abu Ala, put forward as a negotiator by Hannan Ashrawi, in the end was to sideline her as well. The ultimate irony came when Abu Ala presented the agreement to his colleagues in the PLO and Ashrawi complained that anyone who could sign such a document was clearly no resident of the territories.

The track which was supposed to give Peres something to do, which Rabin was prepared to entrust to him because he thought the really important talks were the ones he was controlling himself in Washington, became the only track capable of influencing events, while the impotence and futility of the Washington talks were cruelly exposed. This of all tracks, the one which Rabin had been on the point of scrapping in June, was also the one which earned him and Peres the Nobel Peace Prize, a distinction which they shared with Yasser Arafat.

But Oslo also created prodigious expectations on account of the very image of the signing on 13 September. When I think of what happened on the lawn of the White House I am reminded of an entertaining story by Yehuda Amihai, 'Inverted Love', in which a man and a woman, drunk on the eve of Independence Day and finding themselves in the apartment belonging to one of them, go to bed and make love; the morning after they behave with scrupulous politeness, introducing themselves to each other and parting with a handshake but with no exchange of addresses.

Before the signing of the 1979 agreement between Sadat and Begin, the two leaders had met several times over the previous ten months. Before the signing of the 1994 agreement between Rabin and King Hussein, they themselves and their representatives had been meeting for decades. The agreement between Israel and the PLO was signed at the very first encounter between Arafat and Rabin and the handshake, in reality just the handshake of recognition, was interpreted as the handshake of peacemaking.

As of this moment, at the time that these lines are being written, we have *not* made peace with the PLO; it certainly didn't happen in September 1993, when we had yet to finalise the Gaza–Jericho deal and the interim agreement. The Oslo Accord was an initial agreement on principles which paved the way for the introduction of the interim settlement, but deferred all the sensitive issues to the negotiations on the permanent settlement. The event of 13 September had such an impact, and was so dramatic, that it was taken by the world, as well as by Israeli and Palestinian public opinion, to mean much more than just the beginning of the beginning. Many were under the impression that a peace treaty had been signed. Expectations of it were similar to those of a peace treaty, but this was an agreement incapable of meeting these expectations, especially when it was forced to face the test of violence. 'If there is peace, why can violence not be overcome?' was a question asked on both sides, and it was hard to be satisfied with the reply that in fact there was no peace yet. If this 'inverted peace' were not to have the same ending as Amihai's story, it was imperative to guarantee its continued and rapid progress towards the goal of permanent settlement.

Who, among all the members of the 'Oslo Club', was the architect of Oslo? The phrase 'architect of Oslo' was coined by the press and has been applied to various members of the club, but it seems to me that Oslo did not have an architect at all – if an architect is defined as one who has a clear picture of a structure in his mind, knows exactly what he wants and how to get it and knows what the final outcome will be. I certainly was not the architect of Oslo, although I admit to feeling flattered on occasions when I have heard the phrase applied to me. The decision to open the track and try to reach an understanding with the PLO was indeed mine and it wasn't an easy decision, since I had to take on myself the awesome responsibility of initiating important processes without authorisation from my superiors. From February onward I became part of a team and the responsibility was not mine alone. The fact that the track went ahead is solely to the credit of Yair Hirschfeld and Ron Pundak, since I wasn't prepared to go to Oslo and they were capable of giving the track their unrestricted time and expertise. Their skills and their dedication to the business took us as far as May 1993 when the substantive and (ultimately) fruitful negotiations got under way.

Peres played an irreplaceable role in the Oslo process. He understood the vast potential inherent in this quasi-academic exercise, and from that moment onward he took on himself the central responsibility for steering the track in the direction he considered best. He was the only one who could have persuaded Rabin to give a green light, albeit a flickering one, to this bizarre process, and it was he who, with characteristic willpower, pushed the process forward through its hardest moments to the final signature. His proposal to add Jericho to Gaza was an original solution, doing much to allay Palestinian fears that 'Gaza first' might also prove to be 'Gaza last'.

As Prime Minister, Rabin authorised the continuation of contacts in the Oslo track, and supported the idea of mutual recognition. Without him, the Oslo concept would have become just another instance of missed opportunity, and since there have been so many of these in the Middle East, this one might not even have merited a footnote. He was the 'hero of Oslo', not because he conceived the idea, nor because he was enthusiastic about it, but because – neither of these being the case – it was nevertheless he who took responsibility for the decision and for what followed it, and there can be no doubt that a direct line connects his signing of the agreement and his handshake with Arafat to the bullets fired at him by Yigal Amir.

Uri Savir proved himself a consummate negotiator. He quickly adapted himself to the role, knowing when to stand firm, and how to gain the trust of the other side. He was creative, humane and persuasive, utterly committed to the process, and many of the concepts which later seemed self-evident were in fact the fruit of his vision and understanding. Yoel Singer, the last of the sailors to board the good ship Oslo, was responsible to a very large extent for the achievement of mutual recognition between Israel and the PLO, and for a number of other substantive issues. It was he who convinced Rabin that the track was worth serious consideration, he who persuaded the late Prime Minister to adopt some complex formulas which later proved extremely important. The Oslo Accord could, with only slight exaggeration, be called the 'Singer Accord'.

The Larsens' investment in the process was – and still is – second to none. But neither Terje nor I imagined, when we met in the Tandoori restaurant, that we were setting an earthquake in motion. Stoltenberg ratified the financing of the track before leaving for Yugoslavia, and without financial support the track could not have continued. In retrospect it is hard to believe that the difference between non-agreement and agreement is sometimes a few hundreds of thousands of dollars, but when a track is secret and not officially acknowledged, someone has to pay for airline tickets and hotel accommodation, and it was the Norwegian Foreign Minister who picked up the tab.

Jan Egland pressed for establishment of the track, monitored it from the outset and attended the various meetings in and around Oslo. It is hard to envisage the Oslo track without him. And then of course there was the late Foreign Minister Holst, who understood the potential of the track and turned it, towards the end of his life, into the central concern of his work, seeing the success of the process as his personal success; the final stages, including the exchange of letters of recognition, were made possible only through his involvement and mediation.

On the Palestinian side, Faisal Husseini advocated the establishment of a secret track, Hannan Ashrawi recommended Abu Ala as the man to talk to. Abu Ala, Hasan Asfur and Maher el Kurd all invested much time and effort in the success of the talks, and were still talking to us long after the signing of the agreement. Abu Mazen guided and monitored the negotiations from Tunis, in a role similar to the one that I was playing in Jerusalem. Arafat – like Rabin – took on a very heavy responsibility and no small risk; in his case, the danger consisted not so much in his recognition of Israel as in his agreement to go into an interim settlement without any knowledge of how it would end: would Israel repeat its old ploy and perpetuate the interim period, unwilling to reach agreement before 1999?

None of the members of the 'Oslo Club' – which numbers no more than a couple of dozen, Norwegian, Israeli and Palestinian – can lay claim to the architect's laurels, not only because most of them only joined this exclusive club when the track was paved, but also because none of the founders could foresee the outcome from the outset. Some observers see this outcome as a solution, others see it as a disaster. Only history will be the final judge.

PART THREE

Stockholm

BY OCTOBER OF 1993 it was becoming hard to maintain the level of excitement at further developments in the peace process. New precedents were being set all the time: overtures from Oman, from Qatar, the prospect of seeing an end to the Arab embargo, of establishing diplomatic relations with a dozen countries which either had never recognised us at all or had severed relations after the Yom Kippur War. There was a sense of reverse domino-effect, as if everything was beginning to be resolved after so many years of isolation, alienation and boycott and yet *this* flight to Tunis was particularly exciting.

Tunisia was the first Arab state – besides Egypt – to host the multilateral talks, which in this instance consisted of working groups dealing with the refugee issue, and in particular a group focused on the problem of finding a precise definition of the 'family', in the context of reuniting families. After consulting the Foreign Minister and the Prime Minister I decided to go as head of the delegation, alongside the team leader Dr Yossi Hadass, with the full personnel of the group and a considerable number of media representatives coming along for the ride. I asked Rabin if he had any objection to my meeting Arafat, and he said he had no problem with this. Far from it.

We chartered a special plane and left Ben-Gurion on 11 October, stopping over in Valletta, as Tunisia was not yet prepared to accept direct flights from Tel Aviv, and after a brief but fascinating conversation with the Maltese Foreign Minister, Guido da Marco, travelled on to Tunis military airport.

My first impressions of this sea-port city were quite unlike my impressions of other Arab cities which I had visited: all houses white, all shutters blue, everything spotlessly clean, French culture and French language, an ambience more South European than North African. Never before had an official and public Israeli delegation visited Tunisia, and we had the feeling of being sealed inside a bubble. In addition to the security specialists we had brought with us, there were some fifteen local bodyguards provided by our hosts. We were driven at high speed through streets where all other traffic was halted, and the Hilton Hotel, where all the participants in the working group were staying, became a kind of closed military zone; tourists had been evacuated for the duration and entry was tightly restricted.

For me, Tunis was above all the PLO's capital city. Only seven years before I had been present at a cabinet meeting where it was decided to bomb the PLO's headquarters there. It had been the embodiment of the enemy – an enemy now protecting me.

At the news conference hosted by the local press club, there were hosts of media people and there could be no doubt that the big story was the presence of the Israeli delegation in Tunis, not the holding of multilateral talks on the refugee issue. Even representatives of the most critical Arab papers were very polite in their questioning. A month after the signing of the Oslo Accord, the honeymoon was still holding. I was very optimistic in my answers, a reflection of my genuine feelings.

The Tunisian Foreign Minister, and his deputy whom I knew from previous meetings, delivered the introductory speeches, which for once were not punctuated by mordant criticism of us. Then there was an emotional visit to the Jewish Quarter with its beautiful synagogue, where Rabbi Haim Madar addressed us in the Hebrew of the Old Testament, and a tour of Bourguiba Boulevard, commemorating the man who as early as 1965 was calling for peace with Israel. Later, in the evening, came my meeting with Arafat.

Predictably, the precise time and place were not revealed to us until the last moment. The motorcade raced to his house as if this was a real emergency, sirens shattering the tranquillity of the compound where the PLO leadership resided in spacious villas, and on leaving the vehicle I was almost submerged by a torrent of journalists, camera-crews, Israeli security men, Tunisian security men and even Palestinian security men, some of them graduates of our prisons who conversed in a rather down-to-earth style of Hebrew with their Israeli counterparts, as if nothing could be more natural than all these people finding themselves here together. More echoes of Fellini.

I was accompanied to the meeting by Shlomo Gur, Yossi Gal, who was then serving as deputy director-general for information of the Foreign Ministry, and Orit Shani. In his room Hannan Ashrawi and Akram Hannia were waiting for us.

I felt no trauma shaking Arafat's hand, but it was decidedly strange to be holding such a polite conversation with the man who had been trying to kill us for so many years, whom we had been trying to kill for the same length of time. Now he was going out of his way to play the perfect host, moving his chair to sit beside me, to avoid formality, and urging us to sweeten our tea with honey rather than sugar, this being healthier as well as tastier.

Although we had never met in person, we were not exactly strangers to each other and there was a feeling of conversation continued from a previous occasion. We spoke especially of the psychological problem involved in convincing both peoples that we were doing the right thing, and the need to avoid words or gestures liable to be interpreted by the other side as threatening or hostile. We spoke of the possibility of Jordanian–Palestinian confederation, which he backed enthusiastically, while acknowledging that the Jordanians seemed less keen on the idea. 'As long ago as 1983 we passed a resolution in the Palestinian National Council in favour of such a confederation, and we're committed to it.'

Arafat was very proud of the outcome of the vote of the Central Committee on the Oslo Accord, parallel to our vote in the Knesset. 'We voted just like you,' he said: 'it can't be helped, democracy is democracy...' Sixty per cent of members of the Council, these being 83 per cent of the 107 present, gave him their backing, and it was obviously important to him to show the broad base of support which he enjoyed.

We spoke at length of the prospects of peace with Syria. He reckoned President Assad was ready for peace but only on very stringent conditions, and he suggested that the importance attached by Asad to continuing Syrian influence in Lebanon should be taken into account. As for the el-Hama sector which the Syrians were demanding from Israel, Arafat said, half seriously and half in jest, that these were Palestinian villages, and territory which should in his opinion be awarded to the Palestinians under the terms of the permanent settlement. He believed that substantive progress in talks between Israel and the PLO would improve the prospects of Syrian–Israeli peace.

The four subjects raised by Arafat as being particularly important from his point of view were: release of prisoners, repatriation of exiles, lifting of the closure of Jerusalem and the liberation of Sheikh Yassin. I spoke at some length on the issue of terrorism and the PLO's commitment to renounce it. I told him that the public at home was not *au fait* with the different trends within the Palestinian camp, and terrorism was terrorism, especially if the PLO declined to condemn it. If Israelis believed nothing had changed in the context of terrorism, they wouldn't support the Accord. Arafat replied that he had made a point of denouncing acts of violence during his recent visit to China; he had intended that this statement would be reported in Israel before the vote on the Accord in the Knesset. Israel must know that the PLO had abandoned the use of terrorism and would condemn all acts of terror on the part of others. On this issue Arafat sounded most resolute.

For so long this man had been a symbol, much more a symbol than a man. Watching him now, with the oddly shaped *keffiyeh* on his head and the customary two days' growth of beard, in his habitual khaki fatigues, it was hard to digest the fact that his bodyguards were protecting me too, and we were talking as if standing on the same side of the barricade, confronting the enemies of peace. I had the feeling that if such a meeting as this were possible, anything was possible, and I took a deep breath and asked why he didn't change out of his military gear into civilian clothes, now that we had finally entered a political phase. Silence. After a long pause Hannan replied on his behalf: 'That's how his people see him, how they know him. Without the uniform he'd be a different person.' There was still no response from Arafat but eventually, after another long and awkward pause, we moved to a corner of the room for a more private conversation. We discussed the issue of Israeli soldiers missing in action, and agreed that continued and thorough investigation was required. I then raised another topic: arrangements for the permanent settlement. I pointed out that over the next few years there were bound to be areas of serious disagreement over which compromise would be achieved only with great difficulty, but if it could be shown at this early stage that bridging the gaps was indeed possible, then public opinion on both sides could be reassured, and fears allayed: on the Israeli side, fear of the partition of Jerusalem and return to the 1949 borders; on the Palestinian side, fear lest 'Gaza first' should turn out to be 'Gaza only', meaning no further Israeli withdrawals from the West Bank. I pointed out that examining the issues would not bind either side, but could present us with a more realistic picture of the positions of both sides.

Arafat agreed at once, and asked how I proposed to set up such dialogue. I suggested that Hirschfeld and Pundak would represent me, without involving any others at this stage, and asked him to nominate participants

from his side. He replied that Abu Mazen would be responsible for negotiating the permanent settlement, and that Akram Hannia was the likeliest
interlocutor for our two academics. I suggested setting up a meeting with
them, and he was pleased at the prospect of meeting with two of the Oslo
participants.

This was the beginning of discussion of the permanent settlement. Yair
and Ron turned up within less than twenty-four hours – ready for the
summons, as always. Next day they met Arafat and expressed their willingness to get down to business. This meeting was followed by a convention of Oslo veterans: Terje Larsen, Abu Ala, Yair and Ron, Shlomo Gur
and I sat down together in my room at the Tunis Hilton, less than
100 metres from the unfinished Arab League building. We analysed the
prospects and the risks inherent in the current situation but didn't discuss
the permanent settlement; this was not the appropriate forum.

It was clear to Yair, Ron and me that we couldn't repeat exactly the same
process as before, but in spite of this we reckoned that the principle of
secret and non-binding talks would be the best way of opening up official
and binding talks.

I knew if I reported the 'private' part of the conversation with Arafat to
Peres, he would feel obliged to tell Rabin and I reckoned Rabin would be
reluctant to embark upon discussion of the permanent settlement at such
an early stage. I decided to keep the business under wraps, pending some
really significant development in this track.

But no such development ensued. Abu Mazen remained in Tunis and
suggested several times – through Said Ben Moustafa, then the Tunisian
deputy Foreign Minister and currently Foreign Minister – that I should go
there, but travelling to Tunis was not a practical option for me at that
time, and in the end I didn't meet him until he arrived in the territories.
Almost half a year had passed and nothing had happened. Meanwhile the
'morning after' syndrome began to take effect, as the initial enthusiasm for
the Oslo Accord gave way to incomprehension and even disappointment.
Negotiations over the Gaza–Jericho deal were proceeding at a desultory
pace, and we had the feeling we could advance the interim settlement
only if it were possible to link it with some agreed principles regarding
the permanent settlement. The massacre perpetrated by Baruch Goldstein,
a Jewish fanatic who immigrated from the USA and lived in Karyat Arba,
at the Tombs of the Patriarchs in Hebron, in February 1994, sent the whole

process into reverse and led to the suspension of talks. At a certain stage Rabin was minded to evict the Jewish residents of Hebron to avoid escalation of the crisis, but later he reconsidered this, fearing the tension such a decision was likely to create. For the moment it seemed the process was stalled.

In Vienna, at his own request, Dr Maher el Kurd, formerly of the Palestinian Oslo delegation and confidant of Arafat, met Yair and Ron. He reported that the mood in Tunis was sombre: the Palestinians felt that while there were indeed those in Israel who wanted to reach a permanent settlement, and the sooner the better, there was also a group intent on weakening PLO-Tunis and sabotaging negotiation over the interim settlement.

We decided in the meantime to address the issues on the agenda of the permanent settlement one by one. Parallel work was in progress at the Jaffee Centre, under the supervision of Yossi Alfer, and some of the participants in the debates were responsible for the pamphlets issued by the Centre. The ECF, whose deliberations I chaired, had a concept very similar to that of the Jaffee Centre – an attempt to bypass negotiations and look to the end of the process, rather than planning Israel's opening gambits.

All these debates, sponsored by the German Friedrich Ebert Foundation, were held at the Dan Hotel in Caesarea, over a series of weekends. These were conversations with people involved in the system and with those who had left it in recent years – high-ranking officers in the armed forces and the security services, former senior Foreign Ministry civil servants and university researchers. The talks were very intensive: we would start on Friday evening at five p.m. and conclude twenty-four hours later, having carried on the debate even over meals. The officials of the ECF – Yair Hirschfeld, Ron Pundak and Boaz Karni – guided the debates; at each meeting there was a central lecture, after which the participants would continue with no limit on time. They felt free to say whatever was on their minds – some of the disagreements were predictable, others unexpected – and overall this was an ideal preparation for talks on the permanent settlement.

In the debates, support for the notion of Palestinian–Jordanian confederation was somewhat lukewarm. While a number of academics backed a Jordanian–Palestinian link, it was the security experts who preferred a separate Palestinian state, assisted by Israel and the world at large in the field of economic development and not dependent on Israel for employment. Almost all the participants had reservations about a long interim period which would expose both Israel and the Palestinians to domestic conflict. They proposed to implement the part of the clause in the declaration of principles reading 'as soon as possible' and not to exploit the leeway implied by 'no more than three years after the opening of the final status talks', thereby giving opponents of peace the opportunity to torpedo it.

The feeling of most of the participants was that nothing particularly good was likely to happen in the interim period, that the Israelis and Palestinians knew one another quite adequately by this time and there was no need to pursue closer acquaintance, while Hamas on the one side and fanatics like Baruch Goldstein on the other might well succeed in destroying the process.

The first debate took place on 8 April 1994, and the last on 5 May 1995. We covered all the points addressed in the talks over the permanent settlement and were able to crystallise some other ideas, against the background of the parallel talks taking place in Stockholm (of which more presently). The participants knew of course that they were involved in preparing the ground for the definitive talks which were supposed to begin in May 1996, but they didn't know that this was material we were already using in the secret and non-binding talks.

On the subject of employing Palestinian workers there was serious disagreement. The economists in the group talked of separation, while the security people supported continued employment of Palestinians for the time being, on the assumption that establishment of alternative economic arrangements in the territories proper would be a lengthy process, and Palestinians denied work in Israel were liable to vent their frustration in violence.

Most of the participants had reservations about the notion of Jewish settlements remaining under Arab sovereignty, and recommended the dismantling of the settlements and their transference to areas under Israeli sovereignty. On this issue I took a different line. I thought it would be a mistake to follow the precedent of Yamit in Sinai, demolished prior to the handover to Egypt, and it was not unreasonable that there should be Israeli settlements under Palestinian sovereignty, however incongruous the notion might sound. After all, in 1949 no one expected that the Jewish state would be responsible for the security and welfare of the inhabitants of Arab villages, but that is how it turned out. If the settlers were given the opportunity to choose between staying in their homes and, having received compensation, transferring to an area under Israeli sovereignty, this would be the most reasonable solution. In all probability, the majority would prefer transfer to Israeli sovereignty, while the government would not need to engage in violent conflict with those who remained. In the end this was the objective we agreed on in advance of talks with the Palestinians, although even in our somewhat limited team – Yair, Ron and myself – there wasn't total unanimity on this difficult issue.

The biggest surprise came in discussion of the Jordan Valley. Here we were divided into 'civilians' and former service personnel in a manner both unequivocal and contrary to expectations. While the civilians repeated the traditional concept whereby massive military presence must be guaranteed on the Jordan, backed up by Israeli control of the territory, or even Israeli sovereignty, most former security personnel said this was a discredited and anachronistic myth. They insisted that the Jordan river wasn't a strategic line and that control of it would yield no benefits whatsoever. According to them, it would be possible to monitor the demilitarisation of the West Bank by means of various techniques of intelligence. All that Israel needed to do was sign a peace treaty explicitly addressing the issues of demilitarisation and stating in the clearest possible terms that arming of the Palestinians or – alternatively – appearance in the region of a foreign army would constitute a *casus belli*. Their position was that Israel should concede territory on the West Bank in exchange for strategic depth of some 500 kilometres, extending to the borders of Iraq, a highly advantageous arrangement. 'The Jordan Valley,' said one of the participants, 'is a bridge too far, a logistical burden and a slap in the face to anyone who favours any kind of co-operation between Jordan and the Palestinians.'

This individual, reservist General Yanush Ben Gal, presented the following analysis: occupying a line of future friction has no value in war; it is only useful now, for purposes of routine security. The Maginot Line, the Suez Canal and the Golan Heights all failed in the attempt to delay an invading enemy. When such a military presence exists, the army invests all its resources in troops stationed in the line and has no latitude to engage in strategic planning. In emergency conditions, a line manned by Israeli troops would be likely to turn into a trap, requiring all efforts to be devoted to extricating those soldiers, while the only advantage of having troops there in the first place would be that they could notify HQ a few seconds before the first shell landed on their heads. And if, in spite of everything, there was support for the notion of Jordanian–Palestinian confederation, what kind of confederation would this be, with an Israeli army stuck in the middle of it? If there was to be a presence, it had better be temporary, seeing that its sole function was psychological. In any case, the only solution to the problem of preventing incursion by a foreign army via the West Bank was an intelligence solution. At the end of the day we didn't accept this extreme analysis, because all the time we were faced with the problem of how to convince public opinion, and in particular the opinion of my public, namely Yitzhak Rabin and Shimon Peres. As a result of this, in the academic discussions the Israelis insisted on a significant Israeli presence on the Jordan, but not Israeli sovereignty over the Jordan Valley.

Water was treated by all the participants as an economic issue. This was a very sensitive topic; according to some, disagreement over water was the likeliest cause of future wars in the region. It was perceived as an issue with a price-tag attached, one which could be solved by a fairer system of allocation between agricultural and domestic needs, better piping, exploitation of sewage and desalination of seawater.

There was also general agreement over the sectors in which it would be necessary to extend the frontiers of Israeli sovereignty: the Gush Etzion sector, the Jerusalem sector and the Ariel sector, with very limited adjustments to other places located along the Green line (the 1949 armistice). It was obvious that a certain price would have to be paid for all this, in terms perhaps of a land-passage between Gaza and the West Bank, certain rights to be granted to the Palestinians in the port of Ashdod, or southward expansion of the Gaza Strip in the region of Holot Halutza. This seemed a reasonable price to pay when measured against the fact that the majority of settlers would now be living – for the first time since the Six Day War – in sovereign Israeli territory.

Would it be right also to annex Palestinian villages located in the sectors we would seek to annex to Israel? Here there was genuine discord. While some participants insisted it would be best not to annex a single Palestinian to Israel, even at the price of non-inclusion of a whole area of the West Bank populated by Israelis, others saw no objection to the annexation of a very limited number of Palestinians to Israel, these becoming not Israeli citizens but citizens of the Palestinian state located to the east of us.

The weekend that we devoted to Jerusalem was particularly interesting. We were all acquainted with various plans put forward for solving the problem of this city; indeed some of us had been involved in formulating these plans. One of the outstanding members of the team, who had himself drawn up such a plan, now presented a number of options. He pointed out, rightly, that when members of the public speak of the unity of Jerusalem, most of them do not picture to themselves the municipal limits of the city as annexed to Israel immediately after the Six Day War. It never occurs to the majority of strollers in Jerusalem that villages like Azaria or Shuafat are part of the city. When an Israeli speaks of the unity of Jerusalem he is referring essentially to the Israeli neighbourhoods constructed in the city such as French Hill and Har Gilo, plus the Old City and the Mount of Olives. A number of settlers have dared to suggest, even in public, that Israeli sovereignty be waived in the Palestinian villages annexed to Jerusalem, in exchange for annexation of significant areas of the West Bank – the only problem being that such a process would run counter to what is perceived as the clearest common denominator of Israeli society: the concept of a united Jerusalem under Israeli sovereignty with its present borders, one municipality, the capital of Israel.

These principles still allow considerable freedom of manoeuvre, and options such as Andorra-style dual sovereignty, suspension of sovereignty, deliberate non-implementation of sovereignty, extra-territorial sectors and numerous other variants. In the opinion of our speaker on that occasion, it would be possible to reach a solution to the Jerusalem problem on the basis of certain precepts: a united city, without partitions or borders, in which two communities live – Palestinian and Israeli. The Palestinians would be citizens of the Palestinian state and would vote for its institutions, while the Israelis would vote for the Knesset. The municipal structure would be based on a system of quarters, each quarter being self-administered in the areas which characterise the community living there – education, culture, leisure, personal legal status, minor claims and the like. On the Temple Mount control would be given to the Palestinians and this would, in effect, be a codification of the present system, using existing procedures relating to the Jews. The Palestinian capital could be created, with large-scale international aid, in the sector designated Al-Quds according to Jordanian territorial distribution, which is situated outside the municipal borders of united Jerusalem and comprises such areas as A-Ram, Ras el Amud, Abu Dis and Jabar Mukhabar.

This long debating session opened up other options which, even if rejected by most of the participants, at least served to disprove the claim that 'Nobody is talking about Jerusalem.' After all, we demand the world's recognition of Jerusalem as Israel's capital, and we know that the world's recognition will be withheld until the Palestinians recognise us. Only two countries in the world – Costa Rica and El Salvador – maintain embassies in Jerusalem, thus recognising West Jerusalem as our capital; all the other embassies are located in or around Tel Aviv. Would Israel be prepared, as part of the permanent settlement, to waive the demand for recognition of our capital? Is it in Israel's interest that all the Palestinians living in Jerusalem should be its citizens? Is there any objection on the Israeli side to the notion of the Palestinians of Jerusalem deciding their own cultural and religious way of life? From many other conversations and seminars, but especially from that day in the Dan Caesarea I came away with the feeling that what was being discussed here was no Pandora's Box but an issue to which, given goodwill and determination on both sides, a solution could be found without serious abrogation of principle on either side.

A separate meeting was devoted to the Palestinian refugee problem, – another very sensitive issue, regarded since 1948 as insoluble and yet soluble if both sides were prepared to tackle it. The opening lecture stressed the gravity of the problem as perceived on both sides of the barricade, but also the need of both sides to find a solution: the Palestinian leadership needed to prove to the refugees in neighbouring countries that they weren't being neglected and that the deal which had been agreed affected not just residents of the territories, but the entire Palestinian people; while to Israel it was important that no open wounds should be left untreated and allowed to fester – signing an agreement with one of its central issues unresolved would cast a shadow over the entire deal.

Reservist General Shlomo Gazit, who was presenting us with options for solution of the refugee problem, started by quoting from a conversation with a senior Palestinian official who had told him that in order to solve the problem Israel would need to address the issue openly and accept responsibility for at least part of the problem. Such an admission would be worth more than any number of aid and development projects. In the opinion of this Palestinian, there would be some 2.5 million refugees appealing for compensation, and a significant proportion of this sum could be offset by sale of abandoned property in the territories. Any Palestinian could return to the Palestinian state, but only a few would exercise the option of entering Israel; the majority would prefer rehabilitation, through receipt of international aid, in their current places of domicile.

Gazit himself put forward an alternative solution. Israel would address the plight of the refugees but would not take responsibility for expelling all of them, since there was no historical justification for this. An international organisation should be set up to deal with the settling of the refugees and the provision of aid for their families, Israel being one of the states funding this organisation. Most Palestinians would opt for rehabilitation in the countries where they currently resided, but anyone wanting to do so could live in the Palestinian state. Israel would not take in refugees, but would not prevent the reunification of families, already in progress on a limited scale. When we reached agreement with other Arab states, we would raise the issue of compensation for the Jews who left them to come to Israel. The funds received by Israel would to a great extent defray the cost of compensating the Palestinians.

The suggestion aroused controversy. Some asked whether Israel would really be prepared to accept unlimited immigration into the Palestinian state, some raised doubts as to the prospect of reaching agreement with Arab states on compensation for the Jews, and others had reservations about acknowledging even partial responsibility. But in the end we returned to the principles set out by the lecturer.

The concept which finally emerged, as a result of various deliberations including the marathon debating sessions held in Caesarea, was similar to that which we had crafted vis-à-vis Jerusalem. It was both an ideological and a pragmatic approach: we were not prepared to accept Palestinian refugees in Israel but we would not prevent a future Palestinian state taking in any Palestinians who wanted to live there. As for Jerusalem, we were not prepared to divide it but we wouldn't prevent the Palestinians establishing their capital in Al-Quds, outside the boundaries of united Jerusalem. The dimensions of Al-Quds would not be definitively fixed, but it was clear that *inter alia* it would include Abu Dis, a suburb already defined by the interim agreement as belonging to Area B which had already been handed over to the Palestinians. As for the other issues, the border-lines should be fixed according to demographic, not geographical criteria and should ensure that the majority of Jewish settlers would be under Israeli sovereignty; there would however be no necessity to dismantle existing settlements which would remain in the territory of the Palestinian state. The decision to insist on military presence in the Jordan

Valley was firmly opposed by the majority of the security specialists in the team.

In the wake of the Caesarea debates I set up a meeting with Yair and Ron. All three of us felt that time was running out and we weren't doing enough to exploit it. The slaughter at the Tombs of the Patriarchs and Palestinian terrorist acts had sent the peace process into reverse, just as the perpetrators intended, while the closure imposed on the territories was causing unemployment and serious tension. True, an agreement had just been signed with the Palestinians regarding Gaza and Jericho, but soon the 'morning after' syndrome would take effect and the inhabitants would see that Gaza, after the arrival of the Palestinian leadership, was remarkably similar to Gaza as it had always been. Within two years at the outside we were supposed to be starting negotiations over the permanent settlement, and if we couldn't get the essential arguments clear in our own minds, we would arrive for the start of talks in May 1996 armed with nothing but tired slogans which would only expose the width of the chasm confronting us. We would be open to criticism from both sides: the years that had elapsed had brought us no closer to understanding over the permanent settlement, and hence such a settlement might not be possible at all. In the less than six months remaining before the elections, Likud would exploit the divisions exposed, setting out the Palestinian positions – return to the 1967 borders, Palestinian capital in Jerusalem and repatriation of refugees to Israel – and warning the public that a Rabin government would ultimately adopt these measures in its headlong rush towards peace; we in the Labour Party would have to spend the entire election campaign defending ourselves.

Yair suggested a few possible courses of action, but the three of us were convinced that under present circumstances there could be no more convenient and practical option than discussions with Palestinian academics. Such talks would lay the basis for political negotiations and, if both sides agreed this was a reasonable basis, substantive secret negotiations could begin, lasting a relatively short time and hopefully reaching completion before May 1996. In May 1996, with the start of talks on the permanent settlement, instead of a return to sterile declarations and slogans, a statement of principles for the permanent settlement would be unveiled – including a map showing the permanent borders – and the world would be amazed by the ability of the two sides to reach such a rapid and comprehensive understanding. Rabin and Peres, Arafat and Abu Mazen would initial the statement of principles and the elections in October would effectively be a referendum on the issue. No questions would be asked – it would be a simple matter of opposing or supporting the deal – and on the assumption that a majority of the Israeli public favoured an end to the Israeli–Palestinian dispute, and ultimately an end to the entire Israeli–Arab dispute, Rabin's government would be re-elected and would sign the agreement in full.

But who would we be talking to? I was in Jerusalem, Abu Mazen was in Tunis, we hadn't heard anything from Akram Hannia; everyone was obsessed with setting the Jericho city-limits and the central issue was disappearing over the horizon.

A few weeks after this pessimistic three-sided conversation, we found our interlocutors: two young researchers, Palestinian graduates based in London and involved in the multilateral talks, Dr Ahmed Khalidi and Dr Hussein Agha. Both came to Israel and the territories at the end of spring 1994, expressing their willingness to begin preliminary negotiations. When asked where they would prefer to hold these talks, whether return to Oslo was acceptable to them, they replied that any manoeuvres in Oslo at this time would be seen as highly suspicious. On the other hand, they had a special and positive relationship with the Swedish Foreign Ministry and with the Minister herself, Margarita Af Ugla.

The Swedish Foreign Minister had visited Israel in December 1992 – an impressive lady from an aristocratic family and one of the leading lights of the Swedish Conservative Party. From conversations I had with her I was impressed by her familiarity with the details of the Middle East dispute and her interest in becoming involved. All too often, expressions of willingness to become involved remain just that, polite gestures leading nowhere, but now an opportunity had arisen to test that willingness. A flight to Sweden and a conversation between the Foreign Minister and the researchers were all that was needed to set the Stockholm track in motion. They explained the structure of the talks, the role that Abu Mazen and I would fulfil as supervisors and monitors, and their desire to reach the maximum possible degree of agreement in the space of about a year and present it in documentary form as a basis for substantive political negotiations. The Foreign Minister saw this as a challenge. After all, the Swedes had always resented our decision to go to Oslo, to their allies and greatest rivals. She appointed Ann Dismorr, head of the Middle East desk, to take responsibility for organising the secret talks. A special budget was also allocated to the project and it was decided the first session would take place on 1 September 1994.

We made our preparations. There wasn't the same excitement that had preceded the first meeting in Oslo; we knew that running such a track was well within our ability, we were acquainted with the other side, and the series of debates in Caesarea, as well as numerous conversations between the three of us, had given us the opportunity to refine our positions. At the end of August Yair handed me a very impressive document, addressing the peace agreement which was supposed to be signed before 1999, as a step towards deeper and more comprehensive peace in the region. Immediate peace would bring positive developments such as expansion of the middle classes, democratisation giving legitimacy to leaderships, reduction in defence expenditure and the opportunity to divert resources towards social projects and the narrowing of gaps within society. The document also set out some of the problems associated with peace, in terms of expectations not all of which would be met, and in terms of the exacerbation of social inequalities likely to result from accelerated economic development, and a range of other problems demanding attention from the outset.

The object of the process, as he saw it, was to establish a Middle Eastern Community within fifty years, and he proceeded to set out a very ambitious programme for the next half-century: in the first decade, special emphasis to be placed on regional infrastructure; in the second, focus on tight economic co-operation between Israel, Jordan, the Palestinians, Egypt, Syria and Lebanon, on organisation of regional security, and on the extension of shared infrastructure towards the Gulf and Central Asia; the third decade to see the elimination from the region of weapons of mass destruction and progress towards inter-regional networking between the Middle East and the European Community and the USA; the fourth to see the establishment of the Middle Eastern Community with all its component parts fully developed – economics, infrastructure, culture and defence.

In order to realise this distant objective it was clearly important to find solutions to those issues on the agenda which seemed at that moment most pressing and difficult: crafting a permanent peace, the fixing of borders, cementing relations between the two peoples, guaranteed demilitarisation of the territories evacuated by Israel, installation of various security arrangements, implementation of previous agreements, including economic deals yet to be finalised, agreement on water exploitation, resolution of the Jerusalem problem, and a final settlement of the issue of the refugees, including definition of their rights. Also required were consultation on the involvement of third parties and agreement on Israeli–Palestinian co-operation in the region and on the steps to be taken towards realisation of the vision of peace.

With all this high-powered ammunition Yair and Ron set off for Stockholm, their object being to hold a marathon session at the end of which there would be a first draft of points of agreement and disagreement regarding the principles of the permanent settlement. This meeting took place over three full days and was conducted in a relaxed atmosphere, without a lot of sloganising from the two sides. Ahmed Khalidi is the son of Professor Walid Khalidi, a very well-known Palestinian residing in the USA, considered a moderate but a severe critic of Israel in the past. After the Oslo Accord he became equally critical of the Palestinian leadership, insisting that the deal was seriously flawed from the Palestinian point of view. Hussein Agha is an academic of Lebanese origin, and at this time both men had spent years involved in research at Chatham House in London and had been active in various aspects of the peace process. The meeting with Yair and Ron was not their first encounter with Israelis; it was an almost routine occurrence for them, handled with the pragmatism which was the hallmark of their approach and of their proposals.

The meeting ended on 4 September, and the next day Yair and Ron were already in my office with four documents which had been accepted by all parties. The foursome had agreed to meet every month in Stockholm, and the next session was scheduled for 9 October. One document referred to the Swedish hosts, and constituted agreement that they should be updated from time to time on progress in the talks. A second document spoke in broad and general terms of the ultimate objectives of the negotiations (comprehensive peace, regional stability, and so on). The third document referred to seventeen points which the permanent settlement would need to address, from solution of the refugee problem to defining the political profile of the Palestinian entity; while the fourth was very ambitious and clearly influenced by the draft that Yair had shown me; it referred to six stages in relations between Israel and the Palestinians, from permanent peace to a Middle Eastern Community. We couldn't have expected more than this. It was clear that the first step had been a positive one.

The peace factory was now in full production. The ECF was no longer just a telephone extension in Hirschfeld's house; it occupied a modest office in a rented apartment in Tel Aviv. Every month meetings were held in Stockholm, and between meetings we prepared new draft agreements. In parallel, the ECF was sponsoring further debates in Caesarea, as well as more restricted meetings dealing with specific issues such as water allocation or security arrangements. In comparison with the Oslo days, a great many people were involved in the process – but most were unaware of the fact, not suspecting that their advice and their opinions were helping to draft the permanent settlement between Israel and the Palestinians.

Many drafts passed from hand to hand between us – Yair, Ron and myself – at the end of September and in early October. There were a number of disagreements among us, regarding the possibility of settlements remaining under future Arab sovereignty, also certain security clauses and areas of co-operation with Egypt and Jordan. The issue of Jerusalem occupied us more than any other, and here we constructed a very complicated proposal involving guaranteed Israeli sovereignty in all the municipal territory of a united Jerusalem, with expansion of the city and annexation of additional areas to it. In the end a detailed draft was prepared, ten pages long and dealing with all the seventeen points of the statement of principles, and armed with this Yair and Ron set out for the second Stockholm meeting.

The meetings in Sweden followed a regular pattern. They dealt with drafts, amendments and alternative proposals, and sometimes there was vehement argument over one word or another. Our opposite numbers brought with them a paper regarding solution of the refugee problem, but in most other issues the basis for discussion was papers prepared in Israel. In this respect it was a return to the Oslo model.

In August 1994 official business took me to Denmark, Sweden and Norway. In each of these countries my main concern was to remind them of their obligations as contributors towards the development of Gaza and the West Bank. If enthusiasm for the Oslo Accord were to fade, and with it the willingness to contribute, the Palestinian Authority might well have difficulty paying the salaries of police and other employees. In Sweden I spoke at length with the Foreign Minister, who was aware in general terms of the progress being made in the talks currently under way in her country, and said she attached great importance to them. Elections were imminent in Sweden, and, according to the polls and the general mood, victory of the Socialists seemed assured.

Paradox! My friends in Sweden were Socialists whom I had known since my time as international secretary of the Young Guard of the Labour Party, but what I saw as my life's work was currently in the capable hands of a Conservative government. I couldn't be sure that another government would feel the same enthusiasm for the project. In the Riksdag, the Swedish parliament, I met the foreign affairs committee headed by Pierre Schorri and, later, had a private meeting with Schorri – undoubtedly one of the most talented and outstanding personalities in Swedish politics. Son of a Swedish father and a French mother, he fulfilled a number of functions in the Socialist Party, being particularly active in promoting the party's foreign relations, and my acquaintance with him dated back to conferences of the Socialist International. When I was serving as director-general of the Foreign Ministry, I met him several times in his capacity as deputy to Sten Anderson, the Swedish Foreign Minister. For years he tried to get himself elected to parliament, without success; it was only when his party went into opposition that he achieved this particular goal. Now he was a strong candidate for a ministry – perhaps even the Foreign Affairs portfolio.

I told him about the Stockholm talks. He was very excited, saying he didn't suppose for a moment that a government led by Ingvar Karlson, if and when elected, would cancel Sweden's sponsorship of such an important project; on the contrary, it would treat the Middle East as the leading issue on its agenda. In the meantime, he promised to keep the business secret.

In the elections which took place soon afterwards the Socialists were indeed victorious; the new Foreign Minister was Lena Hilm Wallen, while Pierre Schorri was appointed to a dual role – Minister of International Co-operation and deputy Foreign Minister. He contacted me and announced: 'Whoever needs to know can be told, it's all going ahead, no changes. Keep up the good work!' Sten Anderson, who had been the guiding spirit behind the PLO's decisions in 1988, which had led to the opening of dialogue between the organisation and the USA, was now appointed the Prime Minister's special envoy to the Middle East. He also headed the institute bearing the name of Olaf Palme and the talks were henceforward under dual sponsorship – by the Foreign Ministry and the Palme Institute.

In the run-up to the decision on the award of the Nobel Peace Prize for

1994 there was a sense of latent tension: tension, because Peres and Rabin were natural candidates, and until the last moment it wasn't known whether the prize would be won by a representative of another country or – if it were to be Israel – by one of the two or by both; latent, because no one was prepared to admit he cared.

In the Nobel Committee itself there had been serious dissension. Usually its deliberations are leak-proof, but this time controversy was revealed when one of the committee members, Kora Kristiansen, resigned in protest at the decision in favour of Arafat. It emerged that there had been vigorous debate over two issues: whether to give the prize to two Israelis or just one, and whether Arafat was also entitled to the award. In the course of discussion other names were mentioned, including Uri Savir, Abu Ala, Abu Mazen – and a certain Yossi Beilin. One evening the telephone rang in Jerusalem, and a Norwegian friend asked if I would be willing to accept nomination myself. Apparently, all that was required for candidature was nomination by any member of any of the world's parliaments and the consent of the nominee was not required, although as a matter of courtesy he thought I should be told. He said that the idea came from 'circles' in the committee, with the aim of increasing the number of options available to them. I implored him not to put me up as a candidate. I was sure that Rabin and Peres were the ones who deserved the prize and I didn't relish the prospect of competing with them.

Before the dramatic announcement of the Nobel Committee's decision, it was widely rumoured that Rabin alone was destined to win the prize. When I heard on the Friday morning, 14 October 1994, that there were three winners, Rabin, Peres and Arafat, I considered that justice had been done. The men who had taken on themselves the ultimate political responsibility were now being awarded the world's ultimate accolade. It was also fitting that Oslo, which had entered the language of international politics as a symbol of the peace process, should be the setting for presentation of the prize.

In the event, however, we flew to Oslo with mixed feelings. Any satisfaction we might have felt at the successful transfer of power from ourselves to the Palestinians in Gaza was overshadowed by the horror of a series of recent Hamas terrorist attacks. In October two Israelis were shot dead in a suburb of Jerusalem; in November a soldier was murdered in Netzarim, Rabbi Ami Olami was shot dead in Othniel to the south of Hebron, an eighty-four-year-old woman was beaten to death in an orchard near her home in Kfar Saba – a note found on her body claimed responsibility on behalf of Hamas – and a nineteen-year-old girl-soldier was hacked to death with an axe in Afula. Feelings were running high. Families of the terrorists victims were waiting for us in Oslo and they followed us wherever we went, carrying pictures of their loved ones and making their protests heard, leading to an increase in the level of security surrounding us. It was not a comfortable situation: the Prime Minister and Foreign Minister of Israel arriving in town to receive the Nobel Peace Prize and having to be protected by Norwegian police from their own citizens.

Politically, we were also far from euphoric. Two and a half years after the elections and in spite of the achievements of the Rabin government – peace with Jordan and agreement with the Palestinians – some polls showed equal rating for Rabin and Netanyahu, some even showed a slim majority in Netanyahu's favour. Would the Nobel Peace Prize contribute to the government's longevity? It seemed unlikely.

From Oslo Rabin flew to Japan, while Peres and I went on to Sweden. Alongside the official talks I had discussions with the Swedes who were privy to the secret negotiations, the Foreign Minister, Pierre Schorri and Sten Anderson. They were pleased with the progress that had been made and hoped that within a relatively short period of time the Stockholm track would show the way towards final and definitive negotiations. At this stage the third round of talks had been completed, with an eighteen-clause draft document; the assessment was that gaps had been closed in an appreciable proportion of the clauses, but that a great deal of work remained to be done. Sten promised to visit the region on a regular basis, and he was to keep his word. This affable, white-haired, peace-loving man had devoted much of his energy to the Middle East, both in his term as Foreign Minister and afterwards. His son spent some time on a kibbutz and he himself had links with Israel and had known its leaders since the 1960s; it was only at a relatively late stage in his political career that he became acquainted with some of the Palestinian leaders and began to see a role for himself in promoting conciliation between the two peoples. When he induced the PLO to accept Resolution 242 and renounce terrorism (December 1988), many in Israel saw him as a pro-PLO statesman, granting legitimacy to that organisation in exchange for an empty promise. But times had changed and Israel at the end of 1994 was a different country, where Anderson was a welcome guest.

In Sweden there is a tradition of early retirement from politics; men in their mid- to late fifties are already sorting out their angling gear in anticipation of a long and leisurely retirement. Sten was something of an exception to this trend, and although he considered himself too old to pursue government office, he was always available for special assignments.

On the eve of Santa Lucia (the Swedish festival of light), we sat down to a formal dinner in Stockholm's picturesque City Hall. To the sound of music girls ascended the stairs, dressed in white and with candles on their heads, to dance in celebration of the festival. Returning to my hotel, I noticed lanterns in every window. December. Candles. Lanterns. Nothing to do with Hannukkah and the miracle of the cruse of oil, of course, and yet the resemblance is evidently not accidental. Worship of the light is the most ancient of customs, whatever the religious pretexts attached to it at a later stage. But the contrast was equally striking: from the pastoral tranquillity of Sweden we were returning to the implementation of agreements, to the threat of terrorist attack, to the morning after the party, the morning after the Nobel Peace Prize.

Besides discussing alternative versions of the statement of principles for the permanent settlement, we devoted a lot of time to the issue of the map. Our assessment was that the primary objective was to create an awareness, on both sides, that the arrangements we were discussing were not only new but intended to be permanent; as long as there was no clear frontier, there could be no clear settlement. I reckoned that of all the tough questions on the agenda, including Jerusalem and the refugees, the border issue was by far the most easily soluble, and so it should be addressed without delay. Ron Pundak put a lot of effort into the project, flying over the territory in a light aircraft with an aerial camera, and our objective was simple – annexation of territory to be minimal, annexation of Israelis to be extensive. On the basis of previous work by Dr Yitzhak Beili and by Yossi Alfer, we knew this was feasible.

Regular feedback on some of our ideas, regarding both Jerusalem and the permanent map, was something which I could obtain in meetings of the 'jeans forum', an informal think-tank which I had set up soon after my appointment as deputy Foreign Minister and which, unwittingly, made a substantial contribution to the success of the Stockholm track. Once a month, at 9.30 a.m. on a Friday, we would sit down at a round table, all dressed in jeans, and, fuelled on coffee and biscuits and with no time limit, discuss issues raised by one or other of the participants, some of them controversial and some of them taboo, such as voluntarily reducing our dependence on American aid, or restricting contact with dictatorial regimes. The existence of the forum and the topics discussed were closely guarded secrets; were the veil of secrecy to be lifted this would have become just another departmental talking-shop, with agenda and protocols and pressure to take decisions – not our style at all! Some of the participants were deputy directors-general and veteran Foreign Ministry employees but most were in their thirties and forties, departmental directors who weren't accustomed to being consulted by the Minister or his deputy, but whose sometimes unconventional opinions deserved a hearing. I found these meetings the perfect opportunity to garner fresh ideas and get feedback on my own, although naturally there was never any mention of the existence of the Stockholm track. The map that we had sketched passed the test of the 'jeans forum', albeit in draft form.

On 11 January 1995, in the four-sided meeting in Stockholm, Yair and Ron presented the map to their opposite numbers. The border adjustments were accepted in principle and the central question was: what would be offered in return: anchorage-rights in Ashdod? a corridor linking Gaza with the West Bank? southward extension of the Gaza Strip? One way or the other, we were convinced that the border issue was more readily soluble than the others and it was important to reach agreement on it without delay, since other issues, such as the future of the settlements, were directly linked to the border question. On this point, we made it clear that we had no intention of dismantling settlements situated beyond the border and we would insist on guarantees of their security. We also made progress in reference to the refugees and Jerusalem, which was and remains the most complex problem, and the Palestinians said they wanted their decision-makers and ours to be involved and to be kept abreast of developments, even if knowledge of the existence of a specific Swedish track were to be withheld from them. Political feedback was needed by both sides at this stage.

The feeling of Ahmed and Hussein was that Arafat was building up his position in Gaza and the West Bank in a fashion that would enable him to prepare himself for the permanent settlement, a settlement which could be achieved on the basis of these and other issues and alternatives currently under discussion in this forum. They were disappointed by the cold signals emanating from the Israel–Syria negotiating track. In their opinion, the closer Israel came to peace with Syria, the better the prospect of limiting terrorism, and this in itself would lead to improved relations between Israelis and Palestinians and facilitate progress in formulation of the permanent settlement.

A first step on the political plain in the direction of permanent settlement was a meeting in which I participated along with Haim Divon, who had replaced Shlomo Gur as my office chief and adviser, and Yair and Ron; participating on the Palestinian side were Dr Nabil Shaath and General Yehi Abd e-Razak. This was a weekend session organised by Sten Anderson and Pierre Schorri and it was to take place in Ronberga, formerly a fashionable resort and now a conference centre, some 100 kilometres from Stockholm. After official meetings with the Prime Minister and Foreign Minister I made my way to the site, in the bitter cold of 17 February and – when not making rash forays into the surrounding countryside, where we very nearly perished in the sub-zero temperatures – we spent a long time together trying to crack the problems of the permanent settlement, without referring directly to the Stockholm track.

Typically, such conversations were an opportunity to delve deeper into the experiences and personalities of the other side. Thus for example it was fascinating to hear some of the stories that Yehia Abd el-Razek had to tell. Born in Tantura in 1939, he became commander of the Palestine Liberation Army (PLA) after years of service in the senior ranks of the Jordanian army. He represented a very pragmatic approach to ending the dispute, seemed perfectly prepared to bid 'a farewell to arms', and was particularly interested in a solution involving confederation with Jordan.

Nabil Shaath reckoned that the central problem was how to continue with the process despite the best efforts of extremists on both sides, and how to ensure that the extremists were not given the right of veto over the prospects of peace in the region. He suggested possible options: trying to bypass the interim settlement and instituting negotiations over the permanent settlement; or, alternatively, continuing with the interim settlement in its current form and simultaneously advancing towards signature of the permanent settlement.

Dr Shaath did not reject the notion of separation between Israel and the Palestinian entity, which had begun to gather momentum after the kidnap and murder of the young soldier Nachshon Waxmann, and he said that such separation could be carried out on the basis of agreement with the Palestinians on what should continue to be shared and what should be separate. If, for example, local industries were to be created and employment of various kinds made available to residents of the self-governing territory, there would be no reason for them to carry on working in Israel as though they were Mexican migrant-workers in the USA.

He attached considerable importance to the contacts which were *not* taking place between the Palestinian public and the Israeli public and he asked if Peace Now was capable at this stage of doing anything to foster conciliation at grass-roots level. There was still a widely held feeling that the Oslo agreement was something which leaders had signed and which had not impinged upon the populace.

Shaath wanted to discuss the permanent settlement, but routine day-to-day issues demanded all our attention, leaving scant latitude for longer-term speculation. We proceeded to discuss crossing-points between Gaza and Egypt and between Jericho and Jordan, the release of prisoners, a corridor linking Gaza with the West Bank, the future of Gaza's flower-nurseries and other topics which were the staple fare of debates between representatives of the Palestinian Authority and representatives of the Israeli government.

We agreed to meet again, with participation by Sten Anderson and Pierre Schorri, and such a meeting did in fact take place some months later in Jerusalem. I felt that the bottom line of the discussions could be summed up in two points: willingness on the part of the Palestinians to seek confederation with Jordan and their readiness, in the effort to obtain the kind of border that they coveted, to accept the problematical notion of separation – if accompanied by a binding agreement specifying what belonged to us and what to them.

In tandem with the discussions we were holding in Sweden, the official talks on the interim settlement were continuing in Cairo. At a certain stage these talks had fallen victim to the Washington syndrome: media hype, predetermined positions, confrontation in the conference hall and inconclusive stalemate, presaging neither disintegration nor progress. It was clear that this could not be allowed to continue and another secret negotiating track was initiated forthwith, headed by Uri Savir and Abu Ala, which made progress on the issues of elections to the Council of the Palestinian Authority and redeployment of Israeli forces on the West Bank.

I was afraid of a process whereby the interim settlement would put pressure on the permanent settlement, by means of a redeployment which would ultimately also determine the border, and not vice versa – a situation in which the permanent settlement would be the point of agreement whereby interim arrangements would be decided. This was one of history's typical reversals: in the past it had been the Palestinians demanding to know in advance whither the permanent settlement was leading, to avoid getting bogged down in an unsatisfactory interim settlement; now Israel was in a similar situation.

At this stage Yair, Ron and I held a meeting at which we discussed the possibility of adopting the approach of Faisal Husseini and incorporating it into the interim settlement, viz. to complete redeployment in the West Bank in one phase and in co-ordination with the establishment of a border, agreed by both sides. The border would encompass most of the settlers and would dictate the development plans of both sides, with Israeli settlements continuing to exist in areas controlled by the Palestinian Authority under the terms of the interim settlement. Only in negotiations over the permanent settlement would the nature of the Palestinian entity be determined – part of a federation or confederation with Jordan, or an independent state.

This concept was in accordance with Prime Minister Rabin's approach to the issue of separation. In the deliberations of the committee dealing with separation headed by Police Minister Moshe Shahal it was made clear that anyone wanting separation needs to fix a border, and a border isn't something that gets fixed twice. On the eve of Passover, April 1995, we presented the committee's conclusions to Peres and the resulting controversy, in the government and in the public at large, made the headlines. Hawks and doves split on the issue. There were those who said that any notion of peace was contradicted by the notion of separation between peoples. Peres himself was unwilling to accept the principle of separation, believing that there was no alternative to political and economic co-operation between ourselves and the Palestinians. I took the view that a good border could create good neighbours; Haim Ramon, who had supported separation for years, turned the issue into an ideological banner; Uri Savir had reservations; and the world was wondering just what it all meant. In Likud there were some who claimed that what was really being discussed was a Palestinian state, others who insisted that this showed the bankruptcy of the Oslo process. On the Palestinian side there were some, including Abu Ala, who spurned the idea, others who did not reject it out of hand but said it would be acceptable only if it was the result of Israeli–Palestinian consultation and not a unilateral process.

In the end, the mountains gave birth to a mouse. In spite of all the time and effort put in by the committee, the issue of separation was not even properly debated. The idea was shelved, without announcement or admission from anyone, and was to be revived only after the wave of terrorist atrocities of February–March 1996, when it was Shahal's opinion that non-implementation of separation at an earlier stage had been the greatest missed opportunity of the Rabin government.

My assessment was that if we could reach agreement with the Palestinians on a line of separation, this would amount to solution of a central problem. Remarks made by Husseini in Sweden encouraged me in this direction, and I decided to raise the issue in a conversation with Nabil Shaath which took place on 11 April.

This was at a symposium in the Notre Dame Hotel in Jerusalem, in which Nabil Shaath, Pierre Schorri and I were invited to participate. Pierre had come to Israel in the hope of continuing his conversations with Nabil and with me, and sure enough, when the debating was over and we had parted with warm handshakes, we slipped away – separately – and reconvened in a house in one of the quieter streets of Jerusalem's Rehavia district, where we were joined for lunch by Yair and Ron.

At this meeting it became clear just how high were Palestinian expectations of economic co-operation between Israel and the Palestinians, and how much the success of the political process depended on Palestinian economic development. The Swedes expressed their willingness to help in the financing of economic projects in the Gaza Strip and the West Bank, but they were especially interested in the permanent settlement. We raised the idea of combining permanent with interim settlement and pointed out the advantages from the Israeli and Palestinian perspectives of establishing a border between the Palestinian Authority (even before its final political status had been determined) and Israel, without the need in the meantime to solve the problem of Jerusalem.

There was a weak point in this proposal: detailed attention to the border question was liable to divert the entire negotiation away from the issues of redeployment and elections to the Palestinian Council towards the difficult subject of marking the borders, causing delay to the entire process. On the other hand, fixing a border at this early stage could contribute to the stability of the process. From Israel's viewpoint it would thus be possible to prevent a 'rolling' interim settlement, liable to dictate a less favourable fixed border, since what was to be allotted to the Palestinians as sector A or B, even if only under the terms of the interim settlement, would not, in all probability, become Israeli territory in the permanent settlement. From the Palestinian viewpoint, setting the border would make it very difficult for a different Israeli government to backtrack.

The conversation was interesting and detailed but at the end of it I realised that an attempt to combine interim and permanent settlements would not be practical, if only because of the personalities directing the negotiations. The interim settlement would run its course until agreement was reached; the permanent settlement would have to lead a separate existence.

Political developments in the Palestinian camp were very rapid. Yesterday's allies became today's rivals, those who were influential yesterday lost their influence today. Abu Mazen was in no hurry to go to the territory of the Palestinian Authority; he stayed in Tunis and took to expressing severe criticism of Arafat's policy. According to some accounts this man, who had stood so firmly behind the Oslo process, was forming a rejectionist alliance with Faruk Qaddoumi, the leading opponent of the Oslo Accord in the PLO hierarchy. Others explained that he was simply not impressed by Arafat's political style, and his connection with Qaddoumi was a matter of temporary coincidence of interests.

At a certain stage Nabil Shaath was directing the talks over interim settlement and then Abu Ala's star was again in the ascendant. When Abu Mazen arrived in Ramallah he was welcomed with much pomp and circumstance, but he refused to play any role in the hierarchy, or to stand as a candidate for any office, instead spending a lot of time in Gaza, meeting and advising Arafat. If there had been long-standing tension between Abu Ala and Nabil Shaath, relations between Abu Mazen and Abu Ala were positively frosty after Abu Mazen's arrival in the territories. The latter retained his PLO title of secretary of the organisation's executive committee, in which capacity he signed the interim settlement in September 1995 at the White House. He didn't run in the elections – unlike Nabil Shaath and Abu Ala, who both ran successfully – and was appointed to no ministerial role after the elections, even when a rejectionist like Hannan Ashrawi was persuaded to join Arafat's cabinet. But he was entrusted with the responsibility of negotiating on the permanent settlement, not only in secret talks with us but also in the official talks which began six months after the four academics had completed their work. Later Arafat declared him his number two.

To return to the spring of 1995, from here on the talks on the permanent settlement continued among the foursome in Sweden, with occasional participation by Hasan Asfur, one of the Oslo veterans, now appointed to a central role in the negotiations with Israel, while on our side the talks were joined at a later stage by Dr Nimrod Novik, who had been Peres's policy adviser until 1990. The talks were supervised from behind the scenes by Abu Mazen and myself, meeting from time to time in Jerusalem or Tel Aviv.

Conversations with Abu Mazen (alias Mahmud Abbas) opened up for me another window into the unfamiliar world of the PLO hierarchy. This man, born 1933, who had become very influential in the leadership of the organisation following the murders of Abu Jihad and Abu Iyad, told me of the total ignorance of Israel which used to be characteristic of the leadership of the Palestinian camp. Israel was thought of as all-powerful, as the source of the disaster which had befallen the Palestinian people, as the Devil, as a monolithic society with no distinction to be drawn between moderates and extremists. Foolishly, knowing nothing of the enemy was turned into a virtue, as if wilful ignorance would somehow reduce his potency. Reading material about Israel was interpreted as evidence of Zionist tendencies – horror of horrors – not only among the Palestinian people as a whole but among the leadership, who were supposed by their public to be close and expert observers of the Jewish state.

One day Abu Mazen happened to come across an article describing the demographic composition of Israeli society, and was surprised to read that half of all Israeli citizens came from Arab countries. He had been convinced they were all of East European origin, and was shocked by his own ignorance. At that time, in the early 1970s, he had just been appointed to organise the Fatah wing, and he felt an urgent need to find out more, a lot more, about Israel. Over the next few years he picked up information about Israel from every source available to him and published several books describing the history of Jewish immigration, Israeli–American relations and the peace camp in Israel. He encouraged a series of expatriate Palestinian representatives to make contact with Israel and two of them – Saad Hammami and Isam Sartawi – were murdered for their pains.

Abu Mazen outlined the changes that had occurred in the PLO – from belief in the destruction of Israel to the notion of a Palestinian state alongside Israel – and changes in attitudes to Israel – from willingness to meet only anti-Zionist elements, through interest in Peace Now, to meetings with Moshe Amirav which demonstrated understanding of the need to make contact with those chosen by Israel rather than the PLO's own preferences. The most important change, in his opinion, was the PLO's acceptance of Resolution 242 in 1988, although the resolution referred to the refugee issue and not to the Palestinian national problem.

In one of his books Abu Mazen describes secret contacts with Israel, including a conversation he had in 1988 with a leading member of the Palestine Communist Party, Naim el-Askar. He asked el-Askar if he would be prepared to talk to him without formal restrictions or no-go areas, and he consented to this. 'Do you agree that the *intifada* was created to pressurise the Israelis into withdrawing from Gaza and the West Bank?' asked Abu Mazen. The other concurred immediately. 'Do you think,' Abu Mazen continued in Socratic style, 'that the residents of the West Bank and Gaza will accept our instructions to carry on the *intifada* until the Israelis also leave Haifa, Acre and Jaffa?', and to this el-Askar replied with an emphatic 'No!' – adding: 'If we demanded that, they'd start throwing stones at us!' Here, says Abu Mazen, it was clear we needed to reach a shared consensus, since the time had come to propose alternative solutions to the Palestinian problem and discussions of this kind led to recognition of 242, a giant step for the PLO but interpreted by the Israelis as mere verbal gymnastics.

Abu Mazen told me of the way the Oslo process was regarded in Tunis, of concern lest the two academics represented no official body, of the need to check their contacts, and the significance attached to the admission of Uri Savir, and later of Yoel Singer, to the club. He stressed the need for progress towards permanent settlement, in the clear awareness that neither side would see all its aspirations fulfilled, but that the common denominators were much broader than would be thought by a casual listener to the speeches on both sides.

He preferred to maintain the Swedish track on the basis of continuing talks between the academics in Stockholm on the one hand and talks between the two of us on the other, pending the arrival of a joint draft cooked up by the academics, which we would then need to address, figuring out how best to work together in bringing it to a successful conclusion. From now on the principal activity in the track was to be the exchange of drafts, amending versions and using larger rulers and sharper pencils to reach a proposal on the border issue meeting the requirements of both sides.

The sixth meeting between the four academics took place in Stockholm in mid-May 1995. A year later, final talks with the Palestinian leadership were supposed to begin, and before then the political negotiations should begin and be concluded, so that at the latest by 4 May 1996 it would be possible to present a statement of principles to the people and to the world. Time was running – and not to our advantage. We were convinced that the longer we delayed taking our proposals to the leadership, the less were the chances of the proposals being accepted.

At this meeting we produced a draft which was supposed to bridge the remaining gaps; the title of the paper was 'Parameters for the conclusion of permanent agreement between Israel and the PLO'. In conversations on the basis of this paper it became clear that in some issues, including the border and the refugees, we had come a very long way, but on the Jerusalem question a huge gap remained, capable of leading to the disintegration of the talks or, at the very least, delaying decision on key components into the distant future.

At the next meeting in Sweden, on 16 June, the four academics were joined by Faisal Husseini and myself. This was a session sponsored by the Olaf Palme Institute, a setting in which we knew that confidentiality was assured and we could feel free to exchange opinions and speak frankly. We met – separately and together – with Prime Minister Ingvar Karlson (whose imminent resignation was being widely rumoured) and with the Foreign Minister, Hilm Wallen. Both showed a keen interest in the progress of the track and expressed their satisfaction at the key role being played by Sweden in this ambitious venture.

There is a lot to be said for weekend meetings such as these, without the pressure of telephones ringing or deadlines set in advance, to make way for other meetings or appointments. As usual we discussed current issues, such as the problems involved in granting permits to Palestinian professionals living abroad to work in the West Bank, or allowing residents of the territories across to Jerusalem for purposes of education, employment or hospital treatment, but we soon gravitated towards issues of permanence and addressed ourselves at length to the topics on that agenda.

Husseini's position at this time was somewhat equivocal. On the face of it his dream had been realised – with Israel's recognition of the PLO and Arafat's arrival in Gaza – but in fact he found himself between two stools: because of his status as a resident of Jerusalem he was barred from joining the executive arm of the Palestinian Authority, but on the other hand he wasn't as critical of the Authority as were some, including Hannan Ashrawi. He was called a minister but had never been sworn in as such, and he continued to run Orient House (the building owned by his family which became a centre of Palestinian activities in East Jerusalem) as a semi-official institution visited by VIPs from all over the world – stretching the cord of his relationship with Israel to the limit, without actually breaking it.

With Arafat's arrival it was clear that the centre of gravity was shifting from the 'inside' to the 'outside', although the distinction between them was becoming progressively blurred, and as in any struggle of this kind throughout history there was a lot of resentment on the inside against those who had spent years on the outside and hadn't endured the privations, detentions and interrogations inflicted on their compatriots. If Husseini shared this resentment, he did a good job of hiding it.

This was my first meeting with Husseini and Ahmed, Yair's and Ron's counterparts, and I was very impressed by their professionalism and expertise. The four of them worked as a team, with sober assessment of what could be achieved and what was particularly problematical, and to some extent we found ourselves on opposite sides of the barricade: two politicians confronting four academics, rather than three Israelis versus three Palestinians.

Husseini's assessment was that if we could reach agreement on the future border line and the Palestinian refugees, it would be possible to solve the problem of Jerusalem in such a way that certain points would be left unresolved for the future. Other difficult questions could also be deferred, so long as there was resolution of the border and refugee issues. I remembered a conversation Husseini and I had held some two years previously in July 1993. This was just before the signing of the Oslo Accord, when negotiations had reached a critical phase, and we were both in Moscow for a meeting of the steering committee of the multilateral talks. Husseini had been appointed head of the Palestinian delegation and he invited me to lunch at his hotel.

Conversations between us were always conducted in three languages – English, Hebrew and Arabic – and as usual he was polite and very urbane; the fact that he seemed to be holding something back was also typical of him. He was very pessimistic about the Washington talks, and I asked him what he thought of the idea of leapfrogging the interim settlement and going straight to the permanent settlement. He thought for a moment and then said, 'That would be a mistake. We need time and I think you need time too.'

'But under the terms of the interim settlement', I continued, 'both sides feel they are paying too high a price for no adequate return, and if we can't even put a stop to violence, it will be impossible to implement any permanent settlement.' Husseini did not agree. For a long time he played with his coffee-cup before finally saying: 'Yossi, it's not going to work. The time isn't ripe, and I'm more optimistic than you are about the interim settlement.'

In the two years since then he seemed to have aged a generation. Mutual recognition between Israel and the PLO, the Hebron massacre and Hamas terrorism had put years on all of us. He didn't mention that conversation in Moscow, or repeat what he had said at that time, but the new message was clear: if a Palestinian state were to be established in the West Bank and in Gaza, with borders between it and Israel, it would be possible to leave some subjects open for further discussion. Naturally the logical preference would be for a comprehensive solution to all the issues on the agenda, but this should not mean that a few points could not be deferred to a later, even much later stage. This approach made good sense to me, but it was important to me that these points be kept to the minimum possible; we should not be burdening the next generation with a lot of unfinished business from the Palestinian–Israeli dispute.

The next meeting of the foursome, which took place in the first week of July, brought further progress on several of the eighteen points but vehement disagreement on the Jerusalem issue and some others. It was suggested that agreement on twelve of these points might be sufficient for presentation in May 1996 as a basis for official talks on the permanent solution, leaving Jerusalem and other sensitive issues to wait their turn.

When Yair and Ron returned from Sweden and raised this proposal, I rejected it out of hand. Loose ends were the things that worried me most. I wanted to go to Peres and Rabin with firm ideas about even the most sensitive issues and present them as a basis for negotiation. If they found some of these ideas too firm for their taste and preferred to leave them as loose ends, this would be their decision.

Faisal Husseini was aware of the new proposal and tried to convince me that it was reasonable. We met in the Hague, at a seminar at the Klingendale Institute convened to discuss tripartite co-operation, Jordanian–Palestinian–Israeli. The seminar itself was particularly interesting and I was glad when it emerged from our discussions that fears of Israeli economic domination of the Middle East had subsided to some extent. Jordanians and Palestinians alike expressed desire for co-operation with Israel, their assessment being that they and Israel had genuine shared interests, and Israel understood that neighbours with a healthy economy are better and more stable neighbours.

The pastoral calm of Holland was shattered by the Serbs' attack on Dutch UN troops in former Yugoslavia and this became the leading news story and the focus of political debate. In spite of this, Prime Minister Kok and Foreign Minister van Mierlo found the time to address Middle Eastern issues and when I met them for talks they both expressed willingness to increase Dutch aid to the region and to participate in the economic conference scheduled to take place in October in Jordan.

In a private meeting between myself and Husseini, he suggested the division of the permanent settlement into two parts: the first to be declared in 1996 or 1997 and the second to be implemented ten years later. The border and the refugees would be issues demanding immediate implementation while decisions on Jerusalem, the future of the settlements and final security arrangements could be deferred for a decade. I told him that debating the situation in the territories over a period of ten years would be no easier than agreeing the principles of a comprehensive settlement at the earliest possible opportunity. After all, the Palestinians were not going to accept continuation of the present situation and would demand limitation on the growth of settlements or a freezing of building in Jerusalem; this we could not accept and the controversy would remain and even intensify. Better to take bold decisions now and present them for public consultation. Husseini agreed, but was concerned that such an ambitious project, aimed at resolving the problems of generations, would require much more than the relatively short span of time which we seemed to consider adequate.

This was my last foray into foreign parts during which I was able to combine official business with less official business; a few days later I was appointed Minister of Economics and Planning, and in this role I would need to obtain government permission for every such journey – and report on it afterwards. Henceforward all my meetings, with the Palestinian leadership and with the four academics, were held in Israel. As for the plan of action, I informed the few individuals involved that nothing had changed and the track would continue to operate with the same degree of informality and non-obligation.

The summer was devoted to very intensive negotiation over the interim settlement, with hordes of Israelis and Palestinians descending on the Patio Hotel in Eilat for brainstorming sessions. Peres was there too, and his contribution was crucial, leading ultimately to the acceptance of formulas for the resolution of numerous tough issues such as troop redeployment in Hebron, voting procedures for East Jerusalem's Arabs and the structure of the Council of the Palestinian Authority.

The end of these negotiations was very different from the beginning. Although at the beginning Rabin and Peres were still toying with the idea that elections could be held in the West Bank and Gaza without a decision on Israeli redeployment, it turned out in the end that redeployment would be completed in all eight cities, including Hebron, where the existence of the Jewish enclave demanded a particularly creative solution, leaving a significant proportion of the city under Israeli control. While we had demanded at the outset that voting by the Arabs of East Jerusalem be conducted by post, and the Palestinians insisted on using conventional polling stations, in the end it was agreed that voting would take place in post offices, ballot boxes being returned to a central location for counting; this was a considerable concession on the part of the Palestinians. The number of members of the Council was fixed at eighty-eight, a figure much closer to the core Palestinian demand than to the Israeli proposal, and it was also agreed that the election of the chairman or the president (called 'rais' in English too) would be conducted separately from the election of other representatives and that the Council would effectively be a legislative body, complemented by an executive arm of portfolio holders. This was a substantial concession on Israel's part, considering that the original proposal had been the election of a purely executive council with some thirty members. A whole series of arguments that had bedevilled us since 1979 were resolved during those warm weeks on the Red Sea coast, and Peres left Eilat with a sense of achievement and relief. His wisdom, experience, intuition and creativity had proved themselves once more and the stage was set for the now quasi-routine signing at the White House. The last agreement.

The ceremony took place on 28 September 1995, with all the usual suspects present: Clinton and Christopher, Rabin and Peres, Arafat and

Abu Mazen. This was the most significant agreement ever signed between ourselves and the Palestinians in terms of the changes effected on the ground: elections, establishment of a Council, transfer of powers, Israeli troop withdrawals from major population centres in the territories, introduction of three territorial categories – A (exclusively Palestinian), C (exclusively Israeli) and B (full civil autonomy for the Palestinians, security powers retained by Israel). In fact, under the terms of the agreement Israel transferred a third of the West Bank to Palestinian authority and, although this was an interim agreement, it was obvious that what had been given to them would remain in their hands.

This was also understood by our opponents, who were far from satisfied with the maps they had seen, and when Rabin ascended the podium in the Knesset, on 5 October, to introduce what had been agreed in Washington, he was interrupted and heckled constantly.

But, instead of concentrating exclusively on the interim settlement, the Prime Minister devoted most of his address to the permanent settlement, and his remarks made me very optimistic about the prospects of success in the Stockholm track. Some of what he said was made inaudible by all the heckling, but it was just possible to gain an overall impression. I could hardly bear to wait for the text of the speech to be printed two hours later, and when I finally had a copy before me, I needed to work through the component parts to construct the full mosaic:

> And these are some of the principal changes – not all of them – as we anticipate they will be, and want them to be, in the permanent solution: first and foremost is united Jerusalem, which will also include Maale Adumim and Givat Zeev, as capital of Israel, under Israeli sovereignty ... with recognition of the rights of adherents of other religions, Christianity and Islam, guaranteeing them freedom of access and worship in their holy places, according to their own customs ... the security border for the defence of the State of Israel to be sited in the Jordan Valley, in the broadest sense of the expression ... changes that will include annexation of Gush Etzion, Efrat, Beitar and other settlements most of which are located in the sector to the east of what used to be the 'Green Line' before the Six Day War. Clusters of settlements, ideally based on the model of Gush Katif, would remain in Judaea and Samaria as well.

If these points are taken in conjunction with remarks made by Rabin at this time and in other places, in which he referred to the creation of a

'Palestinian entity' which would be 'less than a state', what emerges is a very clear conception of the permanent settlement: in the Jordan Valley army presence but no annexation, clusters of settlements close to Jerusalem and the Green Line annexed to Israel, Jerusalem united under Israeli sovereignty with respect for the religious rights of Muslims and Christians, and a Palestinian entity which is less than a state in that it is completely demilitarised. If there is added to this a solution to the refugee problem, as an issue entirely outside Israeli sovereign territory, and non-dismantling of the settlements, then the understanding that was taking shape in Stockholm may be said to conform to the Prime Minister's overall conception of the permanent settlement. The fact that Rabin addressed the principles of the permanent settlement in a speech supposedly devoted to the interim settlement was indicative of his keenness to advance the next step.

And what of Peres? I sensed that it was with him of all people that I would face the worst problems in presenting the results of the academic discussions. His conception of the permanent settlement sounded rather different. He made no secret of his preference for a Palestinian state in Gaza, or his belief that the future of the West Bank should be left open, a kind of long-term interim arrangement whereby the territory would be administered by Jordan, Israel and the Palestinian state of Gaza in a manner to be agreed by all parties. Listening to Peres, one gained the impression that his ideal permanent settlement consisted to a great extent of long-term extension of the interim settlement.

These were festival days and I had the leisure for lengthy consultations with the four academics in the run-up to the final draft. The meeting took place in my ministry in Tel Aviv and was also attended by Hasan Asfur. We sat for close on ten solid hours over the map, over the issue of the settlements, over Jerusalem as opposed to Abu Dis. At one moment it seemed that positions were drawing closer; the next the gulf between us looked as wide as ever. Finally I felt we were close to an agreement on principles.

The two Palestinians preferred to go into further detail and only then to agree on a draft which could be put on the table; this would entail a significant lengthening of the timespan. It was especially important to them that the Stockholm track be kept secret until after the elections to the Palestinian Council due to take place on 20 January 1996, on account of the Palestinian concessions. In my opinion we were already behind schedule if we meant to keep the May 1996 deadline, and soon it would be too late. I instructed Yair and Ron not to wait on further detail and confine themselves to getting an agreement on principles.

Drafts came thick and fast: the 20 September draft, the 28 September, the 16 October. Towards the end of October Yair told me that the four of them were ready to present the fruits of their labours to Abu Mazen and to me.

The decisive meeting was held in Tel Aviv, the last day of October 1995. Abu Mazen arrived with Hasan Asfur and the two academics, I was accompanied by Yair and Ron. Abu Mazen was very emotional; when we embraced I saw tears in his eyes. Here for the first time we were touching the most sensitive points of the process. If the Oslo track was the break-through and the forum in which we got to know one another, in the Stockholm track we reached the very heart of the dispute. What was deferred in Oslo was the grist of Stockholm. Topics which to all appearances would never be susceptible to any kind of understanding were agreed here in principle. On the face of it, we had in our hands a document comprising a complete or almost complete solution to a dispute which had lasted at least twenty-eight years – or a century according to some calculations.

The four academics presented the final version. The rules of the game were clear, following the guidelines set out in the conversation held precisely two years previously in Tunis between Arafat and myself. The academics were supposed to reach agreement among themselves regarding the final draft, and inform Abu Mazen and me that as far as they were concerned the document was ready for signing. At the last moment there were still a few disagreements, regarding both the statement of principles and aspects of the border issue, and the two of us, Abu Mazen and I, recommended adjustments which were accepted by the foursome.

From this moment on, the Stockholm document became something to be recommended to the higher political echelons, ripe for presentation to the leaderships: Arafat on the Palestinian side, Rabin and Peres on the Israeli side. After so many years of exchanging slogans and declarations, speeches and promises, we were finally facing a moment of truth – a border line, Palestinian state, united Jerusalem, refugees with no right of return to Israel and exchanges of territory. Could we persuade our leaders to agree to these proposals? Would we encounter appreciation or rejection? At that stage there was no knowing, but it was clear to both of us that 'selling' the deal would be no less tough than any of the negotiations hitherto.

Abu Mazen glanced through the pages again and said that in his opinion if the two sides accepted the paper as a basis for negotiation, about a month would be needed to finalise a signed agreement. We knew that neither side would agree to adopt the document as it stood, and if the two leaderships would accept it as a basis for renewed and accelerated negotiation, this would be the most we could expect to achieve.

I presented the timetable as I saw it. My plan was to arrange a meeting with Peres, and put to him the consensus that had been achieved regarding the statement of principles and the border. If he showed interest in the plan, as I hoped, he would go with me to the Prime Minister and set the agreements before him; and if he wasn't interested, I was sure he wouldn't stop me showing it to Rabin. If the two of them saw the document as a basis for negotiations, despite the criticisms they would undoubtedly express over one point or another, rapid negotiation could begin, either immediately or after the elections in the territories scheduled for 20 January. This negotiation could be conducted as it had started, in the same framework, or through official channels, the only requirement being conclusion before 4 May 1996, the last date for the start of talks on the permanent settlement. That day, instead of the customary exchange of opening positions light-years apart, a key would be provided for the unlocking of all the subjects on the agenda of the permanent settlement, as agreed in the Oslo Accord, point by point.

The agreement would be initialled by both sides, and if in the elections due in October 1996 the Labour Party should win, the agreement could be signed in full. If not, it would be a sign that Israel was not yet ready for a permanent settlement, and the process would take a good deal longer. Abu Mazen agreed with the timetable and promised to take the document to Arafat as soon as possible and try to convince him this was a reasonable basis for negotiations in which neither side was dominating the other, in which both sides were paying an appreciable price but making significant gains in return. Whatever further work might be needed, this was in general terms the right and possibly the only way to reach a settlement. I was about to leave for the USA, and I promised that on my return and after consultations with Rabin and Peres, we would be in touch again.

Next day I flew to the USA, having first scheduled a meeting with Peres at his home for Saturday, 11 November. I told him I had a complicated subject to discuss with him, and I would need two hours. No one could have foreseen the circumstances in which this meeting would take place.

I had planned a longer visit than the three days which would be normal for an American trip (Thursday morning to Saturday evening) as I was also scheduled to attend an event in Los Angeles. I spent a day in Washington, doing the rounds of the State Department and the White House, then went on to a series of meetings with Jewish organisations in New York. On the Saturday Colette Avital, our consul-general in New York, held a brunch-party in my honour, also inviting leaders of the Jewish community and some Israelis who happened to be in town, including renowned novelist Amos Oz. When asked about the situation at home, I said I would feel happier if I could be sure that the peace rally due to take place that day would be well attended and not marred by left–right confrontation.

It was a beautiful New York day, cool and sunny. Amos and I decided to walk to my hotel, where we went up to my room to continue our conversation. Amos was an enthusiastic supporter of rapid progress towards permanent settlement and was one of the few people who could influence both Rabin and Peres, and at one stage I had gone to see him at his home in Arad and heard his impressions of the state of play as it stood in early 1995. Now he asked me for an update. I was glad of the opportunity and proceeded to explain, in considerable detail, the final understanding just reached. Amos was very impressed by the scope and the creativity of the scheme, and promised to lend his support to the effort of persuading Rabin and Peres, should the need arise. He was on the point of leaving when reception called with a message from Orit Shani: 'Your Prime Minister has been attacked.'

It took a while for the news to sink in. *Attacked?* My first thought was that he had been barracked or abused again, but would that be worth a transatlantic call? I switched on CNN and we got the first inklings of what had happened. The next call from Orit confirmed that Rabin had been murdered.

It was impossible to believe it. It seemed like an episode from an implausible melodrama. We're sitting here discussing the most critical phase in the most critical negotiations, wondering how it's all going to be presented to Peres and Rabin – and suddenly we're told that Rabin is dead and the whole picture has been turned upside down at the last moment. We sat there and wept like orphaned children.

It was a sense of deep sorrow tinged with resentment. How could such a thing happen to us! I could see him clearly: angry, smiling, dismissing something with an impatient gesture, in the Knesset, on the hustings – and one particular memory of a helicopter landing at the base-camp of 8 Brigade in the desert, at the end of May 1967, and a man in a peaked cap emerging, the Chief of Staff arriving in person to inspect our dispositions, and the feeling that all is well now he is here.

This wasn't a Kennedy assassination. Not the act of a madman or a publicity-seeker, but political murder in the first degree. Yitzhak Rabin paid with his life for the handshake with Arafat. And now? Was there still a chance of progress? Would Shimon have the stamina to cope with the hatred unleashed, with the backlash? Would he agree to the permanent settlement? And how bizarre it was, sitting in New York and knowing that the whole world's attention was focused on Tel Aviv, seeing on CNN the government of which I was a member gathering in emergency session and unanimously electing Peres as acting Prime Minister. And how strange are the ways of history: Shimon had come to terms with his role as number two, with never again running for the premiership, until one finger on a trigger changes everything and he finds himself back in the role which he performed with such consummate skill ten years earlier, and in cir-cumstances which had never been expected to arise in Israel. And yet arise they did, in Kings of Israel Square of all places, after all those years during which we had been asking: what happens if Hussein goes? What happens if Assad goes? If Arafat goes? And in the end it is Rabin who goes.

Ehud Barak was also in New York, and his aides and mine managed to wangle seats for us on an El Al flight to Israel the same night. The chief steward announced, for the benefit of those who didn't already know, that Rabin had been murdered and that as a mark of respect there would be no in-flight movies or video.

From Ben-Gurion airport I hurried to Peres's office in the Foreign Min-istry. His face said it all. I shook his hand, took a seat and all he said was: 'I miss Yitzhak, miss him a lot.' I couldn't detect the slightest hint of satisfaction that he was back in the Prime Minister's chair, possibly for years to come. He was dejected and depressed; the almost perpetual sparkle in his eyes had disappeared. We discussed the division of the workload involved in meeting the world's leaders, due to arrive the next day for the funeral, and I asked him if our meeting at his house the following Saturday was still on. He assured me there would be no change.

But in fact the circumstances had changed completely. Instead of approaching the first mate, with whose help I might just succeed in convincing the skipper, it was now the skipper I was approaching. As a consequence of Shimon's new role, and in view of recent events, both he and I were surrounded by unprecedented levels of security – to say nothing of media attention. But as always, in the eye of the storm it was quieter and I was able to deliver to the Prime Minister without interruption the long speech that I had composed.

The parameters that I had prepared for this conversation, with Peres and then with Rabin, had also changed. The main political point that I had wanted to impress upon Rabin was that, in view of opinion polls showing equality or even a slight majority in favour of Netanyahu, only a 'bombshell' would break the deadlock. This 'bombshell' could be an agreed-upon plan with the Palestinians which would make it impossible for Likud to raise questions about the future – return of refugees to Israel, reversion to the 1967 borders or partition of Jerusalem.

I arrived at Shimon's house feeling like an army commander seeking cabinet authorisation for an operation, laden down with maps. I spread these out on the table and proceeded to tell him the whole story, starting from the meeting with Arafat in October 1993. I explained that I hadn't briefed him at the time because he would have been obliged to tell Rabin, and Rabin might well have ordered the cancellation or suspension of such a track. As long as they didn't know about the track, I could keep it going. This was a situation I would not have faced had Peres been Prime Minister, because in all probability he would have authorised the track. I told him about the feedback I had received over the course of the year, and the involvement of Amram Mitzna (a former general who had advised us on security issues), Amos Oz and Nimrod Novik.

I set out the rules of the game: this was a paper prepared by two Palestinian and two Israeli researchers. If Peres rejected the suggestions, this would turn out to have been just an academic exercise. If he found it interesting, it could be the basis for negotiation, either immediately or at a later stage – assuming, of course, that the other side also saw it as a basis for such negotiation.

I explained to him the advantages of the document I was putting forward: the River Jordan as a security border with no involvement of any foreign army. There would be hilltop observation posts and anti-aircraft batteries, and an Israeli detachment would be stationed on the river with two commando-launches at its disposal. Israeli–Palestinian patrols would also operate jointly in the vicinity.

More than 100,000 settlers in fifty settlements would be annexed to Israel, while settlements remaining outside the border would not be dismantled and guarantees would be sought for their safety. Israeli citizens finding themselves outside Israel could choose between compensation or staying on under Palestinian sovereignty. Either way they would remain Israeli citizens with the right to vote in Knesset elections.

Jerusalem would remain undivided, with Israel not conceding its full sovereignty over all parts of the city. At this stage the Palestinians would recognise only West Jerusalem as Israel's capital while the disputed status of East Jerusalem would be unresolved pending the convening of a bipartisan committee to study the issue (with no deadline being imposed on its deliberations). On the Temple Mount the Palestinians would be granted an extra-territorial zone, which would in effect be a perpetuation of the present situation, as determined by the Wakf.

The Palestinian capital would be constructed outside the municipal boundaries of Jerusalem, in the sector designated by the Palestinians and Jordanians as Al-Quds and incorporating villages such as Abu Dis. The city would be administered as a series of quarters, enjoying local autonomy in matters of local interest, under the overall civic authority.

The Palestinian state would be demilitarised, and could become part of a Jordanian–Palestinian confederation if Jordan agreed to this; it would include the West Bank, with border arrangements to be agreed with Israel, the Gaza Strip and an extension of the Gaza Strip in the region of Holot Halutza, this last to be a symbolic exchange for the land to be annexed by Israel in the vicinity of the Green Line. Palestinian refugees who chose to do so could settle in the Palestinian state, but refugees would not be admitted to Israeli sovereign territory; an international commission was to be set up under Swedish sponsorship, its purpose being to rehabilitate the Palestinian refugees and assist their economic development. Israel would contribute to the financing of the commission's work, and once the settlement was in place the refugees would have no further claim on Israel.

Alongside this list of proposals, I handed Peres a paper prepared by Nimrod Novik regarding a new deal with the USA, which could accompany the permanent settlement with the Palestinians. This was only an idea, which had not been checked with the Americans. The paper spoke of a memorandum of understanding to include promotion of Israel to 'equivalent NATO status' in areas such as technology and security co-operation, transfer of the American embassy to Jerusalem and a guarantee to uphold Israel's military and economic advantages.

Politically, the murder of Rabin turned everything upside down. My assessment, as I explained to Peres, was that in the short term support for the government would remain solid and opponents would moderate their attacks on it. It was very important not to turn this moment into a time of vengeance and settling scores with the right and the religious; rather, we should be talking to them. I suggested an attempt to reconstitute the previous coalition, this time with the external support of the religious parties and abstention of the National Religious Party in no-confidence votes. And we should try, in parallel, to institute political negotiations with the aim of reaching a permanent agreement to be initialled rather than signed in full. Further negotiations should be pursued with Syria, these too aimed at reaching initialled agreements. The elections due to take place on 29 October 1996 would amount to a referendum on full peace with the Palestinians, with Syria and with Lebanon. There would not at that stage be any questions asked, since the entire picture would have been made clear to the public. If there were no terrorist incidents and if we could complete the troop redeployments in the major Palestinian cities of the West Bank, this would be a glittering conclusion to the Rabin–Peres term. Victory in the elections would, in fact, bring peace to the entire region and if, God forbid, we should fail, we could say that we had done our absolute utmost in the cause of peace over the past four years and we still expected that some at least of our plans would be implemented eventually.

Peres didn't welcome the scheme with open arms. He didn't say a word about the way the talks had been conducted, although he must have found it hard to accept my explanation, he was informed about the Oslo channel two months after its inception. Now it was a story of two years! He agreed that now the remainder of the term should be exploited to the limit and it was worth trying to put together a coalition which would command support from the religious parties, but he intended to use his remaining time in office for implementation of the interim settlement with the Palestinians and trying to get an agreement on principles with the Syrians. He believed that a permanent settlement with the Palestinians was bound to come in time, and fiery speeches at the opening of negotiations with them in May 1996 should not deter us. As for the document I had shown him, he confined himself to saying there were some interesting things in it as well as points he could not accept.

I didn't leave his house with the feeling that all our work had been in vain. On the one hand, I was conscious of an enormous sense of relief, like the removal of a great weight, the moment I told him the whole story; it had not been a comfortable experience keeping such a project secret for so long. On the other hand, I had left the full text of the document in his hands and I knew he would study it thoroughly in his own time. I reckoned he would assent to most of the points raised in it, original proposals capable of resolving the seemingly endless dispute between ourselves and the Palestinians, and after the elections he would give serious consideration to its implementation – perhaps even before them if his other plans came unstuck.

In any case I made haste to tell Yair and Ron, currently chewing their nails at home, that the conversation was over and that at this stage there would be no opening of negotiations on the basis of the document. I asked them to inform the Palestinians of this in order to forestall a different response on their part; even a positive response would not have led to the inception of official negotiation while a negative response would have killed the whole project prematurely. On 11 November, the status of this unsigned document was effectively determined: a consultative paper, to which neither side was committed and which neither side rejected out of hand, which could resurface at some time in the future as a first draft and a basis for negotiation, if and when such negotiation should begin.

The Stockholm document helped me to recognise the lines beyond which the other side would not go, and provided an incentive for trying to build understanding with the religious parties regarding the overall contours of the permanent settlement. My attempts to reach agreement with the NRP and the religious parties were not an unqualified success, largely because of reservations on the part of Meretz; so soon after Rabin's murder, it was felt this was no time to be awarding legitimacy to the religious-extremist camp in Israel.

For my part, the combination of completion of the Stockholm document and Rabin's murder changed my attitude towards the need for continuing dialogue with the rival political camp. I rejected the allegation that we had run too fast in the peace process. Far from it. I had been convinced it was preferable to complete the entire process in one governmental term, following a profound dialogue with the hawkish forces in society, but that's never happened. The document produced in Sweden proved to me that there was something to talk about and only the peace camp could respond effectively to the concerns of the settlers *and* ensure the world's recognition of Jerusalem as capital of Israel. After all, no Likud government was going to annex significant areas of the West Bank unilaterally, for fear of American disapproval; on a bilateral basis, establishing sovereignty would depend on the waiving of Israeli control over most of the West Bank. A Labour government, if it could obtain agreement in the spirit of the Stockholm document, would enable most settlers to live their lives without fear of a future in which they would be uprooted, and without political restrictions on further building or expansion, while for the first time in our history Jerusalem would be recognised as the capital of Israel.

This was the message which I conveyed to members of the NRP (Mafdal) whom I met, members of Likud, settlers from Ofra and Efrat and many others who came to talk with me. It was also the basis of the agreement that I drafted with Rabbi Yoel Ben-Nun on the eve of the elections. Many of my contacts were of the opinion that if these really were the contour lines of the permanent settlement, they could provide the most reasonable solution now that the vision of a Greater Israel, including the West Bank and Gaza, was clearly no longer attainable.

In retrospect, when the question is asked why Peres lost the May 1996 elections to Netanyahu by such a narrow margin, almost any answer will do; as to why he *lost*, there is no question at all. His defeat was the direct result of four terrorist outrages, following seven months of relative calm. This calm had created the feeling that Oslo had been the right course of action; terrorist attacks created the feeling that Oslo had been a terrible mistake, and Likud – rightly from their point of view – turned the terrorism into an ideological banner, raising questions about the partition of Jerusalem and other grim spectres. Would an agreement on the principles of permanence, alongside the Stockholm document, have meant victory for Peres? Or would the very prospect of a Palestinian state with Al-Quds as its capital have caused the polarisation of Israeli society and aroused the electorate to deliver an even greater snub to the Labour government and its leader?

This we shall never know. When Peres succeeded Rabin as Prime Minister, he said that peace was more important to him than elections and if he could promote the peace-making process, elections would be a secondary issue. This was Shimon's genuine feeling and it was mine as well, but in the six months between Rabin's murder and the elections we didn't succeed in advancing the cause of peace beyond implementation of the interim agreement, and in the elections we lost power and with it the prospect of any further progress. When the Likud government took office, it announced as a fundamental principle that there would be no foreign sovereignty west of the Jordan. From that it followed that there could be no permanent solution agreed with the Palestinians. In retrospect, it could be that the risk involved in negotiating on the basis of the Stockholm document was smaller than it seemed in November 1995, and if we could have reached agreement at higher levels, this would have been a giant step forward.

The Stockholm document does not bind anyone – not the previous government nor the present one. We proved to ourselves that goodwill can produce solutions acceptable to both sides.

The best solution for either side is one that the other cannot accept. So, in the end, a solution has to be found whereby each side concedes part of its dream. Not all of it. We cannot have a solution requiring partition of Jerusalem; the Palestinians cannot have a solution without a Palestinian state and a capital at Al-Quds. We cannot accept a situation involving a Palestinian state with an army; the Palestinians cannot accept a situation in which their refugees are left in limbo and their state cannot absorb them. We cannot countenance entitlement of refugees to choose between compensation and return to Jaffa, Haifa or any other place under our sovereignty; the Palestinians cannot countenance an arrangement whereby all Jewish settlements remain under Israeli jurisdiction. We have no use for a solution whereby 140,000 people are evicted from their homes; the Palestinians have no use for a solution whereby Israel annexes most of the West Bank and leaves just a few scattered and isolated sectors at their disposal; and we cannot live with a solution that takes us back to the pre-Six Day War lines without suitable security guarantees.

In the Stockholm track we tried to square this circle. Our aim was to grant to each side what it considered most important, so long as this did not damage the interests of the other. Thus, regarding the refugee issue, the permanent settlement should create a situation where refugee status is no longer the lot of Palestinians anywhere in the world, and on this basis the ultimate solution was presented: refugees who have citizenship (especially those resident in Jordan) will retain their citizenship; others will obtain citizenship of the countries where they currently live, or accept citizenship of the Palestinian state while continuing to reside *in situ* (in Lebanon for example), or be absorbed by the Palestinian state. They will be entitled to compensation from the international organisation that is to be established to replace the existing aid and development agencies, and within a relatively short space of time it should be possible to replace the refugee camps in Gaza, the West Bank and in Lebanon with proper housing.

Resolution 194 of the UN Assembly, determining that the Palestinians may choose between compensation and return (a resolution opposed, incidentally, not only by Israel but also by Arab states and the Palestinians), cannot be implemented. It is true that at the Lausanne Conference in April 1949 Ben-Gurion was prepared to accept 100,000 Palestinian refugees as part of a comprehensive peace, but it was the Arab world which rejected this; you can't come back fifty years later, after so many demographic and political changes have taken place, saying you've changed your mind and is the offer still open please? Anyone seeking to establish two states, one alongside the other, needs to be very wary of anything approaching binationality in either of them.

On the other hand, it isn't realistic to try restricting the number of citizens living in a neighbouring state. The phenomenon of 'quotas' has been a deep wound in our flesh ever since the British bowed to Arab pressure and imposed limits on the number of those entitled to immigrate to Israel. If a Palestinian state comes into existence, it will be impossible to impose immigration quotas on it. I assume that the majority of refugees will not choose to settle in the Palestinian state and will opt for rehabilitation in their places of domicile, but even if there comes a stage where the Palestinian population increases substantially as a result of immigration, I still don't see this as a threat to Israel. We know from our history the ludicrous predictions made in the past concerning the absorption potential of the Jewish state, and we have proved to ourselves and the world that we are capable of accommodating many more than was supposed by the statisticians.

An agreement whereby most of the settlers will be located under Israeli sovereignty will create a totally new situation for them, in which for the first time since 1967 they will be entitled to build as in any other town or village in Israel, without having to obtain special permission or consider the political implications. This is a settlement that can be attained only when Israel gives up most of the territory of the West Bank, while anyone who prefers to retain the status quo will be unable to annex so much as a square centimetre. The situation can be changed for the better only on the basis of mutual agreement.

As for the other settlers, it may be that the majority will choose compensation and transfer to Israeli sovereign territory, but I don't subscribe to the view that living under another sovereignty spells perpetual danger. I well remember the fears expressed over the future of the synagogue and the rabbinical seminary in Jericho; after the transfer of authority to the Palestinians these fears proved groundless, with worshippers and students enjoying unfettered access to their facilities. What currently seems impossible can become eminently practicable in genuinely peaceful conditions.

Transfer of the region of Holot Halutza to the authority of the Palestinian state will enable the overcrowded Gaza Strip to expand a little, providing extra land for the construction of homes. From an Israeli perspective the concession is marginal in comparison with territorial gains in the east, while for residents of the Strip this will be highly advantageous; reducing population-pressure in the Strip will have positive knock-on effects for Israel too.

It is in the context of security arrangements that I see the broadest consensus. Israeli forces stationed along the Jordan will ensure that the river remains Israel's security border and that no foreign army can cross it. Observation posts will enable us to forestall any unexpected assault while the Palestinian state itself will be demilitarised, with only a police force at its disposal. These arrangements meet all our requirements without serious infringement of Palestinian sovereignty.

The settlement regarding Jerusalem is the most complex, the issue itself being the most sensitive. Even the Palestinians are not suggesting the physical partition of the city, a return to the situation preceding the Six Day War. Their demand is for a united city comprising two capitals, West Jerusalem being under our sovereignty and East Jerusalem under theirs. This we cannot accept, and our preferred solution is to allow them to establish their sovereignty in the region of Al-Quds, outside the city limits of Jerusalem as constituted in 1967 and annexed to Israel. Israel will recognise the Palestinian state and its capital; the Palestinians will recognise Jerusalem as the capital of Israel but will sign a protocol of recognition referring to West Jerusalem only, while a bilateral committee will be established to discuss the status of East Jerusalem, without a time-limit. The extra-territorial zone on the Temple Mount will effectively perpetuate the status quo whereby Jews are not permitted to worship on this site, which is administered in accordance with the terms of the Wakf. From the Palestinian viewpoint this is certainly a symbolic achievement, while Israel will obtain Palestinian recognition, and subsequently the world's recognition, of Jerusalem as its capital. It may be assumed that following the agreement all embassies will soon be transferred from Tel Aviv to Jerusalem, and this in itself will have positive effects on the city.

Organising cities by urban quarters is popular in many places in the world. In Jerusalem there are natural quarters, and self-administering communities already exist in several neighbourhoods. The Palestinians will deal with the everyday interests and concerns of their neighbourhoods, as will the residents of other sectors, and above all of this there will be one city, headed by one mayor.

Of course, it is possible to criticise the fact that our sovereignty over the eastern part of the city will remain as it is today, that is imposed by us and recognised only by us, while the indefinite timespan written into the brief of the committee that will decide on the status of the eastern sector is decidedly less comfortable than a solution comprising all the elements. However, it is worth remembering that pending a solution the situation will remain as it is today, unchanged, and any solution agreed by both sides has to be an improvement. Anyone who favours the current situation should not forget that the world doesn't recognise Jerusalem as our capital; it doesn't make life any easier for us when even our best friends still refer in their official communiqués to Tel Aviv as the capital of Israel.

In the end we shall return to the solutions devised in the Stockholm version or something similar. In the end we shall arrive at a permanent solution. The question is – how much time will elapse and how much blood will be spilled before we reach the point that we reached that night in Tel Aviv, less than a week before the bitter and traumatic day of Yitzhak Rabin's murder?

PART FOUR

In Time of Peace

PEOPLE WHO STRIVE for a certain objective, and devote the best of their time and energy to it, tend to see it as the solution to everything. When it is accomplished they are exposed to the 'morning after' syndrome, which follows inevitably, and may well lapse into dejection or dis-illusionment. Even among those who strove for the right to immigrate to this land, paying a high price for their ardent Zionism, not a few became bitterly disappointed when they arrived here, finding themselves with no objective other than arrival itself. A whole generation struggled for the right to establish a state, fought for it in the War of Independence. To many it seemed that establishment of the state was in itself the solution to many severe problems, but, as it turned out, at the same time new problems were created, arising from the very fact that responsibility had been laid upon us. The infant nation had many lessons to learn, and for many the 1950s were a time of profound disappointment.

We must not fall into the trap of thinking that peace solves all problems. It will create a new situation for us, one which is not familiar to us but is familiar to most people in the world. Living in peace and not being a soldier on leave all your life, not turning on the radio every half-hour to check that all is well, not being called up for reserve army service for a month every year, not having to worry about war with Syria, Palestinian uprising or *katyushas* (short range missiles) falling on Karyat Shemona – this isn't a state of bliss, it's just normal.

It cannot be denied: Israel has always thrived in conditions of siege and war. During the Second World War for example the local economy was booming, as full industrial capacity was harnessed to supplying the needs of the British army in the region. Living in a state of emergency con-solidates the sense of mutual dependence, the sense of shared destiny, the willingness to sacrifice yourself or something of yourself for the sake of those around you. The Arab embargo obliged us to work very hard and very shrewdly, to identify faraway markets. Siege conditions and international isolation made us strong and welded us together as a society.

We have lived for many years with a sense of mission: the few against the many, the just against the unjust, the meek against the arrogant, democrats against totalitarians, defenders against attackers. This is the Israeli ethos and on this ethos generations have been raised in this country over the past hundred years.

The army isn't just a burden. It has become a factor of national and personal pride, a factor of our self-definition. Generations are identified by the wars in which they served; your age is determined by your place on the recruitment roster. The army is a fast-track course in what it means to be an Israeli, it has produced a respectable proportion of our leaders, it brings together people from different social backgrounds who would otherwise have no point of contact, it is the most obvious embodiment of the Israeli consensus and an ideal environment for progress and self-improvement. It is a very important customer in the economy, it stimulates research and development and is largely responsible for the fact that Israel's investment in R & D is the highest in the world, relative to its GNP.

Over the years we have become accustomed to the situation in which we live – a small state, built on the ashes of the victims of the Holocaust, representing a people that has suffered more than any other people in the world and thereby has also earned certain rights, including the right not to trust the good intentions of others; a small island in an Arabian sea, unfairly ostracised by the world, whose capital is recognised by almost no other nation, whose exports, if they are to be sold worldwide, must have the 'Produce of Israel' labels removed.

The sense of justice, heroism in war, the need to create something out of nothing and get the better of bans and embargoes – all of these have created an Israel very different from the one envisaged for us by Theodor Herzl. But it is a rare success story, a constant source for the world's headline-writers, sustaining a high standard of living and a higher rate of growth than any other Western nation and still absorbing new immigrants.

We find change disconcerting. We all want to live in peace, but we don't know how to live in peace. Peace is an objective on the way to other objectives. Most people live in peace and in spite of this they aren't happy. The next question must be: what will our lives be like with the advent of peace?

Peace will allow us to live without daily concern for our very survival, without a war every ten years and – hopefully – without the constant threat of terrorism. But the removal of danger also means less mutual dependence, more individualism, less motivation in the army, a tendency towards materialism and a higher risk of falling sick with the maladies of Western affluent society.

Technological progress and open borders mean greater potential for tension, as the gaps between us and our neighbours become evident. A nation which sustains a high standard of living (ranked seventeenth in the world in terms of per-capita income, with every prospect of rising higher up the ladder), alongside much poorer countries, exposes itself to jealousy and perhaps even hostility. Birth rate in the Gaza Strip is the highest in the world, approaching 4.5 per cent per year. If this figure can be matched by the rate of economic growth, the standard of living there will be stable, but on the Israeli side even a marginal rate of growth will be enough to broaden still further the gulf between ourselves and the residents of the territories and the future Palestinian state.

Israel has been the main beneficiary of the peace process. Multinational companies such as Volkswagen or Nestlé are currently investing in Israel simply because the Arab secondary boycott (on firms doing business with Israel) has effectively been lifted. Foreign investments from Japan, from South-East Asia, from Europe and from the USA contribute to employment and to improvements in standards of living, to increased competition in the market-place, to the professionalisation of Israel in the use of its relative advantages, to the ability to invest less in non-durables (energy, food) and to the opportunity to open new industries.

It is easy to invest in Israel. The country has experience of international commerce, while international trade among our neighbours barely accounts for 9 per cent of their economies; it has clear and simple laws regulating investment, a transport infrastructure and modern communications, a professional financial sector. It has people who speak virtually all the world's languages, a standard of education second to none, and a high level of computer-skills. All these advantages could turn out to be our undoing. For our neighbours it is much harder to digest outside aid, to digest investment. They need professional training and changes to their economic structures.

A friend of mine, a senior functionary in one of the neighbouring Arab states, said to me: 'It has to be admitted: our regimes are just not capable of supplying the needs of our peoples.' The solution to this is not a matter of reproof, and certainly has nothing to do with making peace conditional on the conversion of these regimes to Western-style democracies. Nor is it a solution to set Israel up as a model to be emulated, trying to sell the Pioneer Corps or the kibbutz concept to our neighbours. The greatest challenge facing Israel in the twenty-first century will be to devise a system of relations between it and its neighbours that will not be based on arrogance or indifference.

There are no textbook solutions, but there can be no doubt that co-operation and discreet aid will be the name of the game. It will be a process of trial and error. We shall be criticised on the grounds that we don't understand the culture of the region, that we're too Westernised, that we're imposing ourselves. We need to find a golden mean and make a constant effort to give aid but not to intimidate or patronise. Prospects for success in this area will be especially favourable with Jordan, the Palestinian state and Lebanon. We must remember all the time that we live in a tough region, and if we are to survive here we must either live by the sword or foster neighbourly relations and co-operation. We lived by the sword for thirty years before the peace treaty with Egypt; thereafter we combined the two models – a bit of sword and a bit of co-operation. We shall soon reach the stage where we can return the sword to its sheath, while retaining control of the sheath. This we shall do both because the price of living by the sword is a terrible price, and because immunity does not last for ever. But we must be aware – co-operation is no bed of roses either.

We often refer to the European Community as an example to be followed, probably because this is the model most familiar to us. Personally, I find it hard to visualise transference of this model to the Middle East. I tend rather to see a possible framework for the future in the relations of the ASEAN states – Indonesia, Thailand, the Philippines, Singapore, Malaysia, Brunei, Vietnam, Laos, Myanmar – with Australia. Australia is similar to Israel in many respects, being a country with traditions, culture, language and system of government very different from those of its neighbours, but whereas in the past it had a decidedly European orientation, it has recently begun turning towards Asia, preferring not to be a strange plant in its immediate environment.

Many new challenges will face us when the issue of our survival is no longer at the top of our agenda. We shall very quickly be made aware of the gravity of the situation, and peace itself may be a disappointment. But we must not let circumstances grind us down; on the contrary, we should take control of them and mould them to our needs and aspirations. Continuation and consolidation of economic growth, coupled with a process of impoverishment among our neighbours and materialistic life without collective ideals in Israel – this is the worst possible scenario for peacetime. On the other hand, peace is capable of releasing us from many constraints, developing the full potential latent in us and turning Israel into a state which makes a healthy contribution to the development of the region, to the Jewish world and to the resolution of conflicts elsewhere. At the transition between century and century, or millennium and millennium, we shall have the opportunity of fixing the image of the State of Israel in conditions of normality. The important thing is to exploit the sense of mission, which has so long existed in Israeli society, the urge to put ourselves and the world to rights. In these new conditions can we be a light to ourselves and a light to other nations, or shall we abandon the big ambitions, settle back in our armchairs and devote all our creative energy to planning next year's summer holiday?

1

Nationalism

It is easy to criticise the institution of the state. It divides the world, creates enmities, draws artificial borders and stimulates competition between those on either side of them. It puts anthems into the mouths of citizens, with words that exalt and eulogise its unity, puts into their hands a stick and a piece of cloth, with colours arranged sometimes horizontally or diagonally, sometimes vertically, and sends them away to war against someone who sings a different anthem or waves a different piece of cloth. War emanates from the need to defend national honour or a chunk of territory which each of the contesting states sees as its own, to which it has claims dating back for generations. Whosoever sacrifices himself for the flag is a national hero; schoolchildren sing about him and look to him as a model of proper behaviour, and when they grow up they are ready to follow in his footsteps and sacrifice themselves for the honour of their state, to sanctify the youthful blood that has already been spilled for the sake of this honour and for the flag.

In the past states were, effectively, the property of kings and princes; armies were palace guards, the land was royal land. It was only in the seventeenth century, with the end of the Thirty Years War, that the modern state began to take shape, with the transition from ownership to sovereignty and from subjugation to citizenship. Many objected to this. Religious movements sought to divide the world by religions and not by states; Marxism divided the world according to classes, while anarchism rejected the whole paraphernalia, the concept of the nation-state in particular. Internationalists spoke of citizenship of the world, and Zamenhof went so far as to invent a new language, Esperanto, with the object of breaking down barriers and rebuilding the Tower of Babel. Enthusiasts for a united Europe believe in a continent without borders, with a single currency and gradual transference of sovereignty to the central institutions of the Community.

But the state lives on. There are currently some 200 states in the world, more than at any time in the past, and the number is set to rise. When the Iron Curtain collapsed, and the artificial apparatus of the USSR ceased to exist, it turned out that national loyalties had survived intact. It is as if someone has blown the dust from them and they shine as in the past, blaze as in the past, and again children are being born to live by one or another national ethos and already the young are prepared to sacrifice their lives for the sake of the anthem that has been revived, for the flag retrieved from oblivion, and the language that once was relegated to the sidelines and replaced by Russian is restored to its former grandeur.

Terms like 'Bosnia' and 'Herzegovina', which sound as if they belong in the lexicon of the First World War, have returned to the front pages. The Balkan squabbles of past centuries have been revived and revitalised, and again every ethnic group wants a state of its own; families are evicted, children lose their identity, and it is as if Tito never existed. At the end of the twentieth century, enlightened and cultivated people in the heart of Europe are demolishing one another's homes, convinced of the justice of their course, ready to kill or be killed for the sake of the historical collective which never forgets, never forgives, and the body which, once wounded, never heals.

'Who are the champs? Three Platoon!' we used to chant in the army. What kind of pride can be drawn from the fact that you belong to Three Platoon rather than Two – and in the middle of a stretcher-race when you're sweating and thirsty and you've lost all feeling in your feet? And yet for some reason it is very easy to draw a distinction between the collective to which we belong and all the rest. You're born a Jew, and already you're a proud Jew; born an Israeli, you're already a proud Israeli. And although you've made no choices, although you've not achieved anything yet, and although it is all down to chance and you could just as well have been born in an igloo, your pride is in no way impaired. Our national pride is a marriage between extension of personal egotism and willingness to be sacrificed for the sake of the collective.

This pride can be the harbinger of disaster, leading to unnecessary wars, irresponsible decisions and pointless sacrifice – and it can engender healthy competition and constructive aspirations. Then again, national pride can produce excess of self-confidence. Immediately after the Six Day War we in Israel lost all awareness of our own limitations and, instead of adopting the map drawn up by Yigal Allon (who was then a minister of labour) and withdrawing from most of the territories, we stayed put; for six years we didn't believe anyone would dare make war on us. It was a grave mistake going to war in Lebanon, in pursuit of Ariel Sharon's deluded dreams, when the PLO's ceasefire had been holding for eleven months. It was a mistake to stay so long in the Lebanese security zone.

In time of peace, our national pride can foster a sense of mission in Israeli society; our moral and creative values can transform our country into a spiritual centre, playing a vital role in the lives of the Jewish people and earning the respect of the international community.

If nationalism does not turn into the narrow chauvinism according to which anything that the other guy gets is a loss to you, if nationalism means knowing your roots and knowing how to use them to enrich the lives of others, if nationalism means knowing that you're not alone in this world, but part of a great fellowship that understands your language, your allusions, your opinions, what is important to you, part of a historical chain which proves that there is meaning and continuity in the world and that every link is vital to the maintenance of the whole, then nationalism is a positive and an important phenomenon which we are duty-bound to cherish.

2

Foreign Policy

In recent years we have resolved the question 'Who to talk to' and reconciled ourselves to the fact that the PLO is the representative of the Palestinian people and it is to the PLO that we must talk if we want a solution. The question 'What to talk about' we have answered only in part. Just as for a whole generation it seemed impossible that we would find a suitable interlocutor, and for a few years it seemed to us the problem of the interim settlement was insoluble, so today it is the opinion of many that a permanent settlement is unattainable in our generation on account of the gulf between the positions of the two sides.

I am convinced that the document produced by the four academics (outlined in the Third Section dealing with the Stockholm talks) is a reasonable and practical basis for permanent solution, although as a draft agreement it still requires further negotiation and highly detailed consideration. The contour lines of the permanent settlement are becoming clearer.

These measures are supposed to solve problems, some of which are thirty years old, others pushing fifty. They look today like the most complex arrangements imaginable, but I am convinced that in just a few years from now such a solution will be taken for granted and we will have moved on to face a new set of regional and international challenges. Peace with the Palestinians will not be a full stop; it will be another milestone on the road towards the radical changes that the region so urgently needs.

Jordan will play an important role in the permanent settlement – if it chooses to. Its agreement will not be a condition on which a solution of the Palestinian issue depends, but I reckon that all parties involved would see advantages in political confederation between Jordan and the future Palestinian state. Most of the Palestinian residents of Jordan, as well as Palestinians in the West Bank, currently hold Jordanian passports and have family and business ties with Jordan. My impression is that although it was King Hussein who raised the idea of federation as long ago as 1972, and although a year of negotiations between King Hussein and Yasser Arafat, from February 1985 to February 1986, failed to produce agreement, the Palestinians are somewhat keener on the idea than are the Jordanians. However, since both sides clearly stand to benefit from co-operation, this does seem to be the logical way forward.

Such a solution will give expression to Jordan's interest in developing the West Bank and Gaza, as well as to the special responsibility it feels for the Holy Places of Islam in Jerusalem. The confederation will develop over the years in accordance with the system of relations between the partners, and it is indeed possible that there will one day be agreement on joint representation, perhaps even joint membership of the UN. Jordanian–Palestinian confederation could evolve in such a way that it eventually forms part of an economic (definitely *not* political!) confederation comprising Jordan, the Palestinian state and Israel. In my opinion, the territory formerly mandated to Britain, on both sides of the Jordan – which each of the three resident political entities sometimes dreams, or has dreamed in the past, of possessing in its entirety – constitutes the seed of the Middle East conflict and the seed of its solution. The potential for co-operation between these three states, which may in the future also be joined by Lebanon, is great indeed and holds the promise of real prosperity – if we can subdue those dark forces that prefer terror and violence to peace and co-operation, and if we act with imagination and initiative.

Continuation of talks with Syria is vital for completion of the regional picture. Syrian intransigence could deny us the opportunity to advance towards full normalisation in our relations with those states of the Arab League which are outside the orbit of our immediate neighbours. Even if Syria is not inclined towards peace I would still make an effort to keep our contacts alive, since through these contacts it is possible to address current issues and problems which are outside the purview of the direct bilateral talks.

I don't know if Syria wants peace with Israel. I don't know if that is what President Assad wants, and I am not convinced that he is sure himself. He presides over a solid, monolithic regime dominated by Alawites and members of his own family, and like many other leaders he is more concerned with his own survival and that of his regime than with any other issue. We had always thought that the Golan Heights were the apple of his eye, but apparently not so. It could be that, having served as his country's Defence Minister at the time of the Six Day War, he feels a certain residual commitment to our destruction, but there is no public pressure on him to restore the Golan Heights to Syria and the issue is not his priority. Syria could have regained the Heights as early as 19 June 1967, and it is a fact that it rejected the hand that was proffered then, just as it rejected the hand that was proffered in the time of the Rabin–Peres government, despite the formula 'depth of withdrawal equals depth of peace' coined by the late lamented Yitzhak Rabin.

An Arab leader who analysed Assad's priorities for my benefit reckoned that Lebanon was his first priority. Lebanon is the source of both legitimate and illicit revenue, the most prominent businessmen in Syria are Lebanese, and the country occupies a strategic position of vital importance; any settlement that diminishes his stature in Lebanon is sure to be rejected. Contact with the USA is also vital to him, and he attaches the highest importance to having his country's name dropped from the list of states sponsoring terrorism and from the list of states dealing in narcotics; only then will he be eligible to receive American aid. The Golan Heights are the last item on his shopping-list. Of course, it goes without saying that, were there ever to be peace between Syria and Israel, he would expect to receive no less than what was given to the late President Sadat – that is, all the territory and no Jewish settlements on it. However, while a peace deal with Israel could help towards the removal of Syria from the terrorism and narcotics registers, he can't be sure that the Americans would be as generous to Syria as they were to Egypt after the signing of the Camp David Accords. He also fears that peace with Israel would put pressure on Syria to withdraw from Lebanon, and what scares him most is normalisation of relations: economic treaties, Israeli tourists, cultural exchanges – all these are anathema to the hermetically sealed Syrian regime.

In the prolonged negotiations which we held with the Syrians following the Madrid Conference (the latter being most memorable for a crude and intemperate speech from Foreign Minister A-Shara, denouncing Yitzhak Shamir as a terrorist), we sensed their acute discomfort whenever the issue of normalisation was raised. This was shown by their reluctance even to shake an Israeli hand or hold one-to-one conversations with us. The leader of our delegation in the talks was Professor Itamar Rabinowitz, and I remember how jubilant he was when he finally succeeded in getting a smile out of them, offering them coffee from home – infinitely superior, he assured them, to the brand supplied by the US State Department. The discussions in Wye Plantation near Washington did actually feature a one-to-one conversation between the new head of our delegation, Uri Savir, and the leader of the Syrian delegation, Walid Muallam – a rare phenomenon indeed.

In the course of discussion of normalisation issues, the Syrians were invited to use the Internet as a vehicle for co-operation. They immediately said this was impossible, as there were no modems in Syria. 'You have no modems?' asked the Israeli representative in surprise. 'We can supply them to you!' The Syrians smiled. The problem, evidently, was not technical. With a modem you can access the world – precisely what Assad and his government are intent on suppressing.

When I expressed my opinion, early in 1995, that Assad had not taken the strategic decision to make peace with Israel, and that if there were no breakthrough by mid-1995 we would not reach agreement with Syria within the current governmental term of office, I was criticised both at home and in the USA. When Assistant Secretary of State Robert Pelletreau appeared before the Congressional Foreign Relations Committee and was asked to comment on my statement, he said he didn't expect to see papers signed and talks concluded on 1 July 1995. He was right. The negotiations dragged on but led to no solution and the Syrians missed the opportunity to reach agreement with the most moderate government Israel has ever had.

The negotiations weren't a total waste of time. The Savir–Rabinowitz team was definitely a class act, notching up successes on some important points. There was progress on elements of the normalisation programme, and partial understandings were reached on security issues, including reciprocal demilitarisation; but agreement was still far away. And still lurking in the background was Syria's unequivocal demand for Israeli withdrawal to the lines of 4 June 1967, and judging by their behaviour you would think this was a foregone conclusion.

My assessment is that President Assad is much more confused than is evident from his media appearances. He fears for the future of his regime and worries about the ramifications of peace and normalisation with Israel. He has abandoned the policy which rejected any discussion with Israel and replaced it with a policy that does not reject peace on certain conditions, while the Oslo Accord has released him from his undertaking not to reach agreement with Israel in isolation from agreement with the Palestinians. But he has set a very high threshold for agreement with us, as if to say: if Israel accepts these conditions which include, *inter alia*, stringent limitations on normalisation between the two countries, Syria can agree to such a peace; and, if not, it is in Syria's interest to preserve the illusion of talking with Israel, especially for the benefit of the USA and to a certain extent of Europe as well.

If my analysis is correct, Assad was mightily relieved when Benyamin Netanyahu won the 1996 election, but for the upheaval in an Israel prepared to offer substantial compromises, he would have appeared as an intransigent leader unwilling to make concessions in the cause of peace; facing an Israel opposed to compromise, he can once more be the President of a proud Arab nation, insisting on his legal rights, supported by the Arab world and understood by Russia and the West, seeking peace and encountering rejection.

As for the solution: anyone who climbs the Golan Heights and looks down on the Israeli settlements below would tend to think it preferable to hold on to them, rather than giving them up in exchange for peace. This might be true from the perspective of august matrons on a United Jewish Appeal study-tour, or retired generals festooned with medals, but it was much more true thirty years ago than it is today. I reckon that if these visitors were allowed to cross to the Syrian side of the line and inspect the batteries of Scud missiles targeted on Israel, their response might be a little different. I am not saying of course that territory isn't important; you can't live in the air and territory does have strategic value. But if we face danger from Syria, this is a danger of sophisticated weaponry and missiles, not raids mounted from the Golan on kibbutzim and moshavim. That is yesterday's war.

The Yom Kippur War in 1973 proved conclusively that the very fact of controlling territory does not solve Israel's security problem. The Syrians quickly recaptured the Heights, and the settlements there were nothing but an infernal nuisance, trapping their residents and hampering what should have been an orderly retire-and-regroup, prior to reconquest of the Heights. It is almost certain that had we been able to make peace with Syria before 1973 – and it seems this was impossible on account of Syrian intransigence – and if we had withdrawn to the international boundaries in accordance with the decision of the national unity government at the close of the Six Day War, then security in the north would have been much better served, and we would have avoided a situation whereby we didn't have peace, but we had the Heights and they were no use to us.

The Syrian demand for return to the lines of 4 June 1967 is not something we need to countenance. It is an illogical demand, based on the assumption that the prohibition on forcible acquisition of territory is applicable only if Israel does it, while the chunks of no-man's land gobbled up by Syria after the ceasefire of 1949 are being kept. I admit that the demand to dismantle all the settlements on the Heights is more problematical; personally I wouldn't have put them there in the first place, any more than I would have put them in Gaza or the West Bank. Settlements such as these have no security value, and the idea that it is somehow ethical to transfer children's houses to the Heights for the better protection of children's houses in the valley – I rest my case. However, since it has been agreed that there will be no uprooting of settlements in the West Bank and Gaza, I see no valid reason why the Syrians should insist on removal of settlements from the Golan. The Syrians do have one trump card in their hand, and this is the peace treaty with Egypt. Begin's willingness to evict settlers from Sinai created a very problematical precedent, which will bedevil our efforts to keep settlements on the Heights.

Peace with Syria is very important to us. Syria remains the last strategic threat to Israel from its immediate neighbours, and peace with it will have enormous strategic value, to the extent of changing our entire way of life in security terms. Peace with Syria also means peace with Lebanon, and removal of the Hezbollah menace. Comprehensive peace between Israel and its neighbours means the end of all forms of embargo on the part of the Arabs, the possibility of constructing an overland route to Europe, and diplomatic links with Saudi Arabia and the states of the Gulf and North Africa.

The international border has to be the border of the future between the two states. This does justice to both sides, it is logical from the point of view of international law, and no other border will earn the support of the international community. The Golan Heights must be demilitarised, and Israel will need to accept demilitarisation in its own sector, following the example of the demilitarisation of the Negev on the fringes of Sinai to which the Begin government agreed. We shall insist on security pacts, and in this area we can expect to receive technological assistance from the USA; effective electronic intelligence can avoid a lot of arguments between Syria and Israel.

As for the principles of normalisation, it seems to me that here second thoughts are required. From our perspective this has always been the most important issue, and it is only natural to assume that genuine peace means the transfer of goods and people from side to side. I would insist on diplomatic relations, embassies, economic and commercial links, official visits and reciprocal study-trips, but in matters such as tourism and cultural exchanges we can afford to hold back at this stage and not force the pace of convergence.

I would make an effort to turn the Golan Heights into a region of economic co-operation between Syria and Israel, while leaving the settlements *in situ* under Syrian sovereignty. I believe that the Syrians could benefit economically from such co-operation, but I am not sure that they would agree to the proposal, which has been put to them before and rejected.

Just as in the agreement with the Palestinians the border is the key, so in negotiations with Syria too I would put this issue at the centre of the talks. Shortly after the installation of the Rabin government I suggested to Shimon Peres and to Yitzhak Rabin that they should declare the cabinet decision of 19 June 1967 still valid, and offer to open negotiations on the basis of the international border and related security requirements; Peres was sympathetic to the idea, Rabin wanted nothing to do with it, and the border question hovered over the heads of the participants throughout the talks, while the air was full of accurate and inaccurate rumours of possible Israeli concessions on the issue. We presented a list of demands and hinted that, if these were accepted, we would be more flexible on the border question. If there is to be peace with Syria, the border will be the international border. This is known in Israel, understood in Syria, and it is also an open secret in the USA. This being so, it is appropriate that this should be the starting point.

If there is peace with Syria, this will also mean peace with Lebanon. Syria has never recognised Lebanon as a separate state, it keeps a 40,000-strong army garrisoned there, enjoys revenues of between one and two *billion* dollars per year from Lebanon, and decides who rules the country and who will be elected to the various state institutions. Lebanon has not been an independent state since the 1970s. This small country, which used to have a Christian majority as well as the only democratic system in the Arab world, and which had a cultural and commercial identity of its own, has turned during the past twenty years into a Syrian satellite with a Muslim majority, ravaged by war and constituting both a source and a conduit for the international narcotics trade. On account of the talents and skills of its citizens, Lebanon has the potential to tackle the challenges of the future, and in recent years there has been a modest recovery, as its former Prime Minister Rafik Hariri, a billionaire who lived for many years in Saudi Arabia, has succeeded in steering a course between Syria and other forces in his land and in the West. He was the driving spirit behind this recovery.

Lebanon has much to gain from peace and close economic ties with Israel. It is no accident that twenty-five businessmen from Lebanon turned up, admittedly in low profile, at the Middle East Economic Summit in Amman, in October 1995, against the wishes of the Syrians. But, in everything relating to the bilateral or multilateral talks, Lebanon follows Syrian instructions obediently; it must be aware however that its prosperity depends to a great extent on regional co-operation and the Israeli market.

The seriously misguided Israeli invasion of Lebanon in the summer of 1982 easily achieved all of Ariel Sharon's objectives in the Land of the Cedars, but the question was how to end the war and go home. Once it became clear that the fantasy of installing an Israeli-sponsored puppet regime in Lebanon was nothing more than a fantasy, Menachem Begin tried to find excuses for pulling Israeli forces out, since the peace agreement between Israel and Lebanon of 17 May 1983 had never been implemented. The most acceptable formula, accepted by the Labour Party too, was a call for the removal of all foreign troops from Lebanon. If the Syrians left – the government declared – Israel would pull out too. By saying this we gave the Syrians the right of veto over our continued presence in Lebanon, but since they hadn't the slightest intention of leaving, we stayed there too.

When negotiations took place over the establishment of a government of national unity led by Yitzhak Shamir, immediately after Begin's resignation in 1983, there was vigorous debate over the future of Lebanon. The talks were interesting and serious, but over Lebanon it proved impossible to reach agreement. Defence Minister Moshe Arens insisted that the IDF must remain in Lebanon, while Shimon Peres and Yitzhak Rabin were of the view that we could not afford to go on floundering in Lebanese mud and that Israel must find a formula that would enable it to leave Lebanon even if the Syrians stayed there. This was the main issue that prevented the establishment of a national unity government at this stage.

When we returned to power under Peres's leadership, with Rabin as Defence Minister, our first objective was to get out of Lebanon. On 7 November 1984, talks at senior-staff-officer level began in Naqura on the border between Israel and Lebanon, with the object of reaching agreement on Israeli withdrawal, but they dragged on for several months. Israel offered to extend the mandate (given according to the UN security council resolution 425) of the UN Interim Force in Lebanon (UNIFIL) and enable it to operate between the Litani and Awali rivers, as far as the Syrian border; the South Lebanon Army (SLA) commanded by General Lahad would be deployed in the southern sector and within two to three years would be incorporated into the Lebanese Army.

The talks were a failure because of the instructions given by the Syrians to the Lebanese officers with whom we were negotiating. The Americans were reluctant to intervene in Lebanon; Shultz sensed that we were about to get our fingers burned and he didn't want to take responsibility for extricating us. His assistant, Richard Murphy, visited Syria and Lebanon in December 1984. He met the Syrian Foreign Minister A-Shara, as well as Deputy President Haddam, who rejected any redeployment of UNIFIL in south-east Lebanon; he didn't believe that Israel really wanted to withdraw, and hinted that Israel's departure was liable to bring the PLO back to South Lebanon. In Lebanon, Murphy met Prime Minister Rashid Karameh and President Amin Jumayel. They expressed doubt over Syria's desire to see Israel leave, and suggested that withdrawal from Lebanon should be linked with a solution to the Golan Heights issue. Murphy said he didn't think such linkage was possible; his conclusion was that there would be no agreement on withdrawal.

George Neidar, an American of Lebanese origin, a newspaper editor and a frequent visitor to Syria, Lebanon and Israel, met me at the end of December 1984 and told me that the Naqura talks had been forced on Amin Jumayel by the Syrians, and that, although he supported Israeli withdrawal and a fresh deployment of UNIFIL forces, Syria was against this and therefore it would not be implemented. Neidar reckoned Syria was afraid that a solution of the Lebanese problem would diminish its prestige in the area. It wanted to remain the centre of attention and didn't want to be upstaged by a unilateral Israeli withdrawal. He urged me to oppose unilateral withdrawal.

I reported the conversation to the then Prime Minister Shimon Peres, but my personal recommendation was rather different: forget Naqura, get the hell out of Lebanon and do it yesterday.

On 19 December Rabin told the cabinet that he had delivered an ultimatum to the Naqura negotiators: if by 7 January 1985, exactly two months after the start of the talks, no agreement had been reached, Israel would walk out of the talks. Yitzhak Shamir and the finance minister Yitzhak Modai opposed the ultimatum, while Arens said the very notion of unilateral withdrawal was inconceivable. Two days after expiry of the ultimatum, on 9 January, the cabinet was convened for a particularly important session.

This was the most systematic and constructive meeting that I have ever attended. Ten cabinet ministers took part (five from each party) as well as all the Defence Ministry departmental heads. Senior IDF officers showed us maps and outlined four options: the first of these was continued deployment along the Litani river. This was the most confrontational deployment vis-à-vis Damascus; it required substantial manpower, and the safety of the troops could not be guaranteed. The second option was deployment on a new median line, 20 kilometres from the international border, involving a fence and what amounted to local martial law. The third option was withdrawal to the international border, with a role for the SLA and a handful of Israeli advisers in a narrow security strip. The fourth was withdrawal to the international border without a security zone. Most of the generals favoured the option of unilateral withdrawal, to begin immediately and to be completed by the autumn of 1985. The only general who supported deployment on a median line was Orri Orr, the Northern Command supremo.

The ensuing discussions were prolonged and fascinating, transferring from the inner cabinet to full government session, where two lengthy debates took place. Between debates at the Prime Minister's office we had a lot of work to do, talking to Likud ministers and ministers from the other coalition parties and urging them to support unilateral withdrawal. Ezer Weizmann said it was a pity the issue hadn't been subjected to such thorough scrutiny *before* the invasion; it might never have happened. Ariel Sharon was deeply involved at the time in his lawsuit in the USA (over allegations of complicity in the Sabra and Chatila massacres in 1982), but he sent word that his preference was for a 'buffer' solution, with IDF troops stationed only at confrontation-points in the south, and the SLA operating in the central sector. Shamir spoke with near-hysteria of the damage to Israeli prestige in the world. If we folded now, he said, it would be seen as capitulation, surrender, irresponsibility. In the end only two Likud ministers: David Levy and Gideon Patt, joined the Labour ministers and ministers of the other coalition parties and the decision was taken to withdraw in stages to the international border, each stage to be subject to government ratification.

The decision was temporary, and proved yet again that there is nothing more permanent than the temporary. In the Lebanese cockpit nothing changed. Lebanon remained a Syrian satellite; Syria stayed isolated and hints of its collusion in acts of terrorism increased this isolation. The SLA proved incapable of policing the security zone and the IDF had no choice but to reinforce it, with the result that the Lebanon Liaison Unit effectively became a South Lebanon Command.

The line that we had determined at the beginning of 1985 became the *de facto* frontier between Lebanon and the area under our control. The menace of the PLO was replaced by the menace of Hezbollah, sponsored by Iran and supplied with weapons via Syria. Stuck in isolated defensive positions, the IDF became a static army while the residents of Northern Galilee had no respite from the *katyushas*. Incidents followed a predictable pattern: Hezbollah attacks the IDF in the security zone; the IDF responds, calling up air-strikes on villages known to harbour Hezbollah activists and causing civilian casualties; rockets are fired into Galilee.

Since the mid-1980s, every government has evaluated the situation and has been afraid to change anything. All insist they have no interest in controlling a single square centimetre of Lebanese territory, all are in favour of an agreed withdrawal – and there is no agreement.

We have become slaves to national honour. Full and unilateral withdrawal from Lebanon would be seen as unreciprocated concession and would raise questions about the purpose behind our long and debilitating occupation of South Lebanon. We have become slaves in the hands of the Syrians, who fear that our release from the Lebanese burden will deprive them of leverage to be used against us, and expose them to criticism of their own continued presence; for this reason they are not prepared even to hint that Israeli withdrawal would lead to any curtailment of Hezbollah's freedom of action. We have become slaves in the hands of the SLA; whenever the notion of withdrawal from Lebanon is raised the question is asked: how can we abandon the SLA?

And you ask yourself: how has this situation arisen? After all, the IDF is supposed to be there defending northern settlements, not bringing down retaliatory rocket-salvoes on the settlers' heads. The SLA is supposed to be demonstrating its independent capability and preparing the ground for our eventual withdrawal – and we're having to stay there to defend it! Why has the erroneous decision to delay full withdrawal become an article of faith which no one dares to challenge? How many more chapters will be added to this sorry story?

Meanwhile, the breadth of the security zone is less than the range of the *katyusha*, so there is no protection for the Galilee, while in Lebanon IDF and SLA troops are under attack; Hezbollah is proving a more formidable enemy than the PLO ever was. Can we be so sure that Hezbollah's guarantee – not to attack Israel if the IDF leaves Lebanon – is dishonest? Can't we still operate in Lebanon without troops there on the ground? Can't combat helicopters overfly South Lebanon from bases south of the international border?

We have no option but to act and solve the problem, however long negotiations with the Syrians may take, and we must make it clear that our unilateral withdrawal is the issue. We shall need the mediation of a third party (USA? UN?) to ensure that Lebanon keeps its long-standing promise that on Israel's departure the Hezbollah militias will not operate from areas controlled by the Lebanese army. The SLA could then be disbanded, some of its senior commanders being offered asylum in France (if the French government's offer is to be taken seriously) and the remainder being offered financial support and temporary asylum in Israel.

The IDF will pull out of Lebanon for good, with UNIFIL troops moving southward to the international border and the Lebanese Army redeploying its forces in the south in co-ordination with UNIFIL. If there are rocket-attacks on Galilee or attempts at terrorist infiltration, the IDF will be free to act as it sees fit, without providing static targets for Hezbollah in Lebanon. The Americans will be asked to warn Syria against provoking incidents in the border area; it is reasonable to suppose that if Syria is not required to leave Lebanon it will represent Israel's departure as an achievement and, this being so, will see nothing to be gained from unnecessary confrontation with the USA.

We need to construct regional strategic co-operation, and participate in it as an equal among equals; not attempting to dominate the others, not admitted to the club merely as an act of charity. While my preferred model for economic co-operation is that of the ASEAN states, in terms of strategic co-operation the example to be followed is that of the Helsinki Agreement, which led to the inauguration of the OSCE (Organisation for Security and Co-operation in Europe). This is a process which could last for decades, involving discussion of common strategic problems, liaison in intelligence and surveillance measures to counter common threats, joint exercises in which the parties learn to speak one another's military language, and, at a later stage, removal from the region of all weapons of mass destruction. Strategic co-operation doesn't have to be *against* anybody; it should embrace all those who are prepared to make peace with us, while leaving the door open to anyone who might seek to join in the future.

Israeli foreign policy can, in the future, be more ethical and more *Jewish* than it has been up to now. The more accepted we become in the world, the more freedom of choice we shall have, the more discriminating we can be. When half the world wanted nothing to do with us, and even the other half didn't regard us with unqualified admiration, we were forced to associate with other states regarded as pariahs by the international community: we became friends and associates of the Republic of South Africa, we had amicable relations with the Pinochet regime in Chile, with Noriega in Panama, with the government of Burma, among others. Ultimately, as Director General of the Foreign Ministry I persuaded the Israeli government to impose sanctions on South Africa's apartheid regime in 1987.

Since the signing of the Oslo Accord and the ensuing establishment of diplomatic links with some thirty countries, we have felt able to deny Pinochet a visa to visit the country, in spite of repeated requests, and to refrain from recognising Croatia (a decision reversed by Netanyahu's government), on the ground that its president, Tujman, is a Holocaust-denying historian and propagandist; we have cooled our relations with Burma on account of that country's dismal human rights record, and we have blacklisted the four Italian neo-fascist ministers in Berlusconi's government.

Comprehensive peace will release us from the pragmatism, verging on cynicism, into which we have been forced, reluctantly, in the past and which has characterised our foreign policy, especially in the 1970s and 1980s. As a small country, aspiring to represent both Jewish and universal values, we shall make our voice heard where previously we have been silent, on issues such as the behaviour of Indonesia in East Timor. We shall speak out against racism wherever it occurs and denounce any resurgence

of fascism or anti-semitism, without fear of hostile UN votes or international sanctions. We shall not stand aloof from injustice, even when it
is far away from us. For example, in July 1994 we set up a field-hospital
for the treatment of the refugees of Rwanda, saving many lives, and
although our primary motives were humanitarian and altruistic – the relief
of human suffering – it cannot be denied that international appreciation
of our efforts was a bonus.

I don't believe we shall want to give up the Israeli sense of mission.
There are not many Western societies with a motivation and a sense of
mission comparable to Israel's. This is an ideological state founded on the
desire to realise the Zionist dream, and the sense of mission emanates – to
a considerable extent – from the awareness of threat, of the need to train
successive generations in the art of self-defence, fighting our neighbours
at regular intervals.

The wider the orbit of peace becomes, so the sense of mission tends to
evaporate, unless society is presented with objectives other than simple
self-preservation. It is no wonder that Western cultural creativity is
turning, even as the twentieth century draws to a close, to the world wars
as the context in which individual potential is exploited to the full. As
against this, a period of normality and peace poses the risk of lapsing into
complacency or hedonism – unless society is offered a new vision.

Anyone who doesn't have a new vision, and fears the loss of the Israeli
sense of mission, will find himself clinging to the old world, seizing
gleefully on any statement from any Arab leader which suggests that
nothing has really changed in the Middle East. 'The sea is the same sea
and the Arabs are the same Arabs,' said Yitzhak Shamir in one of his more
philosophical moments, giving eloquent expression to the worldview of
someone whose world is of minuscule proportions: all changes are appar-
ent changes and, since nothing is really happening, we must retain the
struggle for survival as the leading item on our agenda; *this* is our mission.

It is no wonder that the right in Israel was so quick to denounce the
concept of a 'New Middle East', an expression coined by Shimon Peres.
Peres was referring, of course, to the creation in the future of a new Middle
East, not describing a change that had already occurred, but his critics
represented him as a day-dreaming fantasist, out of touch with the realities
of Middle Eastern politics. If there is to be a new Middle East, there has to
be a new vision, whereas if old phenomena repeat themselves and if the
old slogans are heard again from the Arab side, then we will know that

all's well and we can return to the warm and comfortable embrace of perpetual conflict.

In time of peace it is much more difficult to sustain the sense of mission. It is easy to explain to somebody why he must fight for his home. Anything else requires a longer explanation, but this is our next test: can we exploit the energy latent in us, the feeling of togetherness that exists in Israeli society more than in any other, and what will be the visions competing for the heart of Israeli society?

I believe that Israel can fulfil an important role in the international community, equivalent to that of countries such as Canada, Denmark, Holland, Sweden and Norway. It has certain specific advantages; being a small country, it is not required to take sides in any international dispute. In terms of standard of living it belongs among the world's top twenty, and is already giving aid to other states, at a level set to increase in the future as our GNP grows. It has military experience second to none, involving organisational skills, the capability to mobilise personnel and resources – and to motivate large numbers of people to work together in the national interest. It has experience of economic co-operation with the Third World. It has relative advantages in terms of numbers of doctors and standards of healthcare, and has a highly successful agricultural sector. Israeli society has an ethos of mission, of the need to do something and not just lead a comfortable life; it has a Jewish tradition of giving and helping.

All this could turn Israel within a few years into a nation that exploits its own painful experience in helping to resolve disputes far from its natural orbit. In recent years we have been asked to mediate between belligerents with whom we had no axe to grind, and have done this with remarkable success. If and when we achieve the peace to which we aspire, we can expand our activity in this field. We can also send volunteers to serve in UN peace-keeping forces and other multinational formations. As in other places in the world so with us, such a mission constitutes a fascinating challenge for men and women of goodwill. We can also extend our involvement in the Third World, especially in Africa, which has been neglected by the West in recent years and where there has been serious erosion of infrastructure, healthcare and living standards. Israeli doctors could work wonders in the African Continent, and Israeli agronomists could help to put food in many hungry mouths.

Israel could become what it wanted to be in the 1960s but wasn't then in a position to be – a bridge between the Third World and the West. In the long term this could be an important contribution to the avoidance of conflict between the hungry world, with its rapidly rising population, and the affluent world, where natural growth is in decline, circumstances which ensure that the gap in living standards between the two is ever widening. A Third World where there is significant improvement in living standards is less likely to engage in such confrontation, with all the negative results that would ensue.

Israel could be a kind of moral maker in all matters relating to human rights. Our tribulations over the past generation robbed us of the opportunity to address such a role; peace will enable us to do as a nation what we have been doing for generations as individuals. This is a vision capable of mobilising whole segments of society and satisfying their aspirations, ensuring that Israel will not lapse into petty-mindedness but will remain a focus of international interest. Some of these activities could also involve Jews from other parts of the world who are willing to work beside us.

Turning Israel into an international focus does not of course need to happen at the expense of tackling domestic problems (to be addressed in Chapter 5 below) such as absorption of immigrants and the reduction of wealth-differentials in our society, at the expense of consolidating links with the Jewish world or at the expense of our regional role. The natural tendency, on hearing of schemes which sound somewhat remote, is to say 'Charity begins at home.' This is always true, and we shall always attend first to poverty in our own backyard, but this need not be our only concern.

I assume, indeed I hope, that in the 'vision market' there will be supply and not just demand, and that there is competition, even opposition, between visions. The moment of truth is approaching, because Israel will have peace and we must not be surprised by it or caught unprepared. Peace, no less than war, requires careful preparation.

There will undoubtedly be criticism of my proposals, and I will readily accept this, welcome it in fact. There is only one form of criticism that I utterly reject, and this is the charge of 'Bolshevism'. I don't propose compulsion, and I don't recommend the creation of a society where everything is geared towards a single objective, and all wear an identical uniform; I don't believe in dialectics, nor in historical determinism. But if no alternatives are suggested, they will not be born of themselves, and if there is no sense that society has a purpose beyond mere self-preservation, then the priceless asset of living in peace is liable to be squandered, giving way to frustration and disappointment.

3

Israel as Part of the Jewish World

After the Holocaust, the Jewish people in the West, especially in the USA, played a central role in the founding and the consolidation of the State of Israel. The Jews of the USA were among those who influenced the decision of President Truman to support the establishment of the state; many of them came to Israel as 'overseas volunteers', fought in the War of Independence and returned – most of them – to America. The United Jewish Appeal (UJA) helped us with the acquisition of weapons and the absorption of mass immigration, with the setting up of agricultural settlements and, later, with improvements in housing. So long as Israel was defending itself and fighting for its economic survival, it was the 'little sister' of the Jews of America. They supported it unconditionally, helped it, sent deputations to it, enthusiastically applauded its Prime Ministers and made it clear they had no intention of going to live there. Senior Israeli officials used to visit the USA on behalf of the Appeal, explaining Israel's economic problems and security concerns, and rich Jews gave thanks to God that they weren't required to send their own children to war and could content themselves with financial contributions.

Although America was and remains the land of unlimited opportunity, it wasn't that easy to be Jewish there, even in the 1950s and 1960s, and there were more than a few restrictions on their involvement in government and in other institutions of the American elite. The link with Israel was a compensation of sorts. Visits to the Prime Minister of Israel, friendly ties with ministers and other important individuals in Israel, gave legitimacy to the leadership of the Jews of America, and status in non-Jewish society. The victory of Israel in the Six Day War turned the 'little sister' into a 'big brother', someone to take pride in. This victory gave the Jews of the USA a sense of closer identity with Israel, as well as pride in being Jewish.

Some thirty years have elapsed since then and the situation has changed, both in the Jewish world and in Israel. Israel has emerged from the deep depression that followed the Yom Kippur War and has entered a period of stability and economic prosperity. In economic terms it is now the equivalent of a middle-ranking European state, meaning it is one of the world's wealthier nations. The collapse of the USSR, the Gulf War, the Madrid process, the Oslo Accord and peace with Jordan have changed the scale of the danger facing Israel; the threat of terrorism, rather than any threat to our survival, is now our primary security concern.

And in the world at large it is much easier to be Jewish. Anti-semitism has not passed, but its manifestations have changed. In Europe, and even more so in the USA, Jews are undergoing a rapid process of integration. They are firmly entrenched in government, in business, in finance, in culture and in higher education. Whereas in the past it suited you to hide your Jewishness, today it is something to be flaunted, not to be ashamed of. In tandem with the process of integration into non-Jewish society there is also, naturally, a process of assimilation. When you live in a ghetto, reviled by those outside, assimilation is not an option. When you live alongside others and are accepted by them, you are much more susceptible to assimilation. The more comfortable the Jews feel in the world, the more the rate of assimilation will rise; in the USA, the percentage of mixed marriages currently exceeds 50 per cent. In other parts of the world the rate of assimilation varies according to the generation of immigrants to which one belongs. In countries such as Canada, South Africa, Argentina and Australia the second generation continues to assert its identity and therefore the rate of assimilation is somewhat lower, but in the transition to the third generation assimilation is definitely increased; distance in years from the first immigrants, combined with accelerated integration into non-Jewish life – the results are all too predictable.

The needs of the communities in the Diaspora are increasing. State welfare benefits are stretched to the limit and, as life-expectancy is prolonged, the burden of caring for the elderly has to be taken up by the community, and this is an expensive burden indeed. Spending on social needs accounts for a growing proportion of the funds raised by the UJA, and a smaller proportion than in the past is spent on Jewish education or is transferred to Israel. The sum reaching this country courtesy of the fund-raising of the UJA and Keren Hajesod – operating outside the USA – amounts to half a per cent of the budget of the State of Israel.

And there is a further development influencing Israel–Diaspora relations. In the past Israel and the Diaspora waged a united campaign to open the doors to Jews seeking asylum from oppressive regimes: the former USSR, Eastern European states, Syria and Yemen. This campaign, in which Israel and the Diaspora worked closely together, has been concluded successfully. There are now no Jews in the world who want to come to Israel but are denied the right to do so.

In short, a series of positive developments has come about in the Diaspora, in Israel and between the two, and it is this very positivity which now threatens the future of their relations: rising standards of living in Israel, improvements in its security, integration of the Jews of America into the upper echelons of society and the opening of doors to Jews fleeing oppressive regimes – all these have led to speculation both in Israel and in the Diaspora as to whether the link needs to be sustained, or is worth sustaining. Even if the question is not raised directly, and lip-service continues to be paid, there can be no doubt that the ties are weakening, and this is a phenomenon worrying to anyone who cares about the continuity of the Jewish people.

In joint sessions with Jews of the USA someone always asks: why is Jewish continuity important? Why is it important to go on being a Jew? My less than totally satisfactory answer is that it is important only to those who consider it important. The religious person could say, perhaps, that it is a matter of obedience to divine ordinance. To the free-thinker, for whom Judaism is a part of his self-definition, it is important that Jewish history – with all its triumph and pain, tragedy and recovery – should be sustained, because in its continuity he sees his own continuity.

We didn't come to Judaism out of choice. We were born Jewish, and the majority of the converts who join us do so not because a flash of inspiration has revealed the truth to them, but because they have decided to marry a certain person. Judaism being a part of us, simply hearing the *Shema* recited in a remote corner of the world is enough to bring tears to our eyes. It is the sense of belonging to a special community and, if this community continues to wither, something inside us will be lost.

Do I have the right, in the name of my selfish desire for the continuity of the Jewish people, to go to Detroit or Sydney and tell a young Jew about to take a non-Jewish wife: Don't do it, you're endangering the continuity of the Jewish people? Has anyone given me this right? And supposing he's in love, head-over-heels in love? And supposing his Jewishness means nothing more to him than the fact that he attended a certain school, belonged to a certain graduation class? The survival of the Jewish people is a function of personal instinct developing into collective instinct and this guarantees shared survival. The issue of assimilation has been to the fore throughout Jewish history, and there can be no doubt that the majority of Jews have been assimilated, although the burgeoning religious lobby has preserved some sense of continuity. Since the age of enlightenment and secularism we have become much more susceptible to assimilation and, as secular Jews, we will not demand return to the synagogue and the keeping of commandments as a means of stemming the tide.

So how is this to be done? One way is by living in Israel. Zionism gives the opportunity to secular Jews to continue being both Jewish and secular in a state of their own where their culture and their education are enshrined and friction with non-Jews will be less of a problem than it is outside the Jewish state. Has this solution succeeded? Many of my American friends tell me that Israel isn't Jewish enough, and assimilation there is liable to be no less rampant than it is in the USA. I reply to them by using the example of *Lag Ba'Omer*. As long as every Israeli child knows when this festival occurs, and as long as the smell of camp-fires fills the air in every corner of Israel, I am content in the knowledge that this is still a Jewish state, where children are familiar with all the festivals in our calendar, not just the Day of Atonement.

As for the future, I can't be certain of anything; but there is no doubt that effort will be required to prevent matters deteriorating further. Among the Jews of the Diaspora, the key to Jewish continuity is education, which tightens the connection with the roots and constructs a higher barrier against assimilation. Of course, private education is expensive, and although it exists in second-generation communities such as those of Canada and Australia, it is unlikely to survive on the same scale in the next generation. In the USA, only children from homes where commitment to Judaism is particularly strong benefit from Jewish education; Sunday schools are just a club for children below bar-mitzvah age, and their alumni seldom learn anything significant about Judaism.

The Jewish establishment feels that the struggle against assimilation is becoming harder and harder, and in the opinion of many of them it may even be impossible. The children of many of the leaders of American Jewry are marrying non-Jews and their grandchildren can be considered Jewish only in the very loosest sense. This generation born of mixed parentage, which never darkens the door of either church or synagogue, is the generation to which the Jewish establishment in the USA is devoting prodigious efforts, striving to keep at least a vestige of its Jewish heritage alive. This seems to be a campaign doomed from the outset, since effective tools are lacking.

The organisational structures of the Jewish people were founded in circumstances totally different from those of today, but out of conservatism and fear of the lack of suitable alternatives they have remained the same – pathetic and irrelevant anachronisms. The World Zionist Organisation (WZO) was founded in 1897. Since then the State of Israel has come into existence; Jews from oppressive regimes have taken refuge in Israel and more will follow, while Jews of the affluent nations stay away and will continue to stay away. In branches of the Zionist movement around the world, veterans of the revisionist Zionist movement argue with veterans of Labour Zionism – and neither side has the slightest intention of coming here. The days when Zionists argued with non-Zionists are long gone. The common denominators which unite all Zionists are love of the State of Israel and absolute determination not to go there. What does it mean to be a Zionist at the end of the twentieth century, when a Jewish state exists but, rather than go there, people attend Zionist Congresses and Zionist action committees? What is the point of inter-party debate outside Israel? Are the efforts of the Zionist movement inducing *anyone* to come here? To all these questions there are clear answers, answers that nobody dares to give.

In 1929 the Jewish Agency for Israel was set up, in a not particularly successful attempt on the part of Chaim Weizmann to involve non-Zionists in the Zionist apparatus. In the end, this organisation bore a remarkable similarity to the WZO. What is significant about the Agency is that it is financed by allocation of funds – the ever decreasing funds – deposited in Israel by the UJA. It isn't a body which represents the Jewish people, and it isn't relevant to anything that is going on here. It is an institution that repels young people interested in the future and the problems of the Jewish people, and its image is that of a smug oligarchy interested only in perpetuating itself.

As the twenty-first century approaches there is an urgent need for a new worldwide Jewish body which will replace both the WZO and the Jewish Agency. Its function will be to represent Jewish communities throughout the world, to elect a world Jewish parliament, to promote continuing dialogue between Israel and the Diaspora on a range of topics of concern to the Jewish people: from attitudes towards neo-fascist parties in democratic regimes to problems of anti-semitism and Holocaust-denial. It will also encourage immigration to Israel and address the issue of Jewish education.

The new organisation (I suggest it be called 'Beit Israel'), would be able to formulate Jewish policy and, among other things, to promote a scheme which I believe has the potential to contribute significantly to Jewish continuity – a birth-right scheme. Every Jewish boy and girl in the world, on reaching the age of seventeen, will receive vouchers for travel to Israel and accommodation there for about a month, in their summer holidays. The plan will comprise a combined course in history of the Jews and history of the State of Israel, and additional programmes according to personal taste, such as music or computer-science. The cost of the scheme, some 300 million dollars per year, will be borne entirely from the funds donated worldwide and currently directed towards welfare programmes in Israel.

Before the visit there will be preparation in the community, and in Israel the visitors will be escorted by young Israelis. After the visit every young person will be asked to complete a follow-up questionnaire, indicating whether he or she would like to visit Israel again, work there, study there, live there – or just find out more about the country.

I see in the birth-right scheme the potential for a new national project which will create impressions and memories among our temporary guests, bringing them closer to their roots and promoting communication between young Diaspora Jews and young Israeli Jews. It isn't a scheme capable of solving the problem of assimilation and it isn't a substitute for Jewish education; what it will do is bring to Israel a high percentage of the world's Jewish youth who would not otherwise come here at all, and whose connections with their Jewish roots are being progressively eroded.

In the previous chapter I referred to the future involvement of Israel in the Third World, especially, though not exclusively, in the contexts of medicine and agriculture. Jewish and Israeli co-operation in such areas could be extremely significant, constituting an additional point of contact between Israel and the Jews of the Diaspora.

I am very concerned about the future of the Jewish people in the Diaspora and their connections with Israel. I fear that, if we leave the situation as it is, we shall be colluding in accelerated assimilation and in mounting alienation between Israel and the Diaspora. The schemes that I have proposed are an attempt to stem the flow, in the hope that it is not too late. What worries me most is the lack of real concern in Israel over what is happening in the Jewish world. Most of us accept the existing objectives and the existing institutions as though they were self-evidently valid. To my mind, it is the need for change which is self-evidently valid.

4

Electoral Reform

The system of proportional representation in Israel was instituted out of a desire to ensure that all the different elements in the population would have a share in the political apparatus. This was a voluntary framework, exerting no pressure on those who didn't want to be a part of it (as, for example, the Orthodox chose not to constitute an element of the 'organised community' of Israeli Jews), and the fact that each group found itself represented by an 'elected assembly' gave legitimacy to the institutions of right and left. Even elections to the Zionist Congress were conducted on a proportional basis, since this was a worldwide body in which each of the participating movements drew its strength from the votes cast within its own community. In the first elections to the Knesset in 1949, Israel was the only state in the world which was a single electoral district and operated a totally proportional system, with the exclusion-threshold set at 1 per cent. As a result of this many parties sprang up in Israel, no party had an overall majority in the Knesset, and ever since then governments have been based on coalitions of parties.

Over the years since the foundation of the state many attempts have been made to change the system to a full or a partial constituency system, not only to ensure representation for those on the periphery but also to create a situation where there are only two parties, one of which will have a sufficient majority to govern without recourse to coalitions.

In the past this was supported by Mapai and the 'general Zionists', while Herut, Mapam and the religious parties resisted the proposal, fearing that the reform would deprive them of representation. None of the attempts at change succeeded, and in the mid-1980s a group of academics led by Professor Uriel Reichmann called for the drafting of an Israeli constitution. The constitution that they proposed comprised several clauses, two of them referring to the electoral system: one suggested the adoption of the German system, whereby sixty members of the Knesset would be elected on a constituency basis and sixty elected from a national list; the other suggested that the Prime Minister be elected directly by the public, in parallel with the Knesset elections.

The unsuccessful attempt to set up a government under Labour leadership in 1990, the wooing of the religious parties and the last-minute defection of two of them created a bad impression. Against a background of public demand for a change to the system and limitation of the power of the religious parties, the idea of direct election of the Prime Minister was selected from among the other proposals set out in the 'Israeli constitution' and put before the Knesset by members of several parties.

In the Labour Party there was vigorous debate over the proposal. Rabin and Peres supported it, both because they felt the need to respond to public demands and because they reckoned this system was likely to favour the Labour candidate; he could rely on the support of the left, including the Arab voters, and, with the additional backing of a segment of the Orthodox camp, might well win the day.

Another group within the party, including Professor Shimon Shitrit and myself, opposed it vehemently and tried, without success, to convince branch members that supporting this system, which did not exist in any other state in the world – neither a presidential nor a parliamentary system – would reduce the power of the major parties and weaken the very principle of the party as a vital democratic link between the individual citizen and the legislature.

In the vote, held at party headquarters, some 60 per cent supported direct election while we, the opponents, were accused of factionalism, and the measure passed into law in 1992 in spite of opposition from the Likud; it was supported, incidentally, by Benyamin Netanyahu. This was the first electoral reform ever to be endorsed by the Knesset, and another (apparently) minor reform was accepted at the same time – raising the exclusion-threshold to 1.5 per cent. As happens in so many such instances, historical paradox came into play: Tehiyya, which had supported the raising of the threshold, was wiped off the political map in the 1992 elections as a result of this, while Labour, which had supported direct election, lost power the very first time that the system was implemented in 1996.

During our term in office I continued to campaign against the decision, and when the Labour Party conference was held in June 1995 I succeeded in getting the issue debated, although this was my only success. By this stage the controversy had degenerated into a squabble between Peres and

Rabin. Peres changed his mind and opposed the new system because of the extra powers it would give the Prime Minister, while Rabin clung to the reform, seeing in the renewal of the debate a vote of no-confidence in his leadership.

At the conference I outlined the arguments against the system: splitting the vote between the Knesset and the premiership would give a bonus to the small parties and diminish the large ones; it would increase the extortive powers of the religious parties, since they would make their demands known before the first round, before the second round (if there was to be a second) and while the coalition was being formed. The Prime Minister would have broad powers, facing a Knesset incapable of applying checks and balances, where he could be overthrown only if sixty-one votes were cast against him – with all the dislocation and disunity which would inevitably ensue. The parties would lose their importance, no longer providing a forum for the crystallisation of positions or a filter for political progress, and could be bypassed altogether, with show-debates replacing proper discussion.

In the end Rabin and Peres preferred not to compete over the issue of direct elections and decided to postpone debate until the conference scheduled for March 1996. It was clear that at such a late stage the system wasn't going to be changed. At the June 1995 conference I was almost a lone voice and the issue was dropped from the agenda. After the murder of Rabin, Peres chose not to revive it, not wanting to be seen trying to change something in which Rabin had believed so strongly.

I still hope it will be possible for me and those who share my views to change this misguided system and implement the following programme: elections to the Knesset will follow the German system, which combines the constituency and proportional principles in a very balanced fashion. The Prime Minister will be the leader of the party that has scored most votes in the election, or will be elected by plenary session of the Knesset in a series of rounds. No-confidence will be an option only if the opposition can put forward a candidate commanding the support of a majority of MKs – the procedure known in the Bundestag as 'constructive no-confidence'. It would be difficult to adopt the high German exclusion percentage (5 per cent), but there is certainly a case for increasing it to 2 or 3 per cent.

It is no accident that in the last years we have experienced two upheavals in the system: direct election of Prime Ministers and 'primaries' to select the candidates put up for election by the major parties. Neither has achieved its objective: direct election was supposed to diminish the extortive powers of the religious parties but has had the effect of increasing them, while the primaries have not reduced the influence of party bosses but have given them added status; they are the dominant figures whom candidates must sweet-talk and cut deals with. The primaries are indeed a departure from the old supervisory committees, where small oligarchies perpetuated themselves, but they are not the absolute opposite, since the opportunities to make deals and fix cosy arrangements remain, especially at district but also at national level. And so the primaries have turned into a new version of the nomination committee, a version which is considerably more expensive and which lays such emphasis on the claims of the competing candidates and their handling of the issues that the primaries are seen as a greater challenge than the elections themselves! Cases of irregularity exposed in the process of the primaries have also made this a problematical system.

It has been suggested that the process be reversed, with the selection of candidates for the Knesset taking place in smaller forums. I don't believe this is either desirable or feasible, but I reckon that some of the maladies of the system could be tackled by means of open primaries, in which anyone who declares he is not a member of another party may participate in selecting a party's candidate for the Knesset. Since this is a system open to abuse by elements who may try to vote in another party's primaries and thereby influence the outcome of the elections, it would be appropriate to hold primaries, in all the parties having an interest in them, on the same day. Another, more radical option is to hold primaries on the same day as the general elections to the Knesset: each elector at the ballot box will choose a voting-slip relating to the party for which he intends to vote, and on this slip he will mark his preferences and thus help to formulate his party's list for the Knesset. In this system there will be complete identity of interest between candidates and their parties, no one will get the chance to influence a list other than the one he is voting for, while opportunities for the striking of deals between party bosses and potential candidates will be reduced.

As for the party, on the one hand it would be a mistake to adopt the American model, whereby there are 'skeleton parties' which operate only in election campaigns and play no role in the intervals between elections; on the other hand, if the party continues with its current pattern of activities it will lose whatever importance it may once have enjoyed. The new party – especially in an era of open primaries to which the number of party members is irrelevant – will be a small party of a few tens of thousands of members, addressing political and social issues on the national agenda. It will, of course, retain institutions such as the conference, the headquarters, central administration, but the basic cell cannot be the branch as currently constituted.

If the German system is indeed adopted and the country is divided into electoral constituencies, local power-bases will be formed in accordance with these districts, but alongside this division it will be necessary to give extra weight to a division that is not geographical but is based on shared interests and common denominators on the ideological level. Elements in the Labour party such as the kibbutzim, Arabs, Druze and certain ideological circles have much more in common than people who happen to live in the same area and are therefore members of the same branch. The organisational base will be transferred from branch level to ballot level, where there will need to be the apparatus to prepare, in the intervals between elections, for the next election.

In time of peace, will the same parties continue to exist? I would not rule this out. The organisational structure exerts a powerful influence, while membership of a party is a factor of self-definition, such that loyalty to a movement is perceived as a virtue in its own right; parties exchange one set of issues for another from time to time and just keep on going. If over the past thirty years the central, virtually the only issue dividing Labour from Likud has been the future of the territories, before 1967 this was, naturally, hardly an issue at all, and matters such as relations with Germany, attitudes towards the trade unions and the kibbutz movement were the divisive ones. And yet there has been no upheaval in the political map of Israel and the only centre party which has emerged (the Democratic Movement for Change) collapsed at the end of its first term of participation in government.

And yet? There is much that is artificial in the personal composition of the various factions in the Knesset, and on many issues such as religion and state, economics or individual freedom there are common denominators between members of different parties – more than is the case within the factions themselves. It is possible therefore that when there is peace and the issue of the future of the settlements has been solved and removed from our national agenda, there will be the opportunity to construct a new map and explore the real division in Israeli society and in every democratic society: between those of conservative–traditional perceptions who seek to preserve structures and values established in the past and those who believe in the need for constant and dynamic change. It is the difference between those who look at the world and say 'Thus was the world created and who are we to change it? We must accept what is and honour what has been before' and those who refuse to accept injustice and inequality and are searching for ways to combat these phenomena. It is possible that we shall yet see in Israel a democratic party confronting a conservative party, each of them being a coalition of groups which will compete among themselves for the support of the first-time voter who has yet to convert party allegiance into a factor of his personal identity.

5

Israeli Society

It is possible that when the peace process is removed from the agenda, some of the parties created in response to the Arab–Israeli conflict (Tsomet, Third Way) will disappear, but the changes in Labour and in Likud will not be so great. It is very possible that the differences between the major parties really are the fundamental differences which divide right from left throughout the world and that their political approach is determined by these differences and not by external or temporary factors.

The left and the right in Israel did not emerge against a background of political differences. At some stages political differences within the left have been greater than those which distinguish it from the right. It is true that the Revisionist Party was founded by Zev Jabotinsky in 1925 as a protest against Chaim Weizmann's policy towards the British, but very soon its political platform was revealed and disputes between the camps focused on matters such as labour relations and the right to strike.

Since then both right and left have come a long way. The left has realised that ownership of the means of production does nothing to promote equality, and the struggle over the need for connections between the Trade Union Federation and the Health Service and union-owned industry has been concluded. Likud has started to take an interest in union affairs, pursuing policies not radically different from those of the Labour Party in the 1998 Histadrut elections, Labour and Likud merged into one list, headed by Amir Peretz, a Labour member of Knesset. The right has become much less extreme, no longer opposing the right to strike, for example; the left too is much less extreme than it was, and when in government it was even more riven by ideological splits than the right. Sometimes it seems that the debate today is between the rival approaches of John Maynard Keynes and Milton Friedman to the supply-and-demand curve, and even this is outside the realm of party politics – hence the blurring of distinctions between left and right in all matters relating to politics and society. But this is a very superficial view.

The truth is that political argument has been straightforward for all of us. The Six Day War left us with territory three times the size of the sovereign State of Israel, and debate on the future of this territory led within a few years to a clear division between the left, willing to concede most of it, and the right, determined to retain it even at the cost of no-peace. As the public debate intensified, other arguments were laid aside, no other issue seeming to command such a level of interest – except in very quiet periods ('Who is a Jew?' in 1970, Black Panthers in 1971).

But the real difference between right and left relates to the question of the equal value of human beings. It is the essence of all essentials. An enlightened person of the right says to themselves, 'We were created different: in the world there are different races and different colours, different sexes, different ages. There will always be "haves" and "have-nots" – and to protest or contend against this would be an absurd and futile exercise. By all means help the weakest members of our society, but don't make the mistake of thinking they will ever be the same as us. Our enemies are different too: they aren't as keen as we are to live in peace, they don't seem to mind being shot to pieces in pursuit of an objective and they're not to be trusted if they offer the hand of friendship – there'll be a dagger concealed in the other hand. That is just the way they are, and it's naive to think otherwise. They are never going to change.'

The person of the left believes in the equal value of all human beings. This is not to say that people are equal, since the differences between them are prodigious, and it isn't even to say they are born equal, since the parameters are set before birth. A pregnant woman in the slums of São Paulo knows the kind of world into which her child will be born, and the same applies to a pregnant woman living in Beverly Hills. But the *value* of these children is the same, and if they were brought up in similar circumstances there would be no difference between them – as has been proved in the case of the 'children of Brazil', adopted by childless couples in Israel. Children are entitled to equal treatment and they should be seen as a worthwhile investment for the future, not allowed to survive on a mere subsistence level. For their sake we should strive to change the face of society so that birth into poverty is not taken for granted, and all have the same opportunity to exploit their potential.

And just as for the left there is no difference between child and child, human being and human being, the notion that the enemy is inferior to yourself, and that anybody can be so 'different' from you that you can't talk to him, is also unacceptable. This does not mean 'peace at any price'. Far from it. It should never be forgotten that blindness in the assessment of an enemy's intentions is liable to lead to disaster, as happened in the days of Chamberlain and Halifax – although it is worth noting that these proponents of 'appeasement' were right-wing British politicians. Making a measured concession for the sake of peace does not necessarily make you a Chamberlain.

Conservatism is an ancient phenomenon, possibly as old as mankind. People are born into a very complex world, they ask many questions and seek, above all, to understand. It is but a short step from understanding the world to accepting it. Generally, when we understand the system we internalise it, enabling ourselves to live within it in a mood of complacency. Were it not so, how would we account for the way that so many generations have for so many years put up with their inferior status and instead of rebelling have endorsed the social system, commending the official line that material progress is irrelevant since true dignity is an inner quality? And how is it that the castes in India, including the caste of the 'untouchables', have accepted and continue to accept the cruel hierarchy which determines their status in the world?

Conservatism has been a great success story. It has succeeded – principally with the aid of religions, which have added a nuance of sanctity to the established order and threatened trouble-makers with divine displeasure – in inducing most of the world to accept its arduous destiny and to believe that order is preferable to equality. There is nothing to be done since it is all 'ordained by Heaven', or life is a bridge to another, better world where those who have known their place during their brief sojourn here below will be rewarded. Or beyond this life you are looking forward to returning in a more successful incarnation, so there is no point in arguing over your present circumstances; you might even consider leaving this life early and moving on as soon as possible to the next, the better stage.

There have, of course, been expressions of discontent such as the slave-uprising led by Spartacus, but leftism as an overall concept was born in the eighteenth century, as an assault on privilege and on those elements in society which maintain privilege. It took a stand against the injustice of class, against the exploitation of women in society and against the gulf between the landlord and the pauper, and it believed that wars emanate, for the most part, from interests alien to the majority of the public. It came forward, in the name of the majority, to demand rights from the privileged ruling minority, but in many cases it was not supported by those whose oppression it sought to uncover.

The left has had its share of failures, the most spectacular of which was the communism of the twentieth century. This was an attempt to impose equality with an iron fist, to disregard the rules of the market, to create a new world while taking from the citizens of this one the right to express themselves or to resist the regime forced upon them. From a historical perspective, this was a very short-lived experiment, but on members of my generation it made a deep and lasting impression: equality can never be achieved by eliminating freedom.

Liberalism emerged as a counterweight to Conservatism, believing in equal rights – including for example the right to vote – and the economics of the free market. The socialism of the late nineteenth century saw liberalism as its rival. It pointed out – correctly – that without equality of opportunity the concept of equal rights is meaningless, and that there is a need for equalisation of conditions and not just the theoretical ability to exercise freedom of expression – the latter also being meaningless if, for example, I cannot read or write. It also supposed – incorrectly – that the free market was its worst enemy, because it put considerations of supply and demand over vital human needs.

During this century there has been increasing convergence between these two important movements. Liberalism has realised the importance of providing conditions as equal as they can possibly be and not being content with the struggle for rights alone, while socialism has realised that fighting for equality without freedom is a contradiction in terms, and for this reason has identified itself with the struggle for implementation of individual rights and for release from colonial subjugation. On the one hand it was Beveridge, a British Liberal, who laid the foundations of the welfare state, and on the other the socialists abandoned their opposition to the market, seeing where this policy was leading and observing the collapse of national economies which had opted for 'five-year plans' and production of 'important' goods, disregarding the role of the market in absorbing or rejecting these commodities.

The liberals and the socialists founded the welfare state. They fought side by side against apartheid, and for the extension of the rights of all elements of the population which had endured privation for generations – women, children, the sick and disabled and other minorities. This joint struggle, in spite of setbacks, has been crowned with undeniable success. Even conservative governments have not tried to deny the achievements of the welfare state and the campaign for civil and human rights. This is a struggle that does not stop at national boundaries, that aspires to change the world, to reduce inequalities between nations and create an international community in which there is less injustice and more opportunity for all to exploit their latent talents.

Full equality will never be achieved; it will remain a remote and impossible objective. We shall narrow the gaps, extend rights, enact laws and pass on the torch of the struggle to the next generation, so that it may try to construct a better world than the one inherited from us, but equality will be elusive for as long as there are differences between people. There will always be the wise and the foolish, the talented and the inept, and, in the absence of misguided attempts to enforce equality, the wise and the talented will always enjoy advantages over the others in terms of prestige and living standards. But continuing effort is required to create a situation where fewer and fewer people are born to an economic destiny which will be theirs throughout life, and where privileges will depend on merit and not on membership of a certain class.

In my view, the left of today should be a blend of socialist and liberal principles, what the British academic Julian Le Grand defined as 'market socialism'. Ownership of the means of production will not promote equality, nor will disregard of the market. No one has yet invented an alternative to the market as a function of supply and demand. The market can serve extreme right-wing perceptions just as it can serve leftist perceptions. The market itself has no ideology.

Social-liberalism believes in the enactment of laws that will guarantee the individual an adequate safety-net, not letting him fall even when times are hardest. It does not consider that these laws, pledging to every individual the provision of education, healthcare, pensions, housing and compensation for conditions such as unemployment and sickness, need to be implemented by the government itself or by government-appointed agencies. Government monopolies spawn extra bureaucracy, declining services and frustration. The solution to this is to develop a 'birth-right society'.

In Chapter 3 I referred to a 'birth-right scheme' as a means of enabling young Jews to visit Israel. This is a part of a more comprehensive concept according to which the function of society is to attend to the rights of its constituent members. The state, or its legislative authority, enacts laws which determine the rights of every individual, according to the values prevalent in the legislature; rights are awarded to the individual by means of vouchers (in concrete or symbolic form). The state is entitled to determine that different individuals will pay in different ways for these vouchers, or that some will receive more vouchers than others, for the same outlay, as their needs are perceived to be greater.

Armed with these vouchers individuals will head for the open market, where service-providers will compete for the custom of the voucher-holders. It will be for the state to decide whether service-providers meet the criteria required, and to check their performance against these criteria on a continuous basis, but here its responsibility will end. The individual may choose between different schools, different health services, different contractors and different pension funds according to his own judgment.

As a counterweight to the effort to increase equality, certain new trends are continually emerging, trends liable to exert a negative influence on the campaign to squeeze differentials; I refer to advances in information technology. We address issues associated with the information super-highway, discuss what should and should not be allowed in terms of information gathering and access, security of databases – and, as far as the majority of the public is concerned, we might just as well be speaking Chinese. The computer revolution is a phenomenon of enormous significance, but in most households it is still a remote concept. The gulf between us and our children is sometimes greater than that between us and our parents, although we prefer to think that the reverse is the case. Technological progress leaves some people way behind, even educated people, and as a result their ability to sustain a decent standard of living is impaired. The volume of information available to us is doubling every six or seven months – apparently a blessing, but one that could become a curse if we don't adapt ourselves to cope with these stunning developments.

The only way to tackle this interesting and difficult challenge is by the constant acquisition of knowledge, meaning the construction of a new system that will enable the individual to learn more and to plan for the extension of his studies in the future, since a large proportion of the knowledge being taught in schools today will be obsolete even before the pupils graduate. Investment in education will yield the highest dividends in terms of equality. A safety-net is essential; those going into retirement and finding their pensions inadequate will suffer, ill-health destroys opportunity, and many people rely on state benefits to keep their heads above water, but all of this is to do with minimum subsistence levels. Education is the key to socio-economic status in a modern society.

I see a case for significant reforms in the Israeli education system, with schooling beginning at an earlier age, even if in the most junior classes the accent is on recreation rather than instruction. Starting school at the age of four, with five full days of schooling per week, will make completion of basic education attainable at the age of sixteen. At this stage pupils can opt for higher education or higher technical training, for which no fees will be charged. By eighteen, most will have completed their academic or vocational education.

At the age of eighteen (or nineteen) national service will begin. A special authority will be responsible for recruiting and assessing each year's intake, a process that will involve women and men, agnostics and believers, Jews and Arabs, although exemptions will be allowed for those pleading religious or conscientious objections to national service. Those remaining may choose between military national service which currently lasts three years, and civilian national service, where the emphasis will be on education, health, environmental quality and other areas of benefit to the community; the state will use special incentives to direct members of this pool towards projects which may be considered particularly important at a given period. Since from this point onward the youngsters will be classed as educated or professional people, their abilities can be better exploited for the benefit of the state, and the experience will be to their own advantage as well. Further down the road, the state will see to it that every citizen has continuing contact with education, to cope with the need to change profession several times in the course of a career. I shall deal with this more fully in addressing the issue of leisure.

In all welfare states there is debate over the issue of the universality of benefits. In the 1940s, 1950s and 1960s universal benefits, meaning those paid at an identical rate at all levels of society for child care, maternity and so on, were regarded as axiomatic. This was a reaction against the time when society was prepared to help only its most destitute members (like the people who used to walk the streets of medieval London wearing caps marked with the letter 'P' for 'pauper'). There was a feeling – a humane feeling – that it was wrong to stigmatise people by giving benefits only to the very weakest.

The problem was the financing. Welfare states proved very expensive. In states where there was rapid growth, it was possible to fund increasing welfare expenditure through direct and indirect taxes charged at existing rates. But if growth was halted and stagnation took hold, extra sources of revenue were required and the only feasible option was to raise rates of tax. The leading welfare states were levying taxes at such high rates that potential investors began looking elsewhere, for places where expansion of production and harder work were not so severely penalised. Benefit payments ceased to be a safety-net and became a way of life for a large section of the population. Aversion to means-testing, and natural generosity, have imposed burdens beyond the capacity of the state. There are nations which have curtailed rights, others which have raised taxes and others which have come to terms with growing budget deficits – and with the resulting negative impact on the rate of inflation, on the stock market and on investment.

In my opinion, there is a case for distinguishing between universality in receipt of services and universality in receipt of benefits. Services such as health and education should be given to all at equal levels, but there is room for variation in the ways that they are financed. In education for example, I consider a full-length school day vital for a number of reasons (including improvement in the training and career opportunities of mothers), but this would be expensive, and I don't rule out the possibility that well-off parents might have to share in the costs, while parents in unfavourable financial circumstances would not be required to pay for this service.

There is no practical justification for a system in which all receive the same child benefits. The cost is awesome, while differentials in living standards remain and are even increasing. It should be relatively easy to reduce the incidence of poverty (calculated as a proportion of average income in Israel), by taking benefits from the higher wage earners and using the saving to increase payments to the less well-off. This could be done by taxing benefits through the national insurance system, and a more radical reform could be effected by requiring all to complete 'income-disclosure' forms. The information thus obtained could provide for fairer taxation of all kinds of earnings, including income from stock dividends which is currently, for no good reason, treated as tax-exempt, while on the other hand 'negative income tax' could be introduced as a supplementary payment to the poorest families.

There is a technical problem here, which I examined in my time as deputy Finance Minister and have been aware of ever since. It has been claimed that, if a duty of income-disclosure is imposed on the whole population, the pipeline will be blocked by a mass of non-vital information, making it impossible to track down the major defaulters and tax-evaders. I don't refute this claim, but I find it hard to believe that in the computer-era on the cusp of the third millennium we can't solve the problem of universal disclosure of income. Such a system could be a factor of social justice, allowing for greater selectivity in benefit payments, giving added income to the weakest and making the kind of budget savings which will obviate the need for tax increases.

Another method of squeezing differentials could be restraint of wages in public companies. The differentials created in recent years in Israeli society, between the workers in a given firm and the management, are higher than those accepted elsewhere in the world. Even if the restraints imposed are lenient, and executive salaries remain several times the average pay of workers in the firm, it will still be a contribution to limiting social differentials in Israel.

Significant changes have taken place recently in the field of industrial relations. Foreign firms investing in Israel often make the system of personal contracts a condition of their investment. Personal contracts prevent the organisation of workers, making strikes and any kind of practical co-operation impossible. Each individual worker has a salary concealed from the others and dependent on the success of his own negotiations with the employer. Most of all, permanence is exchanged for a state of perpetual temporariness, and according to the contract you can be fired at any time without reference to the principles such as 'First in, last out'. These contracts are a widespread phenomenon in the high-tech industries, but are beginning to permeate more traditional firms as well.

Personal contracts are opposed to the traditional conception of trade unions. Indeed, on the face of it, who needs them when there is no collective bargaining and no organisation of workers? The approach used to be that of mutual responsibility, protection of every permanent worker and resistance to his dismissal. Permanence became almost a supreme virtue, and seniority was no less important. Trade unions have often found themselves defending unsuitable workers simply on the ground of their long service in the workplace. Lack of flexibility in dismissing workers means the need to employ supernumerary workers who make no contribution to the success of the operation, and this has an impact on productivity, management efficiency, profits and growth.

Admittedly, personal contracts are a convenient arrangement for some – provided they are young and healthy. Age and infirmity are liable to place the worker in danger of redundancy, after which he will have great difficulty finding alternative employment, and if he appeals to the union he will be told, with a regretful smile, that he can't be helped, having forfeited his rights as a member of the organisation.

Is it possible to turn the clock back and blacklist firms that use personal contracts? Can the issuing of personal contracts in future be prevented? Certainly not. I reckon that the solution in this connection is an effort to integrate collective with personal contracts. It will be up to the union to conduct collective bargaining over the basic conditions of the worker, while allowing every firm which wishes to do so to sign personal contracts with the workforce. The union will protect the worker in the areas covered by the collective contract; everything else is to be between the worker and his employer. As the game progresses and becomes more professional, as firms employ fewer workers, as more people work at home with computers and modems, so the phenomenon of personal contracts will proliferate, and unions would be well advised to adapt themselves to the situation rather than engage in Don Quixote-style warfare.

When the General Federation of Jewish Workers in Eretz Israel (Histadrut) was founded in Haifa in December 1920, it saw itself as an ideological structure rather than as a professional association protecting workers and their rights. After the failure of the attempt to set up a joint party which would include the non-socialist HaPoel HaTzair and the socialist Ahdut HaAvoda it was decided to establish a looser and less formal structure, especially as a result of pressure from young workers of the Third Aliyah (wave of immigration) who didn't care for the factional wrangling of their elder brothers of the Second Aliyah.

The intention of the founders of Histadrut was to turn the Land of Israel, within a few years, into a nation of co-operatives – co-operation in manufacturing, services and commodities. The kibbutzim and the moshavim were the agricultural co-operatives, matched by the urban co-operatives established in industry, transport and supply of consumer goods. The Society of Workers, set up three years after the foundation of the Histadrut, was not, originally, the economic arm of the Histadrut but was intended to be a framework for the lives of workers, an autonomous collective framework comprising the Haganah self-defence force, kindergartens, schools, newspapers, culture, health services, employment and consumer goods. It was only in 1936, when it became clear that the Society of Workers was not going to become an alternative way of life, that the trade union was established on a national basis, as part of the Histadrut.

The Histadrut was a workers' party in the making and a state in the making. But in 1930 Mapai – the Party of Workers of Israel – was established and 1948 saw the foundation of the state. Like many other organisations, the Histadrut failed to recognise the need for radical internal reform, continuing to provide services that were to a great extent beyond its financial capabilities and that could be maintained only with generous support from the government.

Difficulties in sustaining the general health service and pension funds were intensified when Likud governments proved unwilling to support the Histadrut quite so generously, and the ensuing decline was blamed on the Labour Party, perceived as a close ally of the union federation. The status of the Histadrut as both employer and representative became less and less tenable, and the climax came when the Soltam company in Yokneam, owned by the Histadrut, used dogs to disperse protesting workers. Again, it was the Labour Party that took the blame.

When we put forward – both in the Young Guard and in the Mashov caucus in the Labour Party – suggestions for radical reform of the Histadrut, the party accused us of being, of all things, a 'cabal of the new right'. The fact that for eight years I had been a *Davar* journalist, writing extensively on union issues, did nothing to mitigate my guilt; nor were my lectures to university students on the 'History of Israeli Socialism' any defence. To the leadership of the Histadrut I was a 'Thatcherite'.

The crunch came when our group took, to a meeting at party headquarters in 1991, a proposal to separate membership of the Labour Party from membership of the Histadrut. Since at that time any member of the Histadrut was obliged to join the General Health Service, anyone choosing to join a different health service and consequently having to leave the Histadrut was required to resign from the Labour Party, or was at least barred from joining it in future. This seemed to us a very injudicious policy, as many young families were transferring to the Maccabbi Health Service, and we could not afford to disregard this substantial chunk of the electorate.

Most members of the party and Histadrut hierarchies saw in our proposals a fundamental betrayal of the indissoluble knot binding the two organisations, an attempt to demolish all our ideological property. Micha Harish, then secretary-general of the party, who acknowledged the flaws in the present system but feared rejection of our proposal, put forward a compromise solution whereby anyone barred from membership of the Histadrut could be admitted to the Labour Party. To this day, anyone joining the Labour Party but not being a member of the Histadrut must sign an acknowledgment that he has been 'barred' from membership of the Histadrut, even if he has no clear recollection of having ever applied for it.

This was a change typical of a traditional organisation which prefers to deceive itself and not admit the necessity of reform. This episode afforded conclusive proof of the inability of the Histadrut to reform of its own accord. The suggestions that were raised, to convert the Society of Workers into a holding company or to sever connections with the General Health Service, were thrown out. Financial difficulties, lack of relevance and excess of bureaucratisation created the situation where it was easy for a rebel like Haim Ramon to take on the rusty machine of the Histadrut and in elections, watch it simply collapse, presenting him with a decisive and easy victory.

The resignation of Ramon and his colleagues from the Labour Party, and his decision to stand independently in the Histadrut elections, caused problems for those of us who sympathised with his views. We tried to persuade him to change his mind, but he was not to be swayed and he went on to be elected secretary-general of the Histadrut. The revolution that he unleashed in the Histadrut was, in the nature of things, more rapid and far-reaching than the reforms which should have taken place over the years and had not.

I don't share the nostalgia that some feel for the old Histadrut. It had a certain charm and a strong Israeli flavour and a genuine commitment to fight for greater equality and for the rights of the worker; it was also impervious to new ideas, unimaginative, ultimately irrelevant and prone to corruption. But the Histadrut still has a role to play, and its present challenge is to identify this role and define it in terms relevant to the twenty-first century.

I reckon that the Histadrut could still be our foremost civilian corporation, performing a role of unrivalled and unchallenged importance
in Israeli society. It will definitely continue to represent workers, and trade
unionism will continue to be the hub of its activity, with the emphasis on
legal advice and expertise; if this is handled correctly, the organisation has
every prospect of a successful future.

Consumerism is a constantly expanding part of our lives. The market
inundates us with tempting offers – commodities, loans, mortgages, trust
funds – and what is needed is an independent consumer agency that will
recommend, criticise and warn. This is an area in which the Histadrut has
engaged in the past with unimpressive results, but which it could now
convert into a far more central element of its activity. Another issue of
great importance, which has dominated so much discussion in recent
years, is quality of the environment. Its influence on our lives has been
much greater than we used to envisage and it plays a significant role in
the workplace too, affecting the quality of life and even life expectancy.
Here too the Histadrut has a job to do, facing up to the big economic and
political institutions and defending the individual's right to a decent
environment, at work and at play.

The Histadrut must pay more attention to the future labour market and
to non-organised workers. The future employment of Palestinians and
possibly of Jordanians too, and the issue of foreign workers in general,
will oblige it to devise a policy and act accordingly. Mobility of labour is
a new phenomenon for us, although it has long been a feature of life in
other developed countries, and it is set to become increasingly influential
here. The Histadrut's traditional disregard for foreign workers will no
longer be acceptable.

Another issue of increasing importance is leisure. We devote to work
today about half the amount of time that was required of workers a century
ago. In Western countries the working week is some thirty-five hours over
five days, and every year there is holiday entitlement of between one and
two months. At forty-two hours, the Israeli working week is slightly longer,
but we are still left with plenty of leisure time, and we shall have more.

Modern technology requires far fewer hands to operate it, and the drift
from manufacturing to service industries will continue, but here too there
will be fewer hours of work required and the weekend is likely to be
extended. The Histadrut's traditional orientation is towards work and,
besides the establishment of a cultural and educational centre and rec-

reational clubs, it has yet to deal systematically with the issue of leisure. There is a big gap here that it could and should be filling.

There is a catch in the availability of so much leisure. If it isn't exploited by the worker, he will soon find himself in a state of enforced leisure, out of a job. If in the twenty-first century we shall all be changing our trades at least three times before our careers are through, then we should be using every opportunity to prepare for the next challenge. This means we shall have to devote our leisure time, or at least an appreciable portion of it, to acquiring new professional skills. Those who leave this process to the last possible moment – as many undoubtedly will – are going to suffer serious disadvantage. If the state has a role to play in tackling the issue of leisure, it will be the creation of a climate in which service-providers will compete over the exploitation of leisure time, offering the consumer professional training, education, culture, whatever is required. This is another area where the Histadrut could compete successfully, as it gears itself up to face the challenges of the future; it is only by looking forward, and outward, that this organisation will utilise to the full its many advantages – in size, numbers and geographical spread – and not risk lapsing into decline and emasculation.

The kibbutz is the jewel in the crown of the labour movement, although in recent years it has had to endure one of the toughest – if not *the* toughest – crises in its history. The kibbutz was born by accident, when the Zionist movement offered a dozen workers the contract to operate an agricultural collective at Umm Juni (Deganiah). The settlement developed on the basis of shared resources and communal dining, supplemented at a later stage by the building of a children's house and other facilities. Thus the kibbutz came into being, representing a way of life in which the individual concedes a proportion of his individuality, but in return enjoys the full support of the community and needs to take no economic decisions on the personal level, since his sustenance is assured. The continued existence of the kibbutz was guaranteed to a considerable extent by the Zionist movement, and later by the state. Kibbutzim played a pioneering role in the settlement of frontiers, as well as supplying the IDF with some of its best recruits.

In the 1980s many kibbutzim found themselves in crisis as a result of their involvement with the stock market during the years of rampant inflation, and since then the kibbutz movement has been heavily involved in a programme of damage-limitation and recovery. Perhaps it is no accident that the crisis arose seventy years after the inception of the movement. Academic studies have reached the conclusion that the life expectancy of the commune is three generations – or seventy years – since it imposes a certain way of life which only the founders, and in ideal circumstances their children and grandchildren too, are prepared to take on themselves. Will the kibbutz be an exception and survive into the next century and beyond? That is the question. The demise of the kibbutz would be a severe blow not only to the labour movement but to all Israeli society.

The crisis has ruthlessly exposed the weaknesses of the kibbutz. Since its creation was never planned, not in the long term at least, it has retained throughout the years an air of transience, of improvisation. The rights of the kibbutz to the land it occupies have never been determined in law, nor have the rights of the individual to the room or apartment in which he lives.

This wonderful institution – nursery of idealistic youth, always first in line to serve the national interest – has been operating on the flimsiest of financial bases, mainly because it has been assumed it would never be allowed to collapse. The kibbutz does not make the best use of its members: the system of rotation and work-scheduling has ensured equality but is a serious waste of resources, when those who should be devoting their time to commercial and technical projects have to take their turn in the dining-hall or the kitchen. On the face of it there is no unemployment in the kibbutz, but the reality is otherwise: numbers of people are involved in work of no practical significance, just to give them the illusion of useful employment. The industrial projects which finance the kibbutzim have often been chosen very unprofessionally: foodstuffs, textiles and plastics are labour-intensive, low-return commodities, exceedingly hard to sell when the domestic market is saturated.

For many years the kibbutz movement resisted pressure to send its children to universities, both on account of an ideology which saw the university as a bourgeois and unproductive institution, and because limited resources were channelled towards other priorities. The founders of the kibbutzim were, in many cases, educated people who had studied abroad or in Israel before opting for the kibbutz way of life. They maintained that the education given to children on the kibbutz – on a basis of individual tuition and close monitoring of progress – was superior to anything available in high schools or universities. The third generation was not prepared to accept this, and the 1980s and 1990s saw a boom in the number of kibbutz members attending universities, but a whole generation of people – now in their fifties and largely responsible for the economic management of the kibbutz movement – has had no experience of life outside the kibbutz and could not survive in any other environment. The 'fucked-up generation' (their own words, not mine!) represents a mistake for which the entire kibbutz movement is paying a heavy price today.

Also problematical is the range of services and administrative procedures which exist in every kibbutz; in the smaller kibbutzim the system is too big and too expensive and has no justification other than an obsession with autonomy. A change is urgently needed whereby one centralised administrative system will deal with a number of settlements.

The future of the kibbutz is in the balance. The solution is not only financial; even if financial problems can be solved, the hardest questions of all will remain open – will the grandsons and granddaughters consent to maintaining the unique lifestyle devised by the founders? Or can the founders keep the kibbutz alive with the help of outside volunteers alone? Is the increasing proximity of many kibbutzim to towns (a product either of urban expansion or of improved access to private transport) likely to tempt growing numbers of kubbitzniks to try their luck in the towns and enjoy a greater degree of freedom, even if it means doing without the safety-net of the kibbutz?

The answer to these questions is not only an internal kibbutz matter; it is an ideological issue with powerful implications for the character of the kibbutz in the twenty-first century.

The first essential in my opinion is to put an end to the legal limbo of the kibbutz institution and of its members. Legislation is urgently required to clarify the rights of the kibbutz over the land which it occupies, and the rights of individuals to accommodation, pensions and other benefits. The kibbutzim owe this to themselves, and the state owes it to them.

A reform which I would recommend is separation between the kibbutz as a place of work and the kibbutz as a social community offering specific services to its members and demanding specific duties in return. In future very few will be employed in agriculture, and there is no particular justification for siting industrial installations within the precincts of the kibbutz, if half an hour's commuting would enable members to work elsewhere. Outside employment will give opportunities for self-fulfilment in a wider range of activities than are available to the kibbutz itself. Work within the kibbutz will also need to be costed. Many kibbutzim already employ outside workers, and I can envisage a situation where most internal work is done by outsiders while the majority of members commute to employment elsewhere.

Of course, this is not quite as simple as it sounds. Outside the kibbutz, members will earn different salaries. Those on low salaries will live in the kibbutz at a level above their 'capability' and will thus gain significant material benefit from the kibbutz system, while higher earners will live at a level below what they consider themselves entitled to, and may decide to quit the kibbutz for good; those left behind will be the less talented and less flexible, those of limited earning-potential, and the kibbutz itself will be the loser.

A rather complex compromise might be the answer: a system whereby the income earned by the member is not handed over in its entirety to the kibbutz, but a proportion is considered the property of the individual. This amounts to a form of local income tax, which will be charged at a high rate but still leave enough for the individual to enhance his standard of living.

'That's not a kibbutz!' veterans of the movement will protest, and they will not be alone in this. And just what *is* a kibbutz? We weren't given the specifications on Mount Sinai. It was created in response to the needs of the time, and it has a chance of survival if it changes in accordance with changing circumstances. In fact, the process of change has already started. The kibbutz of today, in the majority of cases, is not a remote location visited by a service bus once or twice a day, where most of the activity is agricultural, children live in a children's house, members eat in the dining-hall three times a day, all wear blue or khaki shirts and change into white shirts on Friday, and the highlight of the week is the Tuesday movie, subtitled and screened *al fresco*. These days, children live with their parents, the 'room' has become an 'apartment', fridges enable members to eat at least one daily meal at home if not two, and when they decide to patronise the dining-hall they use vouchers for which they are billed at the end of the month. Some have the use of cars and are already travelling to the nearest town for work or recreation, while jetting off to foreign parts is no longer exceptional. The traditional Saturday-night meetings still take place, but most members would only attend them at gunpoint, preferring to follow proceedings on close-circuit television from the comfort of their armchairs.

The kibbutz is precisely what its members decide it will be. Conservatism is liable to be its doom. Far better to act now, making structural changes and learning from our mistakes as we go along, than to leave it as it is and watch, wringing our hands, as it collapses in ruins.

I acknowledge that the notion of separating the commercial and the social elements is a serious mistake from the ideological standpoint; we have social objectives, and economics and technology are just the means by which we attain them. If a factory for the mass-production of sweaters is running at a loss, there is bound to be someone who thinks the solution is a national rescue campaign, with every citizen who cares (or who feels the cold) buying a sweater; the economic answer is to shut the place down, but this would be seen as insensitivity to the needs of the workers. The real insensitivity, in my opinion, is the attempt to shore up enterprises that have lost their competitive edge and are barely able to pay the minimum wage.

The days of living as a small island surrounded by enemies have passed, hopefully for ever. We don't have to try to make everything ourselves. Israel needs to develop expertise in the field of advanced technology, in research and development, information services, financial services and specialised areas of manufacture – from fashion to processed foods. That is its relative advantage. Investment in Israel should be capital-intensive and not labour-intensive. This will be good for the economy and good for society, encouraging growth and a fairer distribution of resources to the advantage of the less privileged. When labour-intensive enterprises are transferred to Egypt, to Jordan and some day to the Palestinian state, this will be profitable to our neighbours and to ourselves. It would be a mistake to see the transfer of industries that are incapable of paying high wages as taking food from our mouths. It is a fact that the rate of unemployment in Israel has been halved, as a result of growth rather than the artificial creation of job vacancies.

Just as the market is not a term exclusive to capitalism, so too privatisation is not a right-wing concept and opposition to it is not a socialist principle. The effects of privatisation depend on the way it is implemented. If you take a monopoly, the goose that lays the golden eggs, and sell it to a wealthy individual for whose benefit the eggs will henceforward be laid, this is clearly an unjust and socially divisive procedure. On the other hand, if a state-owned company is competing in the market-place and there is no good reason for it to remain in public ownership, and if the state floats it on the stock market, this will be a welcome reduction in the power of central authority and will turn more and more people into property owners.

When I was at the Treasury, Arieh Mintkevitz, chairman of the Securities Authority, produced a report for me comprising a number of recommendations: flotation of a basket of state-owned companies on the stock market, the offer of share options to all citizens, who would have the choice after a year of selling the options for a few hundred shekels, or buying shares at a 20 per cent discount. The scheme was studied at the time by the Bank of Israel and rejected and, although raised on a number of occasions since, has never been implemented.

On the face of it, it is a 'capitalist' notion, but in fact this is the fairest form of privatisation. If privatisation is properly regulated, with guarantees that it will not create monopolies or oligopolies, if it is done by stock-market flotation and not by selling off the family jewels, then it will be a distributor of wealth, not a centraliser. It will be appropriate to encourage pension and provident funds to invest in the market, and to guarantee them a safety-net, of minimal profit, so that they will never collapse and taxation of share dividends will be a useful source of revenue.

I don't underestimate the side-effects of the privatisation process on Israeli society. It is a healthy phenomenon when fewer and fewer of society's interests are under central political control; but, as more influence passes to extra-governmental regulatory bodies, the weight of their burden of responsibility will also increase, and codes of conduct have yet to be devised for them. The influence which multinational corporations are currently capable of exerting on international politics is greater than that of governments, while their mistaken and sometimes unethical policies are less susceptible to public criticism and the process of law than are those of governments and government agencies. In these areas we shall need to operate without the benefit of successful precedents in other societies.

Just as privatisation is capable of squeezing social differentials, so tariff-reform would be a direct contribution to the extension of equality. Any reduction in duties usually runs up against coalitions of industrialists and workers complaining that this is liable to destroy Israeli industry, while all around the world economies seem to know how to defend themselves. As for the industrialists, it has been proved in the past time after time that reduction of duties has led to more rational marketing policies and to increased competition, and at the end of the day has proved beneficial and profitable for industry. As for the broader public, reduction in duties means lower prices, more choice and the opportunity to improve living standards. Free trade forces down the rate of inflation and inflation is, without doubt, the element in the economy most inimical to equality. Although in the short term there will be a threat to inefficient enterprises, those which in the past have been subsidised by the government and protected by a tariff-wall, in the longer term the advantages to individuals, especially those in the poorer strata of society, will be immense.

Israel benefits more than any other country in the world from American aid, aid which exerts an undoubted influence on Israeli society. This comprises 1.8 billion dollars for military aid – compensation for our exclusion from membership of NATO – and 1.2 billion in civilian aid. Dollar-inflation since the mid-1980s has reduced the value of this aid considerably, but we are still talking huge sums of money. It is relatively easy to justify the military aid, bearing in mind the cost of reorganising our forces and defences in preparation for a new era of peace; it is harder to justify civilian aid to a state whose standard of living is relatively high. In fact, the purpose of the civilian aid is to help us repay the loans which we received in the past from the USA, loans which emanated in the main from our defence requirements. In recent years the amount of our annual repayments has been matched by the civilian aid, meaning that we are effectively in balance with the Americans. If the level of these repayments continues to fall, resulting in an increase in our net income from aid, this will be simply unacceptable.

Before the American legislators have their say, we had better act and decide for ourselves to return to the USA all the surplus remaining above our annual repayments. In this manner, civilian aid will continue to decline, and by 2015 should have dried up completely.

I referred in Chapter 3 to the United Jewish Appeal and Keren Hajesod. In Israel there is a need to establish an appeal which will be part of the worldwide fund-raising effort and will emphasise the fact that the future of the Jewish world and Jewish education are important to us too. Contributions reaching Israel will be used, as I suggested previously, to finance a scheme enabling young Jews to visit this country, not directed towards welfare schemes in Israel.

The system of 'Israel bonds' was instituted in the 1950s when Israel was having difficulty borrowing money on the international market and needed the help of Jews who bought its debentures at relatively low rates of interest. As time passed, in order to increase the sums loaned, the bonds commission raised the interest rate and thus in recent years the debentures have become hot properties in banks and professional institutions which have no association whatsoever with Jewish issues, while Israel could have acquired much cheaper loans on the open market.

Obviously, the 'bonds' system has been obliged to defend itself, justifying its continued existence and its multi-million-dollar administration costs, and the claim is that it is supposed to be a safeguard against the 'rainy day' when Israel, God forbid, might find itself unable to borrow from merchant banks. The 'rainy day' justification is typical of institutions established in the period of isolation and embargo, but the time has come for Israel to dispense with this system altogether, even though in recent years it has reduced the interest on debentures and become more selective in the loans it has accepted.

If we do all these things, we shall initiate a process that enables us to see the end of American aid, and we won't need overseas charity for our welfare requirements but will become fund-raisers ourselves. We shall finally be released from a sense that has oppressed Israeli society and distorted our economy for many years – the sense of dependence on the USA and on world Jewry. This is a graduation test which we can and must pass successfully.

6

Dispersion of Population

At the end of the War of Independence we took up our positions on ceasefire lines. For many years we lived not only without a recognised capital but even without official frontiers. Peace with Egypt in 1979 gave us a permanent border in the south; peace with Jordan in 1994 established official borders between Israel and the Hashemite Kingdom. Vis-à-vis the Palestinians we have erased the Green Line, and by May 1999 we were supposed to have fixed a new line. With Syria and with Lebanon our borders remain temporary.

Ben-Gurion's policy was to guarantee the security of the temporary borders by means of dispersion of population. This involved establishing Nahal (Pioneer) settlements, kibbutzim and, especially, hundreds of frontier moshavim, to prevent a situation where Arabs who had fled from Israel during the war might attempt to return, to work their land or to attack Israelis. The object was to create 'facts on the ground', both in territory which since the war had been regarded as no-man's land and along the ceasefire lines, which in due course became armistice lines.

There can be no doubt that this policy combined logic with audacity. It gave a new challenge to the settlement movement and to the young generation, after it seemed that all challenges had passed with victory in the War of Independence. Many young people saw it as their goal to establish and populate Nahal communities, but the majority of those who came to the frontiers did not volunteer to do so. When the great wave of immigration began in 1949, considerable numbers of the new arrivals were sent directly to the moshavim and to the development towns which were established at a later stage. Many of the immigrants had no idea where they were going, most hadn't a clue about agriculture, and they were to resent their treatment by the settlement institutions for years to come.

Population dispersion became official policy, part of the Israeli consensus, although at the outset some were less than convinced. The more dots on the map, the more confident we felt. The 1950s and early 1960s were the years of the development towns, established in both north and south. Ben-Gurion, Levi Eshkol and Pinhas Sapir were the heroes of this time. Ribbons were cut, speeches were delivered, building proceeded at a frantic pace.

In retrospect, there can be no doubt that the establishment of frontier settlements contributed significantly to the definition of undefined borders; equally undisputed is the fact that there was a high price to be paid for population dispersion. Most of the moshavim failed. Their agriculture was not properly developed, they were too homogeneous and exclusive in terms of origin and communal identity, and they offered no solutions to the problems of the second generation; where there were large families, only one of the children could be considered the 'son and heir' and the others were obliged to leave the moshav. The moshav as a long-term way of life was a failure. The few successful settlements of this type have either abandoned agriculture altogether or rely on exceedingly artificial production quotas and subsidies. The principle of mutual dependence no longer operates, and those who criticised the institution of the moshav at the outset, including Ben-Gurion, have been vindicated in many respects.

Distance from the centre made it very hard for the young to reach educational institutions and perpetuated an unsatisfactory level of education which did not equip the young to cope with modern challenges. In the kibbutzim the aforementioned 'fucked-up generation' was emerging at this time, and its plight was particularly serious in the distant periphery, where opportunities of acquiring knowledge in the centre were virtually non-existent. Most of the development towns failed in their objective of raising living and educational standards, and those who continued to live there were idealists who saw population dispersion as a virtue in itself, eccentrics who cultivated a special affection for these newly built structures, or the weaker members of society who knew they would not survive or be accepted anywhere else.

In a significant proportion of these towns numerous changes of population have been experienced. Immigrants arrived, were absorbed, became disillusioned and moved to the centre, while in every such wave a certain percentage remained, making it even harder for the township to acquire its share of the government cake. The promises given to teachers and other valued professionals failed to attract skilled people to the periphery

in sufficient numbers. Government schemes to encourage capital investment transferred many billions of dollars to investors prepared to establish
their businesses in the periphery. Many of these enterprises dealt in commodities such as textiles and processed food, paying low wages and not
requiring a particularly skilled workforce, and after five years of exploiting
every subvention offered them by the state, investors tended to turn their
backs on the development towns. This was a further contribution to the
perpetuation of poverty and of the gulf between these townships and the
centre, and another incentive for skilled and ambitious people to abandon
the township and try their luck in the big city.

The social price paid for the attainment of a legitimate objective was very
high. In some of the development towns whole generations of youngsters
became trapped at an early age in the cheap-labour cycle, missing out
completely on opportunities for higher education. I have no doubt that
many gifted children were neglected and their talents wasted because no
attempt was made to identify them. The system which evolved was very
artificial from an economic perspective: settlements on non-agricultural
land, reliant on poultry farming and on quotas – subsidies by another
name – which raise prices while increasing dependence on production
sectors that present no challenge, certainly no modern challenge. If these
sectors fail, many people will be left destitute and helpless, unable to adapt
themselves to change.

Encouragement of investment in the development towns is also, by
definition, very artificial and is not determined by any relative advantage
of the periphery but by the grants which the state is prepared to give to
those who henceforward will need to travel many more kilometres, pay
for more expensive telephone calls and offer higher salaries to attract
skilled technicians and managerial staff away from the centre of the
country.

The belief that every development town needs to have a large industrial
plant or a number of plants has created an enormous gulf between economic and political considerations. Some townships have become entirely
dependent on one industrial enterprise; where there is no economic justification for the continue existence of this enterprise, the state comes
forward with lavish handouts and all kinds of weird and wonderful promises, just to perpetuate its artificial life which by the nature of things will
not be extended beyond a year or two.

Over the years another fact has become evident: most if not all of the periphery has a decidedly ethnic flavour. There are townships where almost the entire population hails from one country of origin (Morocco, Yemen and others), and it is hard to imagine a phenomenon more inimical to the vision of integration and the 'melting-pot'. Even the immigration from the former USSR, which has changed the picture in some of the townships, is not likely to stay there for long, and most of the new arrivals will transfer to the centre within three to five years.

Is there a case for continuing the policy of population dispersion in the future? A comprehensive peace involving Syria, Lebanon and the Palestinian state will ease the pressure for frontier development. There will be no need to plant settlements along borders which are permanent and recognised by the international community. Roads and existing modes of transport, to say nothing of future developments in transport, will make it possible to solve the perennial problem of separating domicile from workplace. Development towns can be the residential centres, with facilities for the promotion of tourism and other services, while industrial workers can commute to out-of-town commercial estates. Textile and food-processing enterprises which pay their workers only the minimum wage can be gradually transferred to the Palestinian state and to Jordan, to create employment there and boost the profits of their proprietors. Workers in Israel should transfer to industries capable of paying higher salaries; I don't pretend that the process of transition will be simple.

The legislation relating to encouragement of investment needs to be changed so that year by year the grant is decreased by 3 to 4 per cent. Thus the system will be detached in stages from state control, and investors hoping to exploit the opportunities can plan their investments in advance. The role of the state will be focused on education, where there will be a need for higher investment if the periphery and the centre are to be brought closer together. A viable public transport system will be the key, with the accent on expansion of railways rather than on constructing 'trans-Israel' highways, which would damage the environment and soon prove incapable of coping with growing demand. If this can be achieved, it will be possible to change the 'direction of traffic' – with more and more people opting to live in pleasant and quiet surroundings, where there is more room for their children and a decent standard of education, but travelling to work in an area some distance from their place of domicile. Separation between place of domicile and place of work runs counter to the logic bound up in the industrialisation of the development towns and is vital, in my opinion, if a reasonable number of these townships are to be saved from decline.

As for future building projects, I reckon we should execute a 180 degree turn and adopt the programme recommended by the economist Yaakov Sheinin. This programme calls for intensive building in the centre of the country and the gradual transformation of the entire sector into a kind of Manhattan, with appropriate infrastructure and relatively high population density. Alongside development of the centre, there will be continued development of large towns such as Haifa and Beersheba and these will also be the major centres of employment. Those who choose to live in the development towns will find adequate provision of residential, educational and other local services. This is not the time to be building new settlements in the Negev; this sector should be held in reserve for residential needs twenty years hence, when population growth will demand exploitation of the territory.

7

The Arabs of Israel

The Arab minority in Israel is not a candidate for inclusion in the 'melting-pot' – neither in its own eyes nor in the eyes of the Jewish majority. Between the years 1936 and 1948 the Arabs of Eretz Israel were seen as the implacable foes of the Jewish state. The various partition proposals raised during these years spoke of two states to the west of the River Jordan: an Arab state and alongside it a Jewish state with a very large Arab minority. In the War of Independence some 700,000 Arabs fled from the territory which was later to be constituted as the State of Israel, half of them expelled by the IDF and the other half following the orders of the Mufti of Jerusalem and the other leaders who instructed them to leave their homes and move to other places where they could organise themselves and prepare for a triumphant return. Some 150,000 Arabs remained in Israel, and the Jewish state suddenly found itself responsible for the education and welfare of its erstwhile enemies.

This was not easy, and it has become no easier over the years. The Arabs of Israel were given citizenship, but this did not mean that they enjoyed truly equal rights. For eighteen years they lived under conditions of martial law and as a result their freedom of movement was severely curtailed. They had representation in the Knesset, which was effectively determined by Mapai, the party in power. From the outset, the level of development in Arab settlements was way behind that to be found in Jewish settlements, and successive Israeli governments have given no preferential treatment to the Arab segment of the population. As a result, although the gaps have gradually shrunk over the years, they are still far from being closed.

The Arabs of Israel do not serve in the armed forces, partly because the state doesn't recruit them, partly because military service would mean preparation for potential confrontation with their Arab kinsmen, and most if not all of them would prefer to avoid such a predicament. Since in Israel military service has become an admission-ticket to society, the non-service of the Arabs effectively bars them from access to positions of influence. Some work in agriculture, many more are employed as construction workers and foremen, educated individuals tend to be school-teachers and only a few, very few, have managed to transcend these stereotypes and become university lecturers or senior government employees. Opportunities for progress in such areas as entertainment, sport and commerce are rather better, but frustration remains and it is particularly evident among the young and the gifted, who find that education is not the key to equality, to parity with their Jewish con-temporaries. Holders of first, second and even third degrees have no option but to teach in elementary or remedial schools.

The Arabs of Israel have seen significant improvement in their standard of living; it is estimated that their average salary is equivalent to 75 per cent of the average salary in the Jewish sector. Martial law has long since passed into history and the differential which used to exist between Jews and Arabs in the level of child benefit payments has recently been abolished; I am glad that I can claim some of the credit for this – and for the appointment of the first Arab consul-general and the first Arab ambassador, when I was deputy to Shimon Peres at the Foreign Ministry. Hundreds of Arabs are employed today in government departments, there are more than a few Arab judges and, for the first time, an Arab has been appointed chairman of a state-owned corporation. We can afford to feel some satisfaction with the achievements of the past few years, but the very process of closing gaps tends to accentuate the gaps which remain.

Most of Israel's Arabs reside in villages; this is a result of their own preference for living with the extended family – combined with the equally traditional Jewish reluctance to welcome them as neighbours in the larger towns. Both peoples regard mixed marriages as betrayal and apostasy, and although such marriages do take place they are extremely rare. Arab children in the villages learn Hebrew at a relatively late stage of their education, and overall the picture is that of a minority with high birth rate, feeling distinctly under-privileged and riven by conflicting racial and political loyalties.

Peace and equality are the two concepts which have always headed the list of preferences of the Arabs of Israel. It was reckoned that the two were bound together, since a significant proportion of the causes of inequality was rooted in the security situation – the fact that it was impossible to employ Arabs in security-sensitive occupations, to say nothing of the body-searches and roadblocks and other inconveniences directly or indirectly associated with Israel's continuing state of emergency.

The peace process has made life much easier for the Arabs of Israel; many of them now travel to Egypt and to Jordan and some have business interests in these countries. The agreements with the PLO have been greeted with a sigh of relief. On the other hand, the very speed with which the peace process evolved has aroused some criticism; it is alleged, for example, that Israel's principal motive for making deals with the PLO was to avoid the expense of providing Arab villages with running water and modern sanitation, giving the responsibility to someone else. Official willingness to open some doors to the Arabs of Israel has been met with scepticism in certain quarters. In 1993, for the first time two Arab trainee-diplomats were accepted by the Foreign Ministry, but both dropped out of the course after operation 'Accountability' in Lebanon, on the grounds that as Israeli diplomats they would be expected to justify such military actions and this they were not prepared to do. A number of Arab intellectuals have refused to serve as ambassadors of Israel, citing their reluctance to host Independence Day parties or to explain Israeli policy irrespective of the government in power.

Within the Arab communities there have been new developments in recent years. The Islamist movement has gained strength; it is led by resolute young men with communication and leadership skills. On the municipal level their record has been impressive and some have decided to involve themselves with politics at the national level, although the traditional insularity of this group used to be stronger than that of other parties in the Arab sector. Another group, also led by young intellectuals, seeks cultural autonomy for the Arabs of Israel, while the demand to present Israel as the state of all its citizens is heard with increasing frequency among various circles of the Arabs of Israel.

Peace will not solve the problem of Israel's Arab minority. In some respects it will ease tensions, and in others it will raise the issue to a higher position on the national agenda. On the economic level, it will be necessary to continue with a measure of affirmative action, establishing a minimum quota of Arab employees in directorates and other contexts where they are currently under-represented.

It will be possible to solve some of the problems by means of the proposed national service scheme to which I referred in Chapter 5; this would enable the Israeli Arab, like any other citizen, to perform military service, civilian service or no service at all on grounds of religion or conscience. I can envisage the Arabs of Israel working in the service of their community, engaged in projects in other parts of the country, serving in the armed forces at home, or abroad with Israeli units in UN peace-keeping forces. Military or civilian service will give them the admission-ticket to Israeli society which they currently lack, and the combination of comprehensive peace on the one hand and national service on the other can place the relations between Jews and Arabs in Israel on a new footing.

Demands for Arab cultural or even national autonomy or for conversion of Israel to a state of all its citizens will not be granted. Israel is the state of one nation; had it not been a Jewish state, our parents would never have come here in the first place. If you want to live in a conventional state, you can find that elsewhere. The Jewish people is entitled to a state of its own, a fact proved conclusively by the annihilation of the Jews of Europe. Israel will always remain the state of the Jews, of all Jews: as long as the state exists, any Jew in the world is eligible for citizenship. It would be a perversion of historical justice if, just as the Palestinian nation-state is taking shape, Israel were expected by the Arab minority living in its midst to give up its Jewish identity. However, there is nothing in the fact of a Jewish state which should impair any of the rights of Israel's Arabs, and the day must come when there is no function in Israel from which Arabs are debarred, in practice as well as in theory.

The Arab population in Israel today numbers some 850,000. It is a large, important, very interesting and very heterogeneous group. Relations between this group and the Jewish majority will always be special and complex; aversion on both sides to the concept of integration is the dominant factor in these relations, and it is reasonable to assume that in the foreseeable future this aversion will remain.

Most Druze and Circassian males serve in the armed forces, as do some of the Bedouin; among the latter this leads to confusion as to identity – are they Arabs? Palestinians? Israelis? Within the Arab fold there are also important differences in the ways of life of Muslims and Christians; some of the latter who serve in the IDF tend to identify more closely with Israel than with their Muslim brethren. Among the Muslims there are big differences between the group that identifies with the Communist Party, noted for its preponderance of academics and intellectuals, the group that identifies with militant Islam and the pragmatic group which has close links with the leadership of the labour movement.

The status of Arab and Druze women is an important issue on the
agenda of the Arabs of Israel; there are constant demands on the part of
women to play a role in society, rather than being confined to the kitchen
and forbidden any contact with outsiders, even with guests. The struggle
of the Arab and Druze woman for equality in the home and in society
deserves the support of those in Israeli society who believe in the equal
value of all human beings, and who believe that for generations a vast
amount of talent and ability has gone to waste as a result of the sub-
ordination of women.

8

State and Religion

The coming of peace will clear the ground for discussion of issues relating to religion and the state. This has happened in the past, with for example the 'Who is a Jew?' controversies at the tail-end of the 1950s, in the long interlude between the Sinai War and the Six Day War. There can be no doubt that relations between religious and non-religious in Israel are both tense and volatile. All pay lip-service to the status quo, based on a letter from David Ben-Gurion as executive chairman of the Jewish Agency to the worldwide Agudat Israel organisation in 1948, concerning issues of *kashrut* (Jewish religious dietary laws), marriage, the Sabbath and education. The original intention was to freeze the situation as had hitherto existed, in terms of the religious aspects of pre-state Israeli society. For example, in Haifa, which was an Arab–Jewish city, public transport operated on the Sabbath, which was not the case in Tel Aviv; to this day, Haifa is one of the very few places where there is Sabbath public transport. On the other hand technological and cultural changes have led to far-reaching changes in the status quo (many more cinemas and other places of entertainment open on the Sabbath), while these have been matched by a quite massive load of legislation (closure of El Al on Sabbath, prohibition of pig-farming, additional prohibitive dietary regulations) which has shifted the status quo in another direction.

There is no convention or covenant in Israel governing relations between religious and non-religious. The Supreme Court is extremely cautious in its relations with the Chief Rabbinate and prefers not to put them to the test; tensions between the High Court of Justice and the Supreme Rabbinical Court of the Orthodox community arise from time to time, subsiding when other issues take centre-stage.

It is true that Zionism was intended to provide a secular answer to the continuing existence of the Jewish people, but secularism is a very young phenomenon, 200 years old at the most, while religion is ancient and all-pervasive. Just as people cling to nationalism as a means of identifying with a greater collective, so they cling to religion as a cause which will enable them to interpret the world and cope with the problems that are the lot of humankind. Karl Marx could denounce religion as the opium of the masses, and others have said that God is the most ingenious invention of mankind, that men of religion the whole world over have helped to maintain the existing order, institutionalising injustice and oppression, using the promises of reward and punishment to impose obedience – but the fact is that secularism has not succeeded in finding a realistic alternative to religion. Religion kept people busy, instilled discipline and fear of the displeasure of a Higher Providence; secularism liberated people from this fear but gave them no alternative concepts to believe in.

From the secular viewpoint it is easy to accept the religious phenomenon in the spirit of 'live and let live'; from the religious viewpoint it is hard to accept the secular phenomenon, which it regards as heretical and blasphemous. Each side sees the other as a transient phenomenon. Between belief in an external cause guiding all our actions and denial of this, no compromise is available, but there can be agreement on the rules of the game.

The Ultra-Orthodox community is the most extreme of the religious groups in its dealings with the state: it combines religious extremism with extreme anti-nationalism, doesn't recognise Israel, doesn't serve in the IDF, receives no allowances from the state and lives in a world of its own. Other God-fearing folk, associated with Torah Judaism, see the State of Israel as a mistake but are prepared to accept its existence retrospectively: they enjoy its allowances, vote in Knesset elections and are eligible for election themselves, but do not serve in government. Members of the Shas religious party, pious people of Sephardi origin, are more closely identified with the state, voting for and being elected to the Knesset and serving in government. These three groups have religious courts and dietary regulations of their own, and do not accept the jurisdiction of the Chief Rabbinate. National-religious circles mainly around the NRP accept the authority of the Chief Rabbinate and are very closely identified with the state. The non-observant public ranges from traditionalists to those who have nothing to do with religious ritual but still consider themselves as belonging to Judaic culture.

In Israel there are whole areas of life in which the state waives its authority, ceding it to the official religions. The state finances religious agencies and they are responsible for marriage and divorce, for conversion and for burial. Can Israel remain a nation-state, a Jewish state, if there is separation between state and religion? In my opinion, a certain degree of separation is essential, is practicable and poses no threat to the future of Israel as the state of the Jews.

Although Israel has existed some fifty years, the rabbis have made no effort to influence the procedures of the state. They are still living in Exile, still requiring the services of the 'Sabbath goy' and selling *hametz* (bread and flour related food) to an Arab at Passover-time; religious people cannot work on Sabbath even in essential services such as electricity-supply. Devout Judaism lives in a world where it can survive only because there are secularists and non-Jews on hand to guarantee continuation of the business of life.

This is also the case in matrimonial affairs. Free-thinking men are unwilling to accept the fact that they are forbidden to marry a divorced woman if they happen to be of priestly descent or – worse still – the fact that the penalty for illegitimacy is ostracism from the community for ten generations. In Israel there is no possibility of marriage between followers of different religions, not even between Christian and Muslim Arabs. All marriages and all divorces must take place under the aegis of a single religion. In this respect, the Israeli citizen is deprived of a basic right enjoyed in every other democratic state.

Something strange has happened to ultra-Orthodox Judaism in Israel: all its sons are *yeshiva* students. Whereas in Exile, every family included tradesmen and artisans alongside the obligatory seminarian, in Israel every God-fearing youngster is studying in a *yeshiva* (religious higher education institute). This phenomenon of brands snatched from the fire after the Holocaust, this exemption from military service granted by Ben-Gurion to those of devout convictions, has swelled in numbers from hundreds to thousands: a significant portion of the population which does not serve in the army and contributes nothing to the economy. I reckon that the new form of national service – with exemptions – which I recommended in Chapter 5 could lead to a change and give some members of this group the opportunity to serve the community and not just live on its back for ever.

The religious institutions of this country were established decades ago, in conditions very different from those existing today and, like other structures, have failed to adapt to meet changing circumstances.

The Chief Rabbinate was established in 1920 and incorporated into Mandatory law in 1933, with the purpose of representing the religious community vis-à-vis the British administration. Judaism has never accepted papal-style authority, only that of the rabbis of communities, and the installation of the Chief Rabbinate was a secular act rejected by Orthodox Judaism.

The system whereby a Sephardi rabbi and an Ashkenazi rabbi are appointed to officiate jointly was introduced as a temporary measure – a temporary measure which will in the year 2000 be celebrating its eightieth birthday. In accordance with this rule, every congregation in the country numbering more than 6,000 members has an Ashkenazi and a Sephardi rabbi. Since secular Judaism lives in accordance with the precepts of no rabbinate whatsoever, while Orthodox Judaism isn't prepared to obey the Chief Rabbinate, only its own spiritual leadership, the Chief Rabbinate, entirely the creation of a foreign power, serves the national-religious public only. It is a sectarian service in the guise of a comprehensive service.

The religious councils were set up in 1949 with the aim of providing a Jewish religious service. They are financed by the Ministry for Religious Affairs, the local authority and the local rabbinate, but these are blatant political appointments; the status of members of the religious council is equivalent to that of members of the local council, and consequently the leader of the religious council receives the same remuneration as that paid to a mayor.

In 1950 the Law of Return was passed, granting every Jew and every convert the right to come to Israel and acquire immediate citizenship. In 1970 a clause was added entitling the son of a Jew, the grandson of a Jew and their spouses to immigrate and gain immediate citizenship. When the law was promulgated, the legislators were convinced that only genuine Jews would be interested in coming to Israel. A generation on, Israel has the most lax citizenship rules of any free world state, and there are many 'tribes' in the world which claim to be of Jewish origin and are threatening to come here under the terms of the Law of Return. The story of the Falashas in Ethiopia is just one example of this, by no means the only one. Today, if a clan chieftain converts to Judaism, that is enough to make all his sons and grandsons and all their wives eligible for Israeli citizenship. This is not just a hypothetical problem – it has actually happened.

In 1953 the rabbinical courts were established by law. It was the Minister for Religious Affairs at the time, Rabbi Yehuda Leib Fishman-Meiman, who introduced the legislation in the Knesset and in his speech he promised that the rabbinical courts would be accessible to the public and that even secular litigants would prefer them to the civil courts, since their decisions would be humane and reasonable. Fishman-Meiman's vision was not to be realised. Every year there is an increasing gap between the volume of alimony applications presented in the civil courts and the few presented in the rabbinical courts. Most of the *dayyanim* (judges of the religious Jewish courts) are detached from the reality of life in Israel, are afraid of creating precedents and innovations, avoid taking decisions and are incapable of tackling problems such as the adoption of children from abroad or the growing numbers of non-Jews trying to find loopholes in the Law of Return.

In 1953 the State Education Act was passed, but 'trends' in education were not abolished, except that of the labour movement. There was an attempt to establish a 'religious cell' within the state system, but this was not a success. For political reasons Ben-Gurion was unable to abolish the national-religious trend, and in retrospect this has turned out to be a serious mistake. In the state system the volume of religious studies – the Bible and the oral Torah – is constantly diminishing, while the national-religious system has taken a sharp turn in the opposite direction: increasing numbers of Orthodox teachers are employed, separation between boys and girls takes place at an earlier age than used to be the case, and this also applies to the Bnei Akiva youth movement. 'Independent' and 'unofficial recognised' are two types of school maintained by the Orthodox community, with membership growing in accordance with the birth rate of this community, and both are far removed from any involvement with the state.

The tension between the religious and the free-thinkers in Israel will intensify, and is liable to become the central problem on our agenda when the issue of survival seems less critical, but we just don't have the right tools to solve the problem. The religious see the secular as vacuous heretics who must yield to them because they, the religious, are the guardians of eternal values which have proved themselves in the past and will do so again in the future; many secular people resent the fact that they have no option but to turn to the religious sector for purposes of marriage, divorce or burial, and they don't acknowledge the right of the Orthodox to prevent them shopping or enjoying entertainment on the Sabbath, or to seal off public thoroughfares which happen to pass in the vicinity of synagogues. I believe a solution has to be found to this tense situation, and a solution can be found if each side recognises the right of the other to live its life as it pleases, without exercising or suffering coercion. Is it possible that in Israel, in the twenty-first century, a man will still be unable to live without being forced to follow religious procedures, whether he is a Jew or not a Jew?

In the Jewish state, there must be a dominant role for Jewish culture – including study of the history of the Jewish people, Bible, oral Torah and later writings such as the *Maimonides*. Religious ritual is another issue altogether. I am not alone in believing that it is possible to be a consummate Jew without practising ritual, while there are those who declare that being Jewish is meaningless unless the rituals are upheld. One thing is certain: I have no intention of telling the keepers of commandments to stop what they are doing, and I only wish they would show me the same tolerance. Setting up a joint state and state-religious educational system would, I believe, be a significant contribution to the creation of a shared framework, a new national consensus. Some of the teaching would be shared, some separate, but at least the situation would not arise where secular and religious pupils never meet, because from kindergarten to matriculation they live in different worlds.

Every individual in society should be entitled to choose the path he will follow: civil marriage and civil divorce should exist alongside religious marriage and religious divorce, and registration for official purposes will always be civil registration. There can be no doubt this is a radical change, but there is no other way to avoid a future explosion in relations between the secular and the religious, and it will not impair the future of the state as a Jewish state. Currently, people prevented from marrying in this country do so abroad – or do without and just live together. This is not a long-term solution, nor is it an arrangement which the secular majority should be obliged to accept.

Religious services need to be provided by departments established for this purpose in every municipality. There is no need to maintain the religious councils, which are political bodies – with political motivations and a lot of cumbersome apparatus. The departments will supply all religious needs, thereby making considerable budgetary savings and ensuring that services meet appropriate criteria. This will also improve the standing of the religious bodies themselves, which currently gain no advantage from the interaction between the religious councils and the public.

There is no justification for the continuing existence of the Chief Rabbinate. There is definitely a case in favour of local rabbinates, although the anachronistic dualism of a Sephardi and an Ashkenazi rabbi should be abolished. It will be for the state to finance the rabbinates and religious services, and any congregation, belonging to any religion or religious denomination or stream, where a minimal number of members favour the appointment of a leader, will be entitled to the services of such a functionary.

This is not an argument in favour of separating religion from state: the day of rest, *kashrut* in public restaurants, Jewish symbols and Jewish culture, even state funding of religion – all these are worth preserving, and I actually believe that once the era of coercion is over, most citizens will opt for the rites of religious marriage alongside the civil process. The Law of Return will be with us for many generations but we will need to amend it, to prevent its exploitation by those who are not Jews but would like to be citizens of one of the world's most affluent nations. Anyone born Jewish or a convert to Judaism will be admitted to Israel, with his wife and young children, under the terms of the Law of Return; his adult offspring and spouses, grandchildren and spouses, will be subject to the standard immigration regulations.

The changes suggested in this chapter are far from simple. It is possible that some may be accepted, others rejected out of hand. But I have no doubt that in the twenty-first century we shall need to open a new chapter in relations between the religious and the secular in Israel, relations which should no longer be based on regulations inherited from the British Mandate or on structures dating from the foundation of the state. The question – as in other facets of life that I have touched on – is what price must Israeli society pay before change is agreed?

Epilogue

We could have done more in the period of the Rabin–Peres governments. But what we did made it very hard, if not impossible, to turn the clock back. In a television interview the Likud minister Tzachi Hanegbi said that four years of Labour government had been a price almost worth paying for mutual recognition with the PLO; Likud understood how vital this was, but its traditional attitudes would not have allowed it even to contemplate such a move.

The retrospective rewriting of history isn't something that appeals to me, and I tend to treat such claims with scepticism. Besides, saying that you knew a course of action was necessary, but you couldn't bring yourself to do it so you let your political rivals take the responsibility – this isn't something that *I* would choose to boast about.

However, leaving dubious historical analysis aside, it is clear that mutual recognition between Israel and the PLO is an accomplished fact. Even Benyamin Netanyahu, as Prime Minister and as leader of Likud, shook hands with Yasser Arafat, and admitted that the momentum of events since the start of unofficial talks with the PLO was an irresistible force.

A Turkish road (I have heard it said, correctly or otherwise) is a road that you build in order to bypass it. Our Turkish road was the Washington talks, and the bypass took place in Oslo. The road was too exposed to the media, too official, too orderly, whereas the bypass route enabled us to skip the sloganising and talk to the point. On the highway opening statements are presented; on the ring-road you discuss the things that matter.

There is no cause for surprise in the fact that the talks which led to peace with Jordan were secret talks, and they *didn't* take place in Washington; even the discussions preceding the interim settlement with the Palestinians took place in secret, in a limited forum, alongside the official talks with their host of participants. Whereas in centuries past it may have been possible to conduct official political negotiations without blanket coverage on the part of the press, today's decision-makers are obliged to conduct two parallel lines of talks: one purely for the benefit of the media – 'photo opportunities' and all – and one aimed at getting results. In the Syrian track, since 1991 the only talks taking place have been official ones, President Assad having explained, with characteristic cynicism, that secret talks were incompatible with the openness which was such a cherished feature of Syrian democracy and with the accountability demanded of elected leaders by the public ... For this reason there has been no real progress in talks with the Syrians, what little *has* been achieved having emerged from informal conversations held, sometimes with American participation and sometimes without, in Washington and in Wye Plantation.

If there was unacknowledged competition between the Washington talks, the shuttle diplomacy of US Secretary of State Warren Christopher and the Oslo track, Oslo won on account of its uniqueness and its openness. The main lesson I learned from the Oslo process was that change really is possible; that statements along the lines of 'I know that this is exactly what needs to be done, but the public will never accept it' are neither legitimate nor justified. He who believes and is capable of converting his will and his faith into action can not only make changes when the opportunities are created, he can personally contribute to the creation of the opportunities. But change in itself is not enough; you have to ensure that it will take root, once the initial shock has subsided, and in this respect our success was less than impressive.

Hamas was born soon after the outbreak of the *intifada*, and temporary blindness on the part of our security services induced decision-makers to believe that the defeat of the PLO and the victory of this conservative religious organisation would be greatly to Israel's advantage. It was not until the early 1990s that the threat from Hamas was perceived as being infinitely more serious, since its use of violence was indiscriminate and it lacked the pragmatism which had been the hallmark of the PLO in recent years.

When we came to power in 1992 there was a growing fear that Hamas was liable to take over the entire Palestinian camp. Results of elections to student bodies and professional associations showed that the organisation was proliferating, permeating the Palestinian elite and not just those at the lower levels of society who benefited from its welfare programme. The Oslo track – beyond the intention of solving the Israeli–Palestinian dispute, and thereby hastening the end of the wider Israeli–Arab conflict – had the purpose of preventing the domination by Hamas of the whole Palestinian sector. We reckoned that agreement with the representative and internationally recognised Palestinian body would put an end to terrorist acts on the part of groups subject to its authority, and that Arafat would be more successful in confronting Hamas than we had been. The first of these two predictions came true: the PLO called an absolute halt to its own terror campaign and took steps to prevent attacks on the part of other elements, but Arafat believed he could incorporate Hamas into his government, preferring to neutralise its military power by giving it limited political authority. It was only after a series of major terrorist incidents that Arafat changed his tactics, realising that such a coalition would never work, and a crackdown on Hamas was the only answer.

I don't subscribe to the view that last-minute appointments or a different style of election broadcasts would have changed the outcome – although, when the margin is less than 1 per cent, almost anything could be reckoned capable of making a difference, from better organisation and better handling of the news media to more effective make-up in the television studios.

When the terror campaigns were unleashed, the price we paid in blood was heavy indeed. Terrorism did not distinguish between soldiers and civilians, between women and men, between adults and children; no advance warnings were given, targets were selected at random. Ostensibly sane people, intellectuals for the most part, believing fervently in the justice of their cause, produced a bloodbath which left the Israeli electorate wondering if there would ever be an end to regional madness. The Israeli and Palestinian killers Yehie Ayyash, Baruch Goldstein, Hassan Salameh and Yigal Amir succeeded in shifting the balance of political power in Israel, but this was only a step on the way to their ultimate and more ambitious objective – the frustration and destruction of the peace process.

Our most serious mistake was our belief that peace would speak for itself. We assumed that people would automatically associate the peace process with the lifting of the Arab embargo, the boom in investment in Israel, the dramatic fall in unemployment levels, rising living standards, receding prospects of war, the influx of tourists and Israel's emergence from isolation and obloquy into the light of international respect and recognition. Our optimism was misplaced. Instead of associating the peace process with all these indicators of progress, people made the connection between the peace process and the terrorist threat; many accepted the analysis of the right, according to which peace would actually lead to violence, and furthermore our economic prosperity emanated from other causes entirely. Education in the link between peace and other positive developments must be our central objective in the future, and dialogue with those elements in society who see peace as a direct or indirect threat is also vital.

Having embarked on the Oslo process we have no option but to continue it. Ending the process, with a bang or with a whimper, would leave us in a situation worse than the one that prevailed before the Madrid Conference or before the signing of the declaration of principles. Anyone seeking to fob the Palestinians off with some version of 'perpetual autonomy' risks losing all the assets gained by Israel over recent years, since no element in the Arab world or the world at large would support such a move. It is possible, in my opinion, to reach an agreement which will not include return of Palestinian refugees to Israeli sovereign territory, not call for partition of Jerusalem and not demand Israel's withdrawal to the 1967 borders, but there will not be a permanent settlement without a Palestinian state, just as there can be no settlement without PLO involvement. The existence of such a state will also be to Israel's advantage; we shall know for certain with whom we are talking, and at which address. As long as there is no Palestinian sovereignty, what will remain will be the hybrid situation of a semi-independent state on territory illegally occupied according to international law, with Israel accepting ultimate responsibility for everything that happens there – the worst of all worlds. Any arrangement other than the Oslo Accord is liable to plunge Israel into permanent conflict, accompanied by bitter frustration over what should have been done but was not.

Is there a role for the Labour Party while in opposition? What it must *not* do is simply go into hibernation and wait for the creation of the circumstances which will return it to power at the next election. It is important to remember that the Oslo process was begun when we were in opposition, and the economic elements of the declaration of principles were worked out, in all essentials, during the same period of opposition. Peace isn't only the business of governments. In this era of privatisation and limits on government intervention, there is a case for privatising many aspects of the peace process; private initiative has a role to play in promoting education for peace, preparing for future developments in the process and stepping up the pace of dialogue with our Arab neighbours.

It has to be admitted that there is something traumatic about losing power, especially when you are deeply involved in a specific process, when you know what you want to achieve and what can be achieved – and you know the likely consequences of calling it off. On the other hand, in a democracy a spell in opposition is no bad thing; when you are in government, however hard you try you can never really get close to life on the streets and in the market-place. Quite apart from the technical issue of personal protection, and the barrier that this creates between you and the public, you can't even be seen in a bank, in a hospital or a grocery without questions being asked and conclusions drawn – unless of course you're a master of disguise like Harun al-Rashid (who was the famous Islamic Caliph, 786–809, and who disguised himself and went to the market in order to know what the people were talking about). In opposition it is much easier to take the pulse of real life; you also have time to sit and think and prepare yourself for another stint in the driving-seat.

In the last few chapters I have put forward some ideas for the future, all of them based on solid and seasoned ideological foundations – belief in social justice, in the equal value of all human beings, in the need to reduce social differentials, in the obligation to give every individual the opportunity for self-discovery and self-fulfilment. On the basis of these principles, what is proposed is an extension of freedom of choice in all areas – economic, religious, educational – and a concerted effort to remove deprivation. In our modern society, the society of the future, there will be no place for those forms of discrimination which belong in the Dark Ages: discrimination on grounds of sex, age, physical condition, community, religion, race or length of residence in the country.

Israeli society, living in peace, won't only be a just society, but a society which has a purpose and a mission within Israel, in the region and in the world. The precise nature of this purpose will be the subject of the next controversy in Israeli society.

I'm looking forward to it!

Chronology of the Oslo Process

29 April 1992   The first meeting between Terje Larsen and Yossi Beilin in Tel-Aviv.

19 June 1992   A meeting at the American Colony Hotel in East Jerusalem between Terje Larsen, Yossi Beilin, Yair Hirschfeld and Faisel Husseini to decide on the back channel.

9 September 1992   Jan Egland, the Norwegian deputy foreign minister visits the Israeli deputy foreign minister, Yossi Beilin. They decide to operate the back channel between Israelis and Palestinians.

4 December 1992   Yair Hirschfeld and Abu Ala meet in London.

20 January 1993   The first meeting between Yair Hirschfeld, Ron Pundak and Abu Ala and his team takes place in Oslo.

19 August 1993   Uri Savir and Abu Ala sign the Declaration of Principles in Oslo with the attendance of Peres and Holst.

13 September 1993   The signing ceremony in Washington: Shimon Peres and Abu Mazen sign the Declaration of Principles with attendance of President Clinton, Prime Minister Rabin and the Russian Foreign Minister Kosirev.

11 October 1993   The first meeting between Yasser Arafat and Yossi Beilin in Tunis. They decide to begin informal talks on the Final Status. Abu Mazen is designated to be Beilin's partner.

1 September 1994   The beginning of the Stockholm Channel between Ahmed Khalidi, Hussein Agha, Yair Hirschfeld and Ron Pundak.

31 October 1995   The conclusion of the Stockholm talks by a meeting between Abu Mazen and Yossi Beilin with the two teams, in Tel-Aviv.

Glossary

1948 War (War of Independence) The first war between Israel and the Arab states began on the eve of the establishment of the State of Israel and continued until January 1949. The war broke out following the rejection of the Arab states and the Palestinian leadership (represented by the Palestine–Arab Higher Committee) of United Nations General Assembly Resolution 181 of 29 November 1947 that called for the separation of Palestine into two independent states – one Jewish and one Arab – that would be linked economically.

1967 War (Six Day War) The third Israeli–Arab war between Israel and Egypt, Jordan and Syria began on 5 June 1967 and ended on 10 June. During the war, Israel captured the Sinai Peninsula, the Gaza Strip, the West Bank (including East Jerusalem), and the Golan Heights, increasing its geographical size threefold and making Israel responsible for more than one million Palestinian inhabitants of the occupied territories. As part of the Egypt–Israel Peace Treaty of March 1979, Egypt gave up its claim to the Gaza Strip to the Palestinians. On 31 July 1988, Jordan gave up its claim to the West Bank to the Palestinians.

Agudat Israel Agudat Israel is an anti-Zionist religious party which actively participates in Israeli politics. They believe that national Jewish redemption will not occur through the establishment of a democratic secular state, but rather through divine intervention and the founding of a state based on the Torah and Jewish law. Accordingly, Agudat Israel's recognition of the State of Israel is a *de facto* recognition in order to gain resources for the constituents it represents and to guard the rights and interests of religious Jews living in Israel.

Ahdut HaAvoda Ahdut HaAvoda ('Unity of Labour' in Hebrew) was established in 1919 as a Zionist workers' party by the Hebrew Battalion Volunteers of World War I, members of Poalei Zion ('Workers of Zion' in Hebrew) and a broad group of unaffiliates. In 1930, Ahdut HaAvoda united with HaPoel HaTzair and established Mapai – the Israel Workers' Party. Ahdut HaAvoda joined Mapai and Rafi in 1968 to form the Israel Labour Party.

Druze The Druze are a religious sect that broke off from Islam in the beginning of the eleventh century. The founders of the new religion left Egypt and wandered northward, settling along the foot of the Hermon mountain and then spreading westward to the Shuf Mountains, the southern Galil and Mount Carmel, and eastward toward what is today known as Syria. The Druze believe in one god, who will reappear in the form of a person. Their beliefs are shrouded in secrecy and they frown upon those who abandon the community and inter-marry. This has enabled the community to maintain a unique sense of identity. Although the Druze have a strong connection to their land, they have not exhibited any nationalist or separatist aspirations. The Druze remain loyal to the countries in which they live and serve in the army. In the context of the Arab–Israeli conflict, this has meant that Druze often fight against one another. When Israel was established in 1948, there were 13,000 Druze living in Israel. Today there are approximately 90,000.

Hamas Sheikh Ahmed Ismail Yassin founded Hamas, the Palestinian Islamist organisation – an offshoot of the military arm of the Muslim Brotherhood – in the West Bank and Gaza Strip after the breakout of the *intifada* (uprising). Its Charter was published in August 1988, claiming that all of Palestine from 'the sea to the river' is *waqf* (an Islamic religious endowment). Hamas has accepted the principle of Palestinian nationalism as part of the Pan Islamic ideal and has called for *jihad* (holy war) against Israel. Hamas is also against the corrupt and degenerate elements of Palestinian society. Hamas opposed the Israeli–Palestinian Declaration of Principles (DOP) of 13 September 1993 and since then has launched mass terror attacks in Israel, the West Bank, and the Gaza Strip as a means to undermining and ending the peace process. Hamas is viewed as a socio-religious alternative to Arafat's secular regime and its policy of peace making and reconciliation with Israel.

Herut Herut ('freedom' in Hebrew) was a right-wing movement that was established in June 1948 as an offshoot of Etzel. Until the elections for the Fifth Knesset in 1961, Herut ran independently and in 1965,

Herut, together with the Liberal Party formed the Gahal (a Hebrew acronym for the Herut-Liberal bloc) list. In the elections for the Sixth Knesset in 1973, it joined the Likud. Although Herut was the second largest faction in the Knesset since 1955, it did not manage to lead the government until the elections for the Ninth Knesset in 1977. Menachem Begin led Herut until his political retirement in 1983.

Hezbollah (The Party of Allah)   Hezbollah ('Party of God' in Arabic) was established in 1982 as an umbrella organisation for Islamic militants in Lebanon in support of the Iranian Islamic Revolution of 1979 and its ensuing policies. Among its founders was Sheikh Abaas Mussawi, who was elected as head of the party in 1991 and then assassinated by the Israelis in February 1992. The party was created to combat Israeli presence in Lebanon and has launched terrorist attacks both inside and outside of Lebanon. It is staunchly opposed to the existence of the State of Israel, but distinguishes between the present reality and its overall vision. In 1992 and in 1996, the party adopted a political platform and ran in the Lebanese parliamentary elections.

Histadrut   Established in 1920, the Histadrut (The General Federation of Labour) is the largest trade union in Israel. Since its inception, the Histadrut played a central role in developing and planning the economy and assumed the role of the economic branch of Mapai and the Israel Labour Party. Today, however, it focuses less on creating employment opportunities and more on workers' rights.

Israeli Governmental Decision of 19 June 1967   On 19 June 1967, the Israeli government reached a decision regarding the status of the territories occupied by the IDF during the 1967 war. With regard to Egypt, it was decided that a peace treaty would have to be based on the international border according to which the Gaza Strip was considered a part of Israel. With regard to Syria, it was decided that a peace treaty would have to be based on the international border and Israel's security needs. The peace treaty would commit the Syrians to demilitarise the Golan Heights. It was also decided to postpone the discussion regarding Jordan and the refugee problem.

London Agreement   The London Agreement was an unsigned understanding that was reached in a secret meeting in London on 11 April

1987 between King Hussein of the Hashemite Kingdom of Jordan and Shimon Peres, the Minister of Foreign Affairs of Israel. The understanding called for the convening of an international conference on the subject of the Middle East and the beginning of negotiations between an Israeli and a joint Jordanian–Palestinian delegation. Likud Prime Minister Yitzhak Shamir, who was then head of the national unity government as part of a rotational agreement, rejected the agreement and, as a result, it remained unsigned.

Mapai The socialist-Zionist Mapai party (Hebrew acronym for Israel Workers' Party) was created in 1930 by the merging of Ahdut HaAvoda and HaPoel HaTzair (Young Workers Party in Hebrew). From 1930 to 1968, it was not only the dominant labour movement in Israel, but also the central force behind the entire Jewish Yishuv (Jewish community in Palestine) and the World Zionist Movement. Mapai rests its beliefs on the pillar of constructive-socialism, which is based on the ideal of combining the spirit of pioneering with state-pragmatism. Its spiritual leader was Berl Katznelson and its political leader was David Ben-Gurion until 1963. Mapai joined Ahdut HaAvoda and Rafi (a political party formed by David Ben-Gurion in 1965 as a split-off from Mapai) to form the Israel Labour Party in 1968. It was the leader of all government coalitions since the establishment of the state in 1948 until 1977.

Mapam Mapam was founded in 1948 as a socialist-Zionist party. In the beginning, the party's platform had a pro-Soviet slant, but following Joseph Stalin's death, it changed. Even though Mapam worked alongside the Avoda faction between 1969 and 1984 under the umbrella of the Israel Labour Party, their socio-economic basis and orientation was more socialist in character. In 1981, Mapam recognised the Palestinian right to self-determination in the framework of a peace settlement. In 1992, Mapam joined the leftist Meretz Party in a joint slate to the Thirteenth Knesset (Israeli parliament). In February 1997, Mapam joined its forces with Ratz and parts of Shinui to become one official political party.

Multilateral Talks The multilateral talks were an outcome of the Madrid Conference, which was held in Madrid, Spain in the autumn of 1991. On the one hand, bilateral talks between Israel and each of her Arab neighbours took place; and, on the other hand, multilateral talks took place between Israel and the majority of Arab states. The first round of talks opened in Moscow on the 28 January 1992. Five working groups were established in the areas of water, the environment, refugees, economic cooperation, and arms control. The multilateral talks took place in several world capitals, including different Arab cities that agreed to host different Israeli delegations.

Palestinian National Covenant   The Palestinian National Covenant is the basic charter of the PLO that defines its aims. The PLO approved the original version of the charter at its first convention in 1964, which mainly called for the destruction of the State of Israel and the establishment of an Arab–Palestinian state in the entire region of Palestine. The charter was revised by the Palestine National Council in Cairo in July 1968. On 9 September 1993, Arafat pledged in a letter to Yitzhak Rabin that those articles were no longer valid and that the PNC would meet to approve the necessary changes. On the basis of this letter, Israel recognised the PLO and the PNC assembled for a special meeting on 24 April 1996 in order to cancel the problematic clauses.

RATZ (Citizen's Rights Movement)   Shulamit Aloni founded Ratz in August 1973 as a left-wing liberal political party. Ratz concentrated mainly on human rights issues with special attention to women's rights. It also called for a separation of religion and state, an end to occupation, and the Israeli recognition of the Palestinian right to self-determination. In 1992, Ratz joined Meretz in a joint list to the Thirteenth Knesset.

Shinui   The liberal political party Shinui ('change' in Hebrew) was founded in July 1974 by Professor Amnon Rubinstein and Mordechai Virshuvsky, as well as others. The creation of the party stemmed from protest movements demonstrating against Golda Meir and her government's responsibility for the 1973 Yom Kippur War. On an ideological level, Shinui called for giving up the territories in exchange for peace with neighbouring Arab countries; the promise of citizen's rights; and an end to governmental involvement and interference in economic affairs. In 1992, Shinui joined Meretz in a joint list to the Thirteenth Knesset.

Summud   *Summud* stems from the Arabic root 'steadfastness'. In Palestinian mythology, this word denotes the situation of Palestinians living in the West Bank and the Gaza Strip under Israeli occupation, who were mainly passive until December 1987. The PLO differentiated between different situations within the Palestinian population under the Israeli occupation. The *intifada* erupted in 1987, bringing an end to the policy of *summud*. The Palestinian population then passed into the third stage of active resistance.

United Torah Judaism   United Torah Judaism joined the Thirteenth and Fourteenth Knesset. It is a coalition of different anti-Zionist religious political parties that is composed of Agudat Israel and Degel HaTorah. Its overall aim is to establish a religious Jewish state, which is based on the Torah and Jewish law.

UNSCR 242   Following the Six Day War, on 22 November 1967, the United Nations Security Council adopted a British-American initiative, which called for the 'withdrawal of Israeli armed forces from territories occupied' in the Six Day War and the 'right to live in peace within secure and recognized boundaries.'

UNSCR 338   On 22 October 1973, the United Nations Security Council adopted Resolution 338, which called for an immediate cease-fire in the 1973 Yom Kippur War and the implementation of UNSCR 242. This provided the basis for negotiations on achieving peace in the Middle East.

Index

Rabin, Yitzhak: – *cont*
final agreement, 118; enquires about
agreements for end of terrorism, 119–
20; Rubinstein complains of, 124;
accepts recognition of PLO, 127; signs
letter of agreement (September 1993),
127–8; at press briefing on signed
agreement, 128; signs agreement in
Washington, 129–30, 132; and
success of Oslo track, 133, 137; 1994
agreement with Hussein, 135; shares
Nobel Peace Prize, 135, 159–60; and
author's secrecy over permanent
settlement negotiations, 145; and
demilitarisation of Jordan Valley, 149;
and principles of permanent settlement, 154, 175–6, 179; popularity
declines, 160; views on separation,
165; attends signing of last agreement
(September 1995), 174; presents
interim agreement to Knesset, 175;
and Stockholm proposals, 177–8;
murdered, 179–80, 183–6, 189; on
withdrawal from Golan Heights, 203;
and negotiations with Syria, 207;
opposes Israeli military presence in
Lebanon, 208–10; supports electoral
reform, 225–6
Rabinowitz, Itamar, 55, 122, 203
Ramallawi, Nabil, 32
Ramat Yishai, 50
Ramon, Haim: in Labour Party, 12; and
1988 government, 19; in 'Green Village' group, 20; opposes establishment of Palestinian state, 37;
speech on trade unions, 44; in 1992
Knesset, 49; and Labour's 1992 election victory, 53; ministerial post
(1992), 56; link with Tibi, 115; sets up
link between Rabin and Arafat, 125;
favours separation, 165; reforms His-
tadrut, 241
Randell, Dov, 49–50
Ratz Party, 33
Reagan, Ronald, 13, 20, 85
Reichmann, Uriel, 224
Rome: conference on economic issues,
80, 82
Ronberga, Sweden, 163
Ross, Dennis, 61, 93, 114, 120–2
Rubinstein, Amnon, 34
Rubinstein, Eliakim, 45–6, 54–5, 82, 96,
123, 125
Russia: attends December 1992 London
meeting, 60

Rwanda, 214

Sabra massacre (1982), 210
Sadat, Anwar, 2, 40, 135, 203
Saddam Hussein, 36, 39
Safiya, Afif, 26
Saguy, Uri, 119
Salameh, Hassan, 270
Samaria, 24–5, 74
Sanbar, Elias, 82
Sapir, Pinhas, 252
Sarid, Yossi, 34; 'Don't Call Me', 36
Sarpsborg, Norway, 64, 70, 74, 79
Sartawi, Isam, 168
Saudi Arabia, 83, 206
Savir, Uri: heads Israeli delegation to
Oslo, 85–8; and Singer's appointment,
90; and acceptance of Oslo accord, 91;
and seventh round of Oslo talks, 97;
misses eighth round of talks, 102;
declines Palestine amendments at
ninth round of Oslo talks, 105; meets
Norwegians in Jerusalem, 106; and
Holsts' children, 110; criticises Ala,
111; and draft agreements of principle, 112–13; on mutual recognition,
112; and Peres's visit to Norway and
Sweden, 117; signs Oslo agreement,
118; and Israeli ratification of Oslo
agreement, 123; discusses mutual recognition principles in Paris, 127; at
press briefing on signed agreement,
128; and Israeli signing of agreement
in Washington, 129, 132; achievements, 137; proposed for Nobel Peace
Prize, 159; in secret talks with Ala on
interim settlement, 164; views on separation, 165; Mazen on, 169; talks
with Syrians, 203–4
Scheinbaum, Stanley, 19
Schorri, Pierre, 158, 160, 163–4
Shaath, Nabil, 42, 102–3, 106, 163–4,
166–7
Shafi, Haydar Abd el, 44, 46
Shahal, Moshe, 125, 165–6
Shamir, Yitzhak: in 1992 election, 2; suc-
ceeds Peres as Prime Minister, 15;
heads 1988 government, 19, 22;
denounces US negotiations with PLO,
20; Rabin presses for initiative on
Palestinians, 23; accepts ban on contacts with PLO, 25; Taarifi meets, 29;
demands author's dismissal, 30; and
united government (1984), 31–2, 208;
Baker questions, 32; demands Weiz-